The Myth of the Conqueror

The Myth of the Conqueror

Prince Henry Stuart:
A Study of 17th Century Personation

by
J.W. Williamson

AMS PRESS
New York

FIRST AMS PRESS EDITION: 1978

Library of Congress Cataloging in Publication Data

Williamson, Jerry Wayne, 1944-
The myth of the conqueror.

Bibliography: p.
Includes index.
1. Henry Frederick, Prince of Wales, 1594-1612.
2. Great Britain—Princes and princesses—Biography.
3. Great Britain—History—James I, 1603-1625.
I. Title.
DA391.1.H5W47   941.06'1'0924 [B]   77-78318
ISBN 0-404-16004-2

for Gaylan

Contents

ILLUSTRATIONS

Acknowledgments

My most demonstrable debt is owed Barbara Lindsay. Years ago under her instruction at the University of Utah I worked with the Latin elegies written on the occasion of Henry's death. As my interest in the prince and his personality grew, so did Mrs. Lindsay's. In 1973 we collaborated on an article ("Myth of the Conqueror: Prince Henry Stuart and Protestant Militancy," *Journal of Medieval and Renaissance Studies*, 1975, 203-222) in which were advanced some of the ideas developed at length in this book. Mrs. Lindsay and I further planned to collaborate on a book-length treatment of the prince, focusing primarily on his death. I was to do, in the second chapter of that book, a concise biography. As I worked on it, my chapter got somewhat out of hand. My patient collaborator pointed out that I was writing another book altogether, and she insisted that I continue with my own particular exploration of Prince Henry's life and influence. This is the book which resulted: its faults are mine alone, while the virtues it may possess come largely from the continuing interest and advice of my friend and erstwhile partner. She never ceased to encourage my solo effort with the prince; she read each section of the manuscript as it was completed, offering her criticisms and comments with great insight and wit. *Interea fidi parvum cape munus amici.*

I owe much as well to Professors Jack H. Adamson and Harold F. Folland of the University of Utah, under whose instruction I did my first research and writing about Prince Henry. I experienced the best of modern humanism with these two gentlemen, whose own collaborations in biography have been my paradigm for style and integrity. Professor Adamson's students and colleagues were saddened by his sudden death in 1975; the loss to imaginative teaching and scholarship is immeasurable.

For grants to pursue the research and writing of this book, my thanks to Appalachian State University and to the Southeastern Institute of Medieval and Renaissance Studies. At the former I owe particular appreciation to the encouraging support of Herbert Wey, W.C. Strickland, and Loyd Hilton. My fellowship to the latter, at Duke University in 1974, was provided by the National Endowment for the Humanities. I wish to acknowledge in particular the leadership of Professor Dale B.J. Randall, director of the institute. Steve Zwicker of Washington University, St. Louis, a fellow at the institute, contributed much to my study, particularly to my appreciation of royal portraiture.

Among many others who have offered criticism and suggestions, I should like to thank my colleagues, Roger Stilling, Tully Reed, Robert Lysiak, Thomas McGowan, Charles Waterworth, and John Trimpey. I owe special thanks to the directors and able librarians at the British Museum and at the Marriott Library, the University of Utah; Wilson Library, the University of North Carolina at Chapel Hill; Perkins Library, Duke University.

The Infant and the Myth

I

He was born in February 1594, a reassuringly healthy bairn of long body, and baptised six months later to a general acclamation. David Moysie wrote in 1594 that Henry's birth was "a great comfort and maiter of joy to the haill pepill, and movit thame to great triumphe, wantonnes and play, for beanefyres wer sct out, and dancing and playing vsit in all pairtes, as gif the pepill had bein daft for mirthe."[1] This prince who made the "pepill daft for mirthe" was already a potent symbol. For a little country which had been ineffectively led for years by the disruptive and by the weak—by Mary the Whorish Queen and by her son James of the Strange Eye—Henry's masculinity seemed, even untested, a particular gift from God. A prince who so blessed Scotland would no doubt spend his life dedicated to the higher purposes of God and state, and both God and state would in turn bless him.

From his birth Prince Henry was the product of a powerful mythologizing force. Other royal heirs have, of course, been converted into useful symbols by countrymen in need of national images to which to cling in time of crisis or into personal icons by which to order the chaos of change, but the quality of Protestant symbology as it applied to Prince Henry was unusually relentless. It was clear from the beginning that the baby Henry would be a special sort of prince, the focus of an increasingly emotional personation, the player of a national role which Scotsmen, and later Englishmen, fashioned for him. His special task in life would be to fulfill the great labor which the people and the times seemed to demand of him. That mighty feat was no less than the destruction of Catholicism.

It is in that context that small details take on great significance: at his baptism Prince Henry was shown to the ambassadors "lying on

1

his bed of Estate, richly decored, & wrought with brodered worke, containing the story of *Hercules* and his trauels."[2] Henry's early identification with Hercules was only the first in a long succession of comparisons and associations which would follow him all his life, to make it both complex and richly charged with symbolic meaning. A baby's blanket embroidered with images of Hercules was particularly evocative of a new heroic presence in the royal palace. Especially inviting for those Protestants who observed the prince lying in state was the first legendary feat which Hercules performed when he was only an infant: he killed the two venomous snakes which Juno sent to his cradle. The serpents and the bitterly jealous female figure who sent them against Hercules could be easily interpreted in the case of Prince Henry as the Jesuits and seminarians even then being secretly sent into Britain (though hardly on a mission to assassinate the heir of Scotland) by the Whore of Babylon herself. For an age that loved allegory and followed the habit of seeing important people and significant events in terms of well-known mythic patterns, the association of Prince Henry with Hercules seems now hardly remarkable. But, on the other hand, the process by which the prince was personated as Hercules signaled a difference in the allegorizing pattern of the time. The Protestants were quite serious: when they said Henry was a new Hercules come to destroy Rome, they were not merely filling the air with highly embroidered compliments. They meant in a very real sense that Prince Henry was—or should be—a physical and psychological embodiment of what they interpreted the story of Hercules to mean.

Hercules was, first, for the late sixteenth century a universally understood symbol of justice triumphant over tyranny, of virtue triumphant over vice.[3] This was true for both Protestants and Catholics. He was, moreover, the symbol of man become almost divine in his striving, of man transformed into hero by the fearful energies of the divine spark. Hercules was credited in his travels/travails with bringing justice and civilization to the entire western world, just as the figure Bacchus was said to have tamed the East. Thus Spenser linked the two figures in Book V of the *Faerie Queene:*

> Such first was *Bacchus,* that with furious might
> All th'East before vntam'd did ouerronne,
> And wrong repressed, and establisht right,
> Which lawlesse men had formerly fordonne.

> There Iustice first her princely rule begonne.
> Next *Hercules* his like ensample shewed,
> Who all the West with equall conquest wonne,
> And monstrous tyrants with his club subdewed;
> The club of Iustice dread, with kingly powre endewed.[4]

The "club of Iustice" might mean to most Renaissance men a generalized concept of Reason which held in check the base emotions, but to the stout Protestants of Scotland, where the dragon's teeth of religious controversy sprouted thistles, justice meant vengeance, and God's sharp retribution was invariably understood to apply to popery and to its defenders. Prince Henry was heir at his birth already to one Protestant throne, a throne under which dwelt the lions of John Knox, and he was presumed heir to a second reformed kingdom, England, strong enough and wealthy enough to take up God's club against Spain and all the rest of Babylon's brood.

The Hercules myth bore other qualities attractive to the radical Protestant mind. Of the thirty-seven traditional labors of Hercules, the vast majority emphasized the strength and power of masculinity. Even in the second labor, when he begot fifty sons on the fifty daughters of Thespius in one night, love and feminine gentleness got short shrift. The theme was still power and conquest. Hercules was the male demigod whose sexuality was as much a club as the knotty log he carried in his hand. There was nothing about Hercules which suggested a compromise with the feminine, or if there were, it could be easily glossed by the censorious Calvinists or simply ignored. The Protestants needed the image of Hercules' overpowering masculinity for their prospective conquering prince, for Protestantism was the minority religion in Europe and it would not survive the holocaust which everyone saw coming unless it exhibited the sort of masculine hardness that Hercules symbolized. The soft decadence of Italianate manners, the fashions in music and poetry from France—these were the feminine forms which Queen Mary had introduced into Scotland and which King James allowed to continue about him, and these were the signs and shows which the militant Protestants despised. Such courtly delicacies were, quite simply, unmanly. With the images of Hercules and the attempt to lay that persona on Prince Henry, the Scots Protestants would seek to make all such feminine weaknesses anathema to him. And they would succeed. The prince would absorb very quickly the imagery of his assigned role and would show in various ways the influence of the myth in his private life, where the deep vein of anti-feminism in the Hercules myth and in all the conqueror personations subsequently advanced for Henry's use would be mirrored, perhaps unconsciously. At first, of course, decisions were not his to make: he would be literally denied the company of women soon after his baptism, but later, when he might have come to know his own mother as a moderating and softening influence, the imagery of anti-feminism had sunk too deep to be thrown off. Behind all of Henry's later dealings with the female gender would stalk that original image of malevolence out of the myth of Hercules' first labor: Queen Juno envenomed against the male principle. He would never overcome that first implanted prejudice although he would have some opportunity to do so.

A baby swaddled in the energies and symbology of Hercules was no accident, then, and such an association was no mere compliment either. It was a ritual laying on of hands, a transference of *virtu*. And the Hercules persona was not isolated in a bit of tapestry thrown across the baby's cradle. Andrew Melville, a scholar and torch of Scottish Protestantism, wrote a little poem, a *natalia,* celebrating the coming of Henry, but it was no birthday entertainment in the manner of lambkins and hoops. Melville's poem prophesied for the baby Henry two additional labors of Hercules, the conquest of the triple-headed monster Geryon and the fetching of Cerberus from Hades, and predictably a more topical symbology took precedence over the classical: Geryon was in Melville's poem the greasy monster Spain and Cerberus was Rome itself, the watchdog before the gates of Hell:

> ... having laid low proud Spain, bright from your triumph over anointed Geryon, you trample under foot the triple diadem of the Cerberus of Rome, who duplicates the din of Hell with fearsome thunderings from the Capitoline crag.[5]

The club of Hercules might weigh heavily in the chubby hands of a baby barely six months old, but Melville and his fellow Protestants apparently saw nothing inappropriate in creating such a role for their prince.

II

But while the Scots poets were about their wholly pleasant business of creating the personation which Henry would don for the rest of his life, King James had been busied with the far less heroic labor of helping insure that he and his new son would one day sit on the throne of England. The baptism was delayed and postponed repeatedly as James the proud father waited for both the completion of a new Chapel Royal at Stirling Castle and for the arrival of a sufficient number of foreign ambassadors to swell his son's hour. The English proved especially troublesome, as Queen Elizabeth and her ministers made James wait and wait most unregally. While the other ambassadors feasted at James's considerable expense, spending the summer days in Scottish entertainments devised for their delectation while awaiting the longed-for English, Queen Elizabeth was dallying over the simple selection of an ambassador. The Earl of Cumberland was finally chosen, but as he was preparing to leave London, he fell ill, and Elizabeth shifted the responsibility to Robert Radcliffe, fifth Earl of Sussex. The switch, carried out with the maddening leisure which Elizabeth favored when James was pressing her for haste, forced the king to postpone the baptism from August 11 to August 18, but a mere week was not enough time for the Earl of Sussex to gather bag and baggage for the journey. Reluctantly, James again postponed the ceremony to August 25. The Danish ambassador, who had been waiting in Scotland already for weeks, began to complain that the repeated delays would put his home-bound ships on the North Sea in the midst of autumn storms. At last, on August 27, the Earl of Sussex arrived in great state at Edinburgh, on Scottish soil at last but still some thirty-five or forty miles from Stirling Castle where the king and his infant son waited. James suggested that the English ambassador could surely be at Stirling on the twenty-eighth for the baptism, but the ambassador replied that he was inconvenienced by the slow pace of his baggage, which had not yet arrived in the capital. King James, with infinite patience, agreed then on August 29 for the ceremony. But the baptism had to be put off yet another day: the Earl of Sussex moved with the glacial assurance that the inconvenience he occasioned in the name of Queen Elizabeth would be accepted in Scotland with obsequious gratitude. But ironic was King James's patience in the face of the theatrical delays visited on him by Elizabeth and by her ambassador. James wished, of course, to tie his son's fortunes quite firmly to the English throne —the *benedictus* of Queen Elizabeth's proxy over the infant's head would do much to establish the bond between the two thrones—but James might have worried less, for young Henry's star was destined to rise by the irresistible pull of forces much stronger than the symbolic blessing of a queen whose glory had become paste and cosmetics.[6]

As the day for the christening approached, King James ordered the lion brought from Holyroodhouse to Stirling, to add an extra measure of emblematic energy to the spectacle, and he sent heralds into the countryside "charging all the sundry our soverign Lords leiges of what estate or degree soever they be of to set apart their particular feuds, quarrels, and grudges and keep good peace during the time of the baptism."[7] On the day appointed, the English ambassador, Queen Elizabeth's vicarious eyes and hands, bore the infant into the newly completed Chapel Royal where Henry was in good Christian manner anointed and proclaimed. If Scots poets had already identified Henry as a Hercules, the preacher appointed for that day, Patrick Galloway, was no less eager to find a fitting personality and precedent with which to enwrap the baby, though the Reverend Galloway chose fittingly from the Old Testament rather than from classical legend. He preached to the assembled ambassdors from Genesis 21:

> Now ye Lord visited Sarah, as he had said, and did vnto her according as he had promised.
> For Sarah conceiued, & bare Abraham a sonne in his olde age, at the same season that God tolde him.
> And Abraham called his sonnes name that was borne vnto him, which Sarah barre him, Izhak.
> Then Abraham circumcised Izhak his sonne, when he was eight daies olde as God had commanded him.
> So Abraham was an hundreth yere olde, when his sonne Izhak was borne vnto him.[8]

In these scriptures, as in the Hercules tapestry and in Andrew Melville's *natalia,* there was much of symbolic import. *For Sarah conceiued, & bare Abraham a sonne in his olde age.* The temporal application was oblique but nevertheless telling. King James had not been an avid match-maker for himself. He had displayed not much interest in yoking himself to any woman, and when the marriage to Anne of Denmark had finally been negotiated and the royal couple brought together, despite the machinations of storms in the North Sea and the curses of witches, there had intervened four dismaying years without a pregnancy. The birth of Prince Henry did seem, then, like the blessing brought to Abraham's old age. Further, Isaac symbolized in Old Testament hermeneutics a type of Christ, sent precisely at the moment the race of holy Abraham seemed destined to die without issue. Isaac was the promised son, his birth prophesied by angels, the blessed child who sprang from a womb thought barren (or, in the case of James, from loins rumored impotent) and who was at birth marked for God's work. The comparisons between Isaac and Henry were as inviting as those which linked Hercules and Henry, and the Reverend Galloway did not hesitate to conjure mightily with the persona of the Old Testament figure. Henry as a parallel to Isaac was the royal son who would pour oil on the rocks of Scotland to make them spring up soldiers for the Lord. And as with the Hercules myth, with its deeply embedded strain of anti-feminism, there was in the Isaac persona another implicit image which would characterize the conduct and direction of Henry's life: it was the child Isaac who went like a lamb to be slaughtered for God. As with every type of Christ, this end in self-sacrifice was inevitable, and this too the young Henry would absorb as he grew. Prince Henry did not consciously march toward self-immolation for the cause of reformed religion; rather, he lived by a code and according to a myth which made implicit the inevitability of martyrdom. If the logic of that final end was never conscious in Henry's mind, it was likely also unconscious in the minds of the Protestants who created the role. Having encouraged Henry to become their conquering Christ figure, they chose to focus on the idea of triumph rather than on the necessity of martyrdom. As long as Henry remained a growing prince, ever approaching his hour of destiny, there was no problem in ignoring that part of the myth which called for the shedding of the prince's blood. Thus the personation of Prince Henry grew, with those seeds present from the very beginning which were to form the key elements of his conqueror myth: his utter freedom from the softening influence of femininity and his Christ-like dedication to the causes of God. Other male parallels would join those of Hercules and Isaac; always Henry would be associated with heroic deeds and energies fed from the very font of holiness, energies sufficient to conquer monsters, raise up nations, and battle hell itself.

In this highly charged atmosphere of image-making, the celebration of Henry's birth continued. In the flat meadows beneath the towering basalt spur on which Stirling Castle perches, the king and his lords played on horseback a masque of Christians and Turks. The ladies looked on from the high battlements at the tilting of plumes and pennants, and though Henry was certainly too young to behold and understand the pageant, it too was played with a pertinent symbology. For many Protestants, whose ambitions for Henry outran the sun, the Catholic world would be only the first triumph, before the prince moved on to finish what the Crusades had left unfinished. Below on the sward the Duke of Lennox, dressed as a Turk, bit the dust symbolically before the superior Christian lance of King James.

III

The final banquet honoring Henry's baptism was replete with devices, masques, personages classical and allegorical, learned speeches, and songs fantastical, most of it of the king's own invention and most of it therefore different in tone and intent from the militant Protestant myth. The prince was present, though hardly a participant, at the highest table, to which came a dazzling progression of mechanized carts and contrivances which bore in the feast and the subsequent entertainments. One chariot was dedicated to the meaning of Henry's birth and on it rode Ceres, Fecundity, Faith, Concord, Liberality, and Perseverance,[9] a peculiar combination of old fertility symbols and new Christian virtues. This device represented most decidedly King James's own contribution to the symbology of his son's birth, and with its introduction we come to a problem about which some important distinctions must be drawn. How was it that King James's own programme for his son differed from the dominant Protestant myth? And why did the conqueror role prove a more powerful influence on Henry than the role which King James was here suggesting for his son, the bringer of fertility and abundance?

To begin, King James had never been an especial friend of militant Protestantism. To be sure, he had been reared on the strict Calvinism of George Buchanan, but he had also been reared to be jealous of his rights and prerogatives, and radical Protestantism implied a threat to the rule of magistrates, bishops, and inevitably kings. Why, then, would James stand by and allow the Puritans to pre-empt his son as their symbol? The most obvious answer is that he was simply powerless to stop the Protestant mythologizing process. He had long ago learned the futility of trying to rein in the mavericks who had inherited their blunt tongues and tough minds from John Knox. They would not compromise, so James had to learn to be somewhat adept at it. But I do not mean to suggest that James would have stopped the Protestant mythologizing of his son if he had possessed the power to do so, for likely he perceived in that process no clear threat and no encroachment. On the contrary, the universal rejoicing of Scottish Presbyterianism at Henry's birth, and the mythic forecasts of greatness for the prince, would have seemed to James like a blessing. To have suddenly focused on his household the good wishes of the entire nation was a condition to be marveled at and encouraged. Let them name his son a Hercules, an Isaac, anything they liked. The compliments were appreciated. What James did not realize, of course, was the difference behind the complimentary impulse. These Scotsmen who anointed Henry with mythic names, who called him to stand forth in borrowed robes, were trying to awaken a lion. They would eventually succeed, and by the time James perceived the danger implicit in the mythic role, both for his son and for his realm, he would indeed be too late and too powerless to turn the myth around.

At Henry's baptism, then, cause for alarm was nowhere evident in his nascent conqueror myth, although all the dichotomies were present to forecast what one day would be cause for alarm. James might have observed the dichotomy readily enough if he had known what to look for: while the king's own masques and devices for the prince's baptism celebrated fertility and abundance (the domestic virtues which carried much implication of the feminine strongly wedded to a tamed masculinity), the militant Protestants spoke only of warriors and conquerors and heroes who characteristically shattered the grain to win the battle. James was a man of peace, had dedicated his life to it, and saw in his mind's eye his own private myth as Europe's Peacemaker. It was an irony of history, however, that this man of peace should be tied to first one and then two kingdoms which were dominated by belligerence, old antipathies toward Spain, and a general dyspepsia which tended to call James's love of peace nothing more than craven fear. So while James spun out his pleasant masques of fertility to celebrate his son's christening, he did not understand the bloody thoughts which stood just behind the complimentary images of the Protestants. Had he understood them, he likely would have conducted Henry's youth far differently, for in many ways James played an unwitting ally to the forces that shaped Henry to the harsh outlines of the conqueror role.

Why did the prince become so thoroughly susceptible to the

conqueror personation while rejecting the fertility myth? We can only speculate. Perhaps the role as God's warrior simply captured his imagination more immediately and forcefully; the vagueness of an indwelling and benevolent symbol of fertility, which James dramatized for the celebrations of the baptism, must have seemed far less attractive. The conqueror myth implied movement, action, color, speed; the fertility myth involved color enough, the greens of growth rather than the reds of battle, but it also necessitated being firmly rooted, hence denying the promise of the leaping battlehorse and the charging army. Perhaps the growing prince was simply led to adopt his myth of the conqueror because of the personality and conviction of the men offering it to him. Nowhere have there existed men who spoke with more power of personal conviction than the militant Protestants of Scotland and England. They could not be ignored, and they were easy to believe because they demanded agreement. James, however, was perhaps no match as a spokesman for an alternative princely role; he was pedantic rather than convincing. But more than that, King James and those others who perhaps shared his lack of aggressive warmongering simply did not understand the necessity of presenting their programme to the prince as one side of some crucial national debate. Moderate men, loyalists and Anglo-Catholics simply did not understand that a debate was underway, that while they pictured Prince Henry in the vaguely pleasant role of the Renaissance courtier, the militant Protestants were well advanced toward the goal of turning him irrevocably into an instrument for their aggressions and their ambitions.

Thus, King James's own vision for his son as harbinger of abundance and concord, as seconder and preserver of the general peace which he as king intended to establish for Great Britain, that vision never became Prince Henry's. The king's baptismal masque might celebrate his own view of his son's future role, and the entertainments might divert the ambassadors of Europe, but Ceres and Fecundity formed images that would never touch Prince Henry's armor-clad determination to make himself Catholicism's conqueror.

IV

Out of the keen anticipation which attended Henry at his birth and baptism flowed almost ten years of childhood marked by a no less electric atmosphere of expectation, as the royal Stuarts waited to move south to the throne of England. At the heart of Henry's personation among the Scottish Presbyterians was the tacit assumption that he was born heir to England as well as to Scotland. Officially, Queen Elizabeth had no heir and steadfastly refused to name one (do not "require me in mine own life to set my winding sheet before my eyes," she declared pettishly to those who urged her, for the good of the realm, to name James as her successor), but no man in Scotland doubted that the throne belonged on Elizabeth's death to the Stuarts of Scotland, though many men in England wished it otherwise. So, the prophets intoned, Prince Henry will unite England and Scotland in a holy league of reformed religion. With this in mind, Walter Quin, a Dubliner who had become one of Henry's tutors, called Prince Henry the heir of old Britain's legendary Arthur ("Ille tibi ARTHVRI sceptrum, cum sede, parabit" [Arthur's scepter, with his throne, shall be prepared for you]);[10] a prince so armed with the mystic scepter of King Arthur could drive back the pagans from the shore, and Master Quin hardly needed to remind everyone who the pagans were. The king himself lectured his son at the age of five on the proper dignity of an heir apparent: you "shall be King of moe countries then this."[11] James meant that prediction to apply equally to himself, though he scarcely understood at that time how his little heir would want to use his share of the patrimony.

Few royal sons have been so assiduously prepared for a future role in a foreign country. Almost from the time he could walk alone, Henry's training was rigorously complete in the arts, exercises, and graces of the princely. James, who had been separated from his mother as an infant, duplicated that educational program with his son, though with quite different results. Women were soon "put from about his Highness" while James recruited "divers of good sort ... to attend upon his Person,"[12] men like Adam Newton, a classical scholar, who became Henry's chief tutor, and Sir David Murray, a poet-knight of Sir Philip Sidney's mold, who was appointed Henry's Gentleman of the Bedchamber. These two men had in hand the prince's most intimate education from the beginning. They constantly reminded Henry of the military role which stood before him, and he was pushed to excel, especially in all sorts of athletic and military exercises; he pushed himself. Between his birth and 1603 he grew quite remarkably strong and coordinated, a self-confident horseman, a skilled wielder of rapier, sword, and pike. He showed an early inclination for all the trappings of warfare, a delight which seemed at times to border on the obsessive. He enjoyed particularly standing by while cannon of all sizes were fired off. This shooting of "pieces both small and great," which the master gunners of the army took delight in performing for such an eager young prince, became such a frequent diversion for Henry that the drain on shot and powder threatened to drain the treasury as well and deplete the precious supplies. The firing of cannon was diplomatically curtailed, and Henry took solace in the warlike sounds of drum and trumpet.[13]

King James himself wrote a prescription for Henry's behavior, *Basilikon Doron, or His Majesty's Instructions to his Dearest Son,* in which he gave his version of the usual Renaissance advice on "how to become a perfite King indeede."[14] James could speak knowledgeably on that subject, not so much from the practice thereof but from his voluminous reading; he was ever capable of confusing the excursions of scholarship with reality, a contradiction destined one day to announce itself to his son's critical eye. But more ironic than James's own evident shortcomings as "a perfite King indeede" were his quite unintentional contributions to Henry's military persona. The last thing which the king would wish to encourage in his son was aggressiveness, especially of the variety praised by the pugnacious Protestants, but that is likely what James did in sum inspire with his *Basilikon Doron.* The pronounced distrust of women—though caused in the king by reasons other than a warrior's mystique of chastity— was clear in the *Basilikon* and would enter Henry's mind programmed to fit the Protestant myth of himself. This condition of almost obsessive male exclusivity had already been much fostered when James took his son out of the keeping of women and denied the boy the company of his mother. With other children the outcome of such segregation might have produced far different results, but in Prince Henry the absence of feminine influence seemed to contribute to the sort of male code of silent pain that the militant Protestants could rejoice in. The accounts and anecdotes which survive of the prince's childhood are full of the sorts of detailed incidents which become part of legend or hagiography. Once he stumbled and injured both hands severely, but though they bled, and "the smart which he felt wrung from him some teares: yet did he rise up in the meane time smyling, and as it were dissembling his hurt." Or, badly hurt on the shin, he denied any pain and soon "ran up and downe playing as before." When he was "scarcely seauen yeares of age, a boy of good courage almost a yeare older" fell "by accident to buffets with him," but the prince got the upper hand and "loued the same boy euer after the better for his courage."[15]

James said in the *Basilikon* that women of different religions were special demons for a ruling prince—"what can all these worldly respects auaile, when a man shall finde himselfe coupled with a diuel, to be one flesh with him, and the halfe marrow in his bed?"—primarily because a Catholic queen in a Protestant land bred more religious contention than royal heirs: "Disagreement in Religion bringeth euer with it ... a dissention among your subiects."[16] Though, once again, James himself was chief offender in failing to control his wife and in preventing religious dissention—Queen Anne became a practicing Catholic some time after her marriage to him and kept mass priests, to the horror of the Protestants—Prince Henry would learn the lesson the *Basilikon* taught and maintain its truth long after James would wish him to forget it.

The most important contribution which James made to Henry's developing myth, however, was surely in the matter of the king's portrait of the ideal prince: "First of all things, learne to know and loue that God, whom-to ye haue a double obligation; first, for that he made you a man; and next, for that he made you a little God to sit on his Throne, and rule ouer other men."[17] Here was the prescription for arrogance that James would have cause to rue, though likely he never blamed himself as part of his son's education in arrogance. In the passage from the *Basilikon* just quoted, the pride of manhood and the implied disdain of the feminine come just before the crowning notion of the "little God." James could not have said more to encourage in his son the assumption of the mythic role that would make him later the champion of the English Puritans, the very men who would much oppose King James while hailing his son.

Toward the end of this period of Henry's life—shortly before the death of Queen Elizabeth in 1603—King James received a notorious letter from Pope Clement VIII which, when its contents became known in Scotland and England, confirmed to the militant Protestants their conviction that Henry was indeed the conquering hero for whom they had sighed. According to the popular account, the pope had offered James "such sums of money, as might secure and establish him in the throne of England," if he would transfer the education of the prince to the wisdom of the Holy See. The pope, it appeared, wished to have "in his power so important a pledge as the Prince."[18] Though motives and effects were doubtless exaggerated by Protestants who thought of the pope as of the devil himself, Clement did indeed offer King James what appeared to be a bribe. The accepted interpretation was that even in Rome the birth and childhood of Henry had been noted and correctly analyzed as a potent future threat to the Catholic world. Pope Clement's inopportune and clumsy offer of cash to James seemed to prove the mystical role ahead of Prince Henry and served further to agitate the Protestants into training their future hero with an undiluted stream of propaganda.

V

The organization and content of Prince Henry's childhood was perhaps not unlike the education of many another royal heir—except in the complete exclusion of women from the process—but the outcome was uniquely and intensely a triumph for the single-minded myth. The boy was denied a domestic life, with its contours of both father and mother; he was led, rather, down the lone road toward his conqueror role. James believed the boy his own possession; Queen Anne fought for her mother's rights and seemed for a time to win them; she thought Henry belonged to her. But the truth would become clear enough by 1603 that Prince Henry belonged to neither father or mother, had forgotten perhaps how to love them, for he was son by that time of a much more demanding and exciting parent, his own myth of the conqueror. The year of Queen Elizabeth's death was the year when he would step out before the world's eye, almost ten years old but far older in terms of self-assurance and bearing and purpose. King James would be too preoccupied with his own assumption of the English throne to notice fully that a second light destined to rival his own had also arrived with him in England. Perhaps Queen Anne alone, only recently reunited with the son so long denied her presence, realized that nine years of education in the royal nursery had changed her infant son into a prematurely serious knight set already on a holy quest. The relationship between King James and Queen Anne in Scotland, the emotional storms which constantly broke and which were usually bred out of rivalry for the possession of Prince Henry—the very lack of a normal domestic setting in which the boy might grow up—ought to have produced woeful effects in a child Henry's age. But the fact was that Henry was insulated by his myth from the disruptions his parents caused; already the prince had begun to separate—or rather make indistinguishable—his private life and the life of his myth. He would, for example, bring to his own later life and character an iron grip of self-control, so unlike both his parents. To understand fully the contrast between Henry and his mother and father, and to appreciate his first, tentative exercise of youthful power, we must examine more fully the relationship between James and Anne and Henry as the pivotal year 1603 approached.

James, the proud but increasingly baffled father, sought companionship all his life, the society of like-minded men who hunted the day in close, sweaty comradeship and watched the night through the philosophical haze of good wine. There were always those he could purchase to stand by him in the uneasy hours and those multitudes who trailed after and beat down the grain in their eagerness to be with him on the hunt, but the few loyal and trusted friends who loved him for his own sake were difficult to find, even more difficult to keep. He could have hoped for nothing more sublime than that Henry, son of his own loins, would be one of those who loved unsolicited. It was not to be. The strategies devised by the militant Protestants to turn the prince into a national symbol also turned the little hero a few more degrees away from the ordinary, more mundane objects of affection.

James did his best to set himself up in his son's eyes as sole authority and sole parent. Anne of Denmark was, of course, the indignant and frequently hysterical victim of the king's anti-female policy. She was a friendless alien in a cold land. Her temperament was anything but thoughtful, and Scotland offered so few diversions. She found herself marooned in a rocky desert where the club of males which gathered about her husband excluded her from both the beerhall revelry and the pedantic discussions. Unable to establish herself through witty discourse or ornamental attendance at the drinking bouts or learned debates, she took the only other direction which her limited intelligence told her might serve. She became pettish, she hatched pathetic little plots, she coquetted with lairds out of favor, she threw tantrums. Until the birth of her first son, she had not imagined she could enjoy any identity within the state other than the center of disquiet, but Henry had suddenly flooded her life with attention and love. King James made quick work, however, to end her brief aura of importance.

James had no understanding of nor appreciation for women; he bred his royal progeny by necessity from the womb of one of that sex, but he was enough of a scholar to know that philosophical opinion ran heavily against women as creatures of more than utilitarian purpose. They were silly and mindless, full of the humorous miasma which made right reason a foreigner to their brains and which could, indeed, infect the rationality of reasonable men, should they wander unaneled into the influence of those sirens. He pronounced his summation about women for Prince Henry in the *Basilikon:* they were "beautie without bountie, wealth without wisdome, and great friendship without grace and honestie . . . the deceitfull masques of infinite miseries."[19] Clearly, the keeping and education of the future hope of Scotland and England could not be entrusted to a woman, especially one who so unfortunately justified the king in his negative attitude. So almost immediately after his baptism, Henry had been taken away from Queen Anne and placed into the custody of the Earl of Mar. Just as suddenly as she had found a new identity with the birth of her son, Queen Anne had lost it, or rather had it ripped from her, and the Earl of Mar was quite thorough in keeping the letter of James's law.

She became an indefatigable intriguer, working her plots against Mar with whatever broken driftwood the currents of the court cast within her grasp. Around the time of Henry's first birthday, she began in earnest her petitions to James, coupled with maneuvers to discredit Mar. The diplomatic dispatches between Scotland and England during the months of March, April, May, June, and July of 1595 alluded repeatedly to Queen Anne's battle.[20] Her pressure on the king for custody of her son was reported as constant, but no more constant than James's adamant, and by now reinforced, resolve that he had made the correct decision in removing Henry from Anne's company and keeping. The doors of Stirling Castle, where Henry was kept, were tightened against her. On July 12, 1595, a dispatch mentioned that the queen was "something crazed" in her frustration. One day later, one of the Earl of Mar's servants was murdered mysteriously, and suspicions encircled the queen. Obviously, the domestic war had come to threaten the tranquility of the state, and James, always sensitive to threats of violence, took stronger measures to quell his wife. The king wrote to the Earl of Mar, making it clear that his custody of Prince Henry was not only to be considered a permanent arrangement; it was also to be looked upon as a matter of state security:

> Milorde of Mar. Because in the suretie of my sonne con-
> sistis my suretie and that I have concreditid unto you
> the chairge of his keiping upon the trust I have of youre
> honestie, this present thairfore sall be ane warrande unto
> you not to delyver him out of youre handis except I
> commande you with my awin mouth, and being in sikke
> cumpanie as I my self sall best lyke of, otheruayes not
> to delyver him for any chairge or message that can cum
> from me. And in kayce God call me at any tyme that
> nather for Quene nor Estaites pleasure ye delyver
> him. . . .[21]

The finality of that letter did for a time wither Anne's spirit. James took some pity on her, wished her to know that within his love (such as it was) she had wide latitude to gambol and play, but matters of state were not her province, and the welfare of the prince was most certainly a matter of state. During the autumn following the conflagration of July, Queen Anne became pregnant again. A reassuring, though thin, contentment settled over the royal household.

The next child born to Anne was a daughter, Elizabeth, and a second girl and two boys (one of whom survived and was named Charles) followed that daughter, but the nagging hurt over Henry would not go away. Again in the spring of 1600 Anne renewed her petitions for the custody of Henry, now six years old, but she subsided again almost as quickly, as she came full term with her third pregnancy (this one Prince Charles). Anne's relationship with James now seemed dangerously unstable, and she was able increasingly to draw the king into the troughs and crests of her waterish personality. On October 28, 1600, an observer at court reported a "strange kindness" between the king and queen, yet three days later "high words" were passing between them. News of all this inevitably reached England, where men gossiped over the domestic trials of the Scotsman who was surely marked by destiny to be the next King of England. John Chamberlain wrote to Dudley Carleton on December 22: "The Scottish king hath another sonne; we listen still for newes from thence as yf there were some tempest abrewing."[22]

In January, 1602, Anne gave birth to a third son, Duke Robert, and pathetically engulfed the whole court in her anxiety that he too would be snatched from her like the others. (Charles, like Henry, had been placed under the sole custody of a trusted lord as soon as convenient after his birth.) In her anticipation of the inevitable she reopened the old wound of Henry's sequestration, but then the infant boy, Duke Robert, died in June. One way or another the fates seemed arrayed against her. Cruelly, the hand of husband or the hand of God seemed always ready to reach out and separate this woman from her children. As late as February 28, 1603, only a month before Queen Elizabeth's death, John Chamberlain wrote to Dudley Carleton news of the continuing strife between Anne and James: "New troubles arise dayly in Scotland, but the worst of all is the domesticall daungers and hartbreaking that the Kinge findes in his owne house."[23]

The long awaited death of Queen Elizabeth in March of 1603 seemed in the whirl of activity to give Queen Anne the occasion and opportunity to be reunited with her children—especially with Prince Henry—while King James began his progress south to take possession of his throne. In this fortuitous break in the regimen of the king's isolation of Henry, the boy himself was to be the chief instrument of his liberation. He would call his mother to come to him, whether out of some surviving fragment of childhood memory or out of a genuine residue of affection, or perhaps more likely out of a rather disinterested curiosity about his mother and about his own ability to command.

James departed for his new throne in England on April 5, leaving his queen and his children behind in Scotland to follow him presently when he should summon. With him went the chief Scottish lords, among them the Earl of Mar, who left Prince Henry in the custody of his family and retainers. Before leaving Scottish soil, King James thought it fitting to admonish his son rather sternly about his behavior in the months to come. He first apologized to Henry: "That I see you not before my pairting, impute it to this greate occasion, quhairin tyme is so precious." But the king was not in such a hurry that he failed to warn Henry no less than three times in the course of his letter to be "not insolent," suggesting that arrogance had indeed become the prince's most distinguishing trait: "Lett not this news make you proude or insolent. For a Kings sonne and heire was ye before, and na maire are ye yett. . . . Be therefore merrie, but not insolent. Keepe a greatness, but *sine fastu*. Be resolute, but not willfull."[24]

Almost immediately the prince sat down and wrote to his

mother, an act of presumption if not of arrogance, for as he wrote he knew he was violating the king's express commission given to the Earl of Mar. The prince's letter to his mother (transcribed below; see facsimile, Fig. 1) certainly mentioned "great greif and displeasure" at being so long denied her presence. But how are we to interpret Henry's groping communication? It may be indeed a testament to deep and abiding love, an anguished cry of a child for his mother. This is surely how Anne interpreted the letter. But her first impression, like ours, may have been subject to a set of assumptions and expectations somewhat irrelevant for a prince who had by this time put aside much of his childhood for the sake of an adult role. I am inclined to see in the letter more curiosity than poignant love, more a childish exploration of forbidden perimeters, now that the authority figure was conveniently on his way to England. The fact that Queen Anne's emotional reunion with her son, prompted by this very letter, produced no enduring relationship between mother and son suggests that Henry's impulse in writing was rather seriously misinterpreted by a mother who had been starved for love and recognition.

> Madame and most honoured Mother my humble seruice remembred, having occasion to wryte to ye Kings Maiestie my father by this accident quhich hes fallin out of lait, I thoght it became me of my dewtie <to wryte> by writt also to congratulat vnto yor Ma: the happy succes of that great turne almost aboue mens expectation. The q^{ch} I besech God to blesse in the proceedings as he hes done <w^t> in ye beginning, to the gretter increasse of your Ma:^{ties} honour and contentment. And seing by his Ma:^{teis} departing I will lose that benefite q^{ch} I had by his frequent visitation, I mon humblie request yor Ma/ to supplie that inlaik by yor presence, quhich I have <cause greatter> the more iust causse to crave, that I haue wanted it so lang to my great greif and displeasure, to the end that yor Ma. by sight may have <q^{ch}> as I hope the gritter mater to love ^{me}/and I lykewyse may be encouraged to go forduart in well doing and to honour yor ma/ with all dew reuerence as apperteins to me quho is
>
> Yo^r Ma most obedient and
> duetifull sone
> Henry[25]

Queen Anne scarcely needed the inducement. She hurried to Stirling Castle, hoping to find the defenses down and penetrable now that its ruling earl had gone south with the king. But at Stirling, Anne encountered an even more implacable foe, the dowager Countess of Mar, the earl's redoubtable mother. She would not budge; she had the king's commission, she said, not to deliver Henry, *nather for Quene nor Estaites pleasure,* and indeed she had that commission in writing under the king's own hand. So close to her goal and yet affronted once again, Anne fell into a rage and then into a fever. At the time of her siege of Stirling she was once again pregnant, and those at the castle, fearing the outcome and their own parts in any subsequent royal wrath, sent riders posthaste to overtake the king and his party. The Earl of Mar was subsequently sent back into Scotland to placate the queen and turn her aside from her desire, as she had in the past been so often turned aside. But Anne clung to the volcanic rock of Stirling; the sight of her old enemy Mar and the sound of the pledges and denials brought from the king's own lips only drove her more into her rage. According to one report, Anne flew into a fury, cursed the king and his ministers, "and four months gone with child as she was, she beat her own belly."[26] The company at Stirling, accustomed as they were to Anne's histrionics, had seen nothing like this. She vowed that if James denied her the keeping of her son, then by the God of the High Kirk she would deny the life of his brat now within her womb. The fearful speeches were nothing to the sequent events: Anne miscarried the child and lay, all thought, at the point of death herself. Riders were sent posthaste once again to inform the king, and he puzzled over the innovations of this determined woman. England beckoned him on, yet behind him squalled a storm which had boiled down on him along the Great North Road. Wearily he sent the Duke of Lennox back to Stirling with the royal decision: the war was at an end. Queen Anne could take possession of her prize.

James wrote a letter to Anne on this occasion which was a mixture of complaints, stern warnings, whining excuses, defense of himself and of the Earl of Mar, and above all, an admonition that Anne owed both James and Henry the respect of queenly deportment. "And thairfore," James wrote, " I say over againe leave these womanlie aprehensions, for I thanke God I carrie that love and respecte unto you quhiche be the law of God and nature I ought to do to

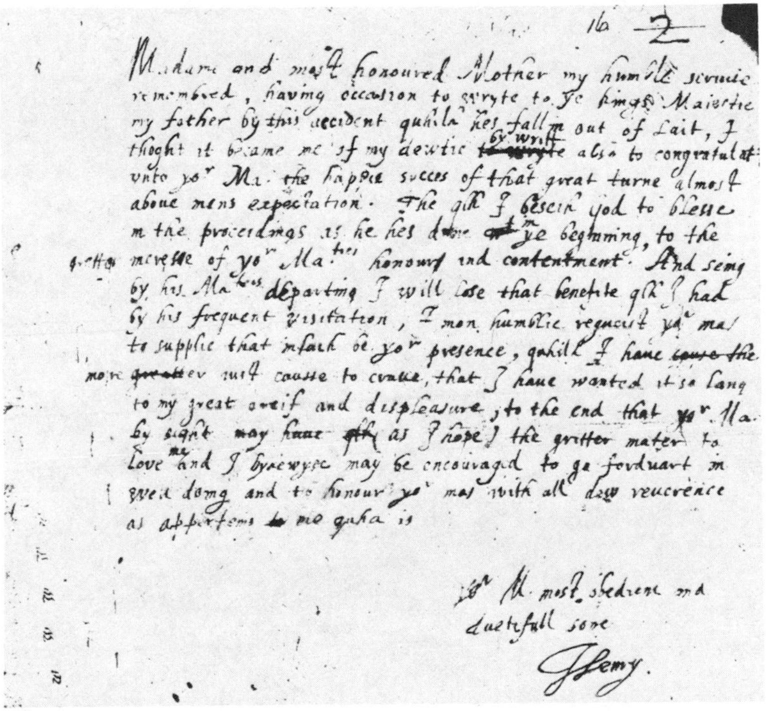

16

Madame and most honoured Mother my humble service
remembred, having occasion to wryte to ye kings Maiestie
my father by this accident quhilk hes fallin out of Lait, I
thoght it became me of my dewtie by writt also to congratulat
unto yor Ma the happie succes of that great turne almost
above mens expectation. The quhilk I besech God to blesse
in the proceedings as he hes done in ye beginning, to the
greater increase of yor Maties honour and contentment. And seing
by his Maties departing I will lose that benefite quhilk I had
by his frequent visitation, I man humblie request yor Ma
to supplie that insafar be yor presence, quhilk I have
more ever will cause to crave, that I have wanted it so lang
to my great greif and displeasure, to the end that yor Ma
by sight may have (as I hope) the gritter mater to
love me and I lykewyse may be encouraged to go fordwart in
weill doing and to honour yor Ma with all dew reverence
as appertenis to me quha is

Yor M. most obedient and
duetifull sone
Henry.

Figure 1. Henry's manuscript letter to his mother. Harleian MS. 7007, fol. 16. Reproduced by permission of the British Library Board.

my wyfe and mother of my children. . . .'' But then he closed his letter snappishly: "As for youre dooleweede wearing it is utterlie impertinent at this time."[27] The queen's "dole-weeds," her mourning blacks donned to mark her miscarriage during the siege of Stirling, did indeed suggest a temperament somewhat too theatrical. James was concerned about wooing the English in every way; his queen might too easily become a spectacle rather than part of his pageant. James was also worried about his son and heir now in the company of the queen, but there was no cause for worry on that score.

Miraculously, the queen recovered her strength within a month, put off her blacks, and was ready to travel south with her son by her side. In many ways the progress south for mother and son was more triumphant than the king's own journey. Henry seemed to inspire an equally intense reaction among the people; he was England's first Prince of Wales in more than fifty years and no less the center of hope than he had been to the Scots. This was his first time on public display, and as the waves of adulation broke before him, he had the first real indication that the prophecies made in his name were in fact true. A prince so welcomed must perforce be some sort of savior.

Anne, finally coming into a kingdom which knew how to entertain a queen, could feel that half the interest bestowed on Henry belonged to her. But apparently the expected happiness of mother and son reunited at long last proved especially ephemeral. Within a month of their arrival in England, a great cooling off was noted between Anne and Henry. The Venetian ambassador observed on August 27: "The Queen has received a large number of valuable jewels from the King, the palace of Nonsuch, and an income of forty thousand crowns a year, they say, so that should she be left a widow, she will be independent of her son."[28] Anne apparently learned enough about Henry on their trip into England to realize that the normal affections of his childhood had been alchemized into other energies. This disappointment was more easily overcome, however, than had been the original separation in the bleak fastnesses of Scotland. She was soon dancing and masquing and entertaining from her purse the finest poets in England, building a reputation among Prince Henry's admirers for frivolousness and the expensive entertainments which Scottish frugality had denied her.

VI

More important than anything else that accompanied Prince Henry into England in 1603 was his myth of the conqueror. The Scots poets bade farewell to their Hercules, their Achilles, their Alexander and Caesar, and lectured England concerning the anointed presence that was coming. Significantly perhaps, Sir Thomas Craig, after holding up the conquerors of the past as examples for Prince Henry to imitate in his new kingdom of England, advised Henry in Latin verses that he should seek the hearts and loves of his subjects rather than arouse their fears.[29] How the prince was supposed to personate the gods and demigods of war without simultaneously rousing apprehension and anxiety, Sir Thomas did not explain.

But fears for what this growing prince might undertake in the name of a godly crusade against Catholicism seemed hardly justified in the spring of 1603. Indeed, the logical consequence of the adulation seemed never to have been recognized. The warrior persona had preceded Henry into England where the poets there picked it up as innocent praise. Some of those who immediately contributed to the myth of the conqueror would later see their mistake and would considerably alter their manner of speaking to and about Henry. One such was Ben Jonson, himself a Catholic and no warmongerer. He found, however, that the form and substance of any address to Prince Henry had already developed a curiously rigid formula. In his entertainment written for the reception of the queen and the prince at Althorp, Jonson tagged on the requisite compliments to Henry, dressing them in the prescribed garb of the military myth:

> Shine bright and fixed as the Artick starre:
> And when slow Time hath made you fit for warre,
> Looke ouer the strict Ocean, and thinke where
> You may but lead vs forth, that grow vp here
> Against a day, when our officious swords
> Shall speake our action better then our words.[30]

Jonson added these rather stiff lines to a masque-like entertainment which featured Queen Mab, her fairies and satyres, the entire green world of English countryside. That the address to Prince Henry should stand completely divorced from the world of fertility was symbolic. Jonson was correct in sensing in the prince an aura which simply would not blend well with the poet's vision of nature and benevolent spirits. Here Jonson was content to write his poetic tribute to the prince as a separate appendage, but later, when Jonson fully understood the unhealthy direction of the prince's conqueror myth, he would make an effort to integrate Henry into the green world in order to suggest that the warrior persona should be replaced with the mask of fertility and abundance. But Jonson's change in attitude would come too late to produce a corresponding change in Henry. The prince's course had been fixed even before he came to Althorp.

And he was helped along that path by scores of writers who, unlike Jonson, found nothing in the conqueror myth to doubt. On the assumption that Henry's function for reformed religion would be carried forward by flame and sword, his arrival in England was greeted most characteristically by religious and controversialist tracts which burned with the same anticipation which had structured Henry's myth among the Scots. Books like the English translation of Philippe de Mornay's *A worke concerning the truenesse of Christian religion*, which bore a pious dedication by the publisher Thomas Wilcocks, and Thomas Winter's translation of the French Huguenot Du Bartas' *Third Dayes creation*, testified well to the wholesale adoption of Henry by the English Puritan community. Wilcocks looked to Henry as to one made "chiefly for the Churches, good."[31] These characteristic volumes with their intense prefaces addressed to the prince were more than just the ordinary flattery or the indiscriminating search for a beneficent patron. They spoke for a large body of co-religionists and expressed their collective hopes which were placed in Henry, thus extending and enlarging the mythic role which had begun in Scotland. With the strictly religious writers there joined their natural allies, soldiers and veterans of the Spanish wars, in preaching the necessity of a holy crusade against Catholic Europe. Barnaby Rich, for example, expressed a wish parallel to the hopes of the Puritan preachers that Henry would resurrect the military might of England while awakening her spiritual zeal.[32] Thus the religious and the warlike united to forge more links in the chain of Henry's myth.

Notes to Chapter 1

1. David Moysie, *Memoirs of the Affairs of Scotland*, ed. James Dennistoun (Edinburgh: Bannatyne Club, 1830), 113.

2. *A True Report of the Baptisme of Henry Fredericke, Prince of Wales* (London, 1603), sig. [B 4]. An inventory of James V of Scot-

land lists "7 Stikkis of tapessarie of antik work of the histories of Venus, Pallas, Hercules, Mars, Bachus, and the Moder of the Erd." It was perhaps one of these tapestries that was used at the time of Henry's baptism. See Edmund Spenser, *Works,* variorum ed. by Greenlaw, Osgood, and Padelford (Baltimore, 1932-49), III, 397.

3. See Eugene M. Waith, *The Herculean Hero* (New York, 1962), *passim;* Edmund Spenser, *Works,* variorum ed., V, 162; DeWitt T. Starnes and Ernest W. Talbert, *Classical Myth and Legend in Renaissance Dictionaries* (Chapel Hill, 1955), *passim.*

4. Book V, Canto I, stanza ii.

5. Andrew Melville, *Principis Scoti-Britannorum natalia*(Edinburgh, 1594), sig. 2^V:

> . . . fastu donec Iberico
> Latè subacto sub pedibus premas,
> Clarus triumpho delibuti
> Geronis, triplicem tiaram,
> Qua nunc revinctus tempora Cerberus
> Romanus atra conduplicat face
> De rupe Tarpeia fragores
> Tartareos tonitru tremendo: . . .

English translation by Barbara N. Lindsay. See B. N. Lindsay and J.W. Williamson, "Myth of the Conqueror: Prince Henry Stuart and Protestant Militancy," *Journal of Medieval and Renaissance Studies,* 5(1975), 203-222.

6. For the political maneuvers occasioned by Henry's birth and the series of delays in the christening, see Thomas Birch, *The Life of Henry, Prince of Wales* (London, 1760), 3 ff; *A True Reportarie;* and the relevant dates in *Calendar of State Papers Relating to Scotland* (London, 1858), II (1589-1603).

7. *Letters to King James the Sixth* (Edinburgh: Maitland Club, 1835).

8. Here and throughout, all biblical quotations are from the Geneva Bible, 1560.

9. Described in *A True Report,* sigs. C 3^V-[D 3].

10. Walter Quin, *Sertvm poeticum, in honorem Iacobi sexti* (Edinburgh, 1600), sig. B 4^V.

11. *Basilikon Doron,* in *The Political Works of James I,* ed. Charles Howard McIlwain (Cambridge: Harvard University Press, 1918), 28.

12. Sir Charles Cornwallis, *The life and death of our late most incomparable and heroique prince, Henry prince of Wales* (London, 1641), sigs. A 6-A 6^V. These details and others of his youth are sum-

marized by Elkin Calhoun Wilson, *Prince Henry and English Litera-*
ture (Ithaca, 1946), 5-7, 11-12.

13. Details drawn from Cornwallis; Birch; W. H., *The true pic-*
ture and relation of Prince Henry (Leyden, 1634); and *The Autobi-*
ography of Phineas Pett, ed. W. G. Perrin, *Publications of the Navy*
Records Society, vol. 51 (London, 1918).

14. From the dedicatory sonnet attached to the 1599 edition
of the *Basilikon*.

15. Drawn from W. H., *The true picture and relation of Prince*
Henry, sigs. A 3-A 3^V, quoted by E. C. Wilson, 11-12.

16. *Basilikon*, ed. McIlwain, 35.

17. *Ibid.*, 12.

18. Birch, 22.

19. *Basilikon*, 35.

20. See especially *C.S.P., Scotland*, II (1589-1603), *passim*.

21. *Report on the Manuscripts of the Earl of Mar and Kellie*,
Historical Manuscripts Commission (London, 1904), 43-44.

22. *The Letters of John Chamberlain*, ed. Norman E. McClure,
Memoirs of the American Philosophical Society (Philadelphia, 1939),
I, 113.

23. *Ibid.*, I, 187.

24. The letter is printed in Edward Edwards, *The Lives of the*
Founders of the British Museum (London, 1870), I, 157-158; and
with differences in Birch, 25-26.

25. Harleian MS. 7007, fol. 16. I have indicated Henry's cancellations with broken brackets.

26. *Calendar of State Papers and Manuscripts, Relating to Eng-*
lish Affairs, Existing in the Archives and Collections of Venice (London, 1900), X (1603-1607), par. 66. Birch deals with Anne's assault
on Stirling Castle, 29-30.

27. *Hist. MSS. Comm. E. of Mar*, x. A letter from Anne to
James prior to her success in obtaining Henry is printed in *Letters to*
James the Sixth. It is hastily written, with many cancellations and
inter-lineations.

28. *C.S.P., Venetian*, X (1603-1607), par. 118.

29. Sir Thomas Craig, *Ad serenissimum Britanniarum principem*
Henricum (Edinburgh, 1603), summarized by E. C. Wilson, 15 n.

30. *Ben Jonson*, ed. C. H. Herford, Percy Simpson, and Evelyn
Simpson (Oxford, 1941), VII, 131.

31. Philippe de Mornay, *A worke concerning the trueness of*
Christian religion, trans. Sir Philip Sidney and Arthur Golding (Lon-
don, 1604), sig. A 4^V. See also the dedications in Guillaume de
Saluste du Bartas, *The third dayes creation*, trans. Thomas Winter

(London, 1604); Saluste du Bartas, *Bartas: his deuine weekes and works*, trans. Joshua Sylvester (London, 1605); and Gui Du Faur, Seigneur de Pibrac, *Tetrastica. Or, the quadrains of Guy de Faur*, trans. J. Sylvester (London, 1605); Hugh Broughton, *Familia Davidis* (Amsterdam, 1605), *A Comment vpon Coheleth or Ecclesiastes* (London, 1605), and *A replie vpon the R.R.F.Th. Winton for heads of his divinity in his sermon and survey* (Amsterdam, 1605); Henoch Clapham, *Doctor Andros his prosopopeia answered, for removing of Catholike scandale* (Middelburg, 1605).

32. Barnaby Rich, *A souldiers wishe to Britons welfare* (London, 1604) and *The fruites of long experience* [Part 2 of *A souldiers wishe*] (London, 1604).

The Myth
Comes to England

I

Within two months of his arrival in England, Prince Henry was invested with the Order of the Garter, and despite his youth he bore himself with a grace and dignity which the English thought altogether fitting for their highest ceremony of knighthood. He was commended for his "quick witty answers, princely carriage, and reverend obeisance at the altar,"[1] all of which let the councillors of England know that in Henry they had found a future king of great promise, and incidentally, a quite startling contrast to the royal Stuart who was in fact the king. James was, in his new English kingdom, a puzzled virtuoso of gaffes, missed cues, offending speeches and gestures, and unsavory language and habits; by contrast the son, young Henry, was a gazelle. "I have visited the Princes at Oatlands," wrote the Venetian Ambassador, Scaramelli, to his principals in Venice a month after the ceremony of the Garter: "The Prince is ten years old [he was actually nine], little of body, and quick of spirit. He is ceremonious beyond his years, and with great gravity he covered and bade me be covered. Through an interpreter he gave me a long discourse on his exercises, dancing, tennis, the chase."[2]

A leading court painter, Robert Peake, was engaged that summer and brought down to Oatlands south of London to paint Henry's first official portrait. Peake apparently sensed in his young sitter a revolutionary fervor; the old Elizabethan style of portraiture—lifeless, immobile faces trapped in airless interiors—obviously would not do in capturing the spirit and assurance which radiated from this royal boy. Obvious also was the need for some grander symbology to mark the occasion of Henry's coming, so Peake devised an innovative pro-

gramme for his portrait of the prince (see Fig. 2). Instead of a suffocating interior, Peake drew on the pastoral setting of the Oatlands
palace and placed his prince outdoors, engaged in the symbolic hunt
for the stag—the first royal hunting portrait in the history of English
painting. The painting spoke a rich symbolic language, but probably
the most immediately accessible symbolism—and probably the first
which would suggest itself to the seventeenth-century viewers of the
painting—was the sacramental initiation of the hero.[3] The stag was
universally associated in the Renaissance mind with the panting and
thirsting of the soul after righteousness, so that the hunt for the stag
—especially by a royal or saintly figure—was understood as a first
step toward holiness or triumph. Significantly, Peake added to the
background of his painting several other deer which ran in a distant
meadow that was connected to the foreground by a path and a
bridge over a stream. Presumably, Prince Henry, having won his
first sacramental honors (the loving conquest of his new Kingdom of
England) would go forth to a succession of royal "hunts." His holy
destiny beckoned from the distance.

The sword which the prince held unsheathed also carried quite
traditional associations with Truth and Justice; to the Protestants,
especially, the sword was symbolic of St. Paul's Christian "spirit,"
which came directly from the Word of God: "And take the helmet
of saluation, and the sworde of ye Spirit, which is the worde of
God" (Eph. 6.17). Around his neck Henry wore the George medallion (see Fig. 3, detail) which represented in jewelled relief St.
George riding down the dragon. The legend was ancient, the Christian symbology well established: St George was the Holy Church
triumphant over paganism. But at least since the days of Edmund
Spenser, who had made great use of St. George in the *Faerie Queene,*
there was readily available a Protestant interpretation of the symbol:
St. George was the Reformed Religion driving its lance down the
throat of Roman Catholicism.[4] In one sense at least Prince Henry,
in Peake's portrait, stood over the slain stag and duplicated the
action of the George medallion. Admittedly, this interpretation
gives the sacramental aura of the painting a slightly strident edge,
but Peake seems to have deliberately sought the intensification in
the way he personified Henry himself: the stance of the legs, placed
wide apart, and the old-fashioned bonnet were visual echoes of the

Figure 2. Painting by Robert Peake, the Elder, dated 1603, showing Henry and Sir John Harington. The Metropolitan Museum of Art. Purchase, 1944, Joseph Pulitzer Bequest.

Figure 3. Detail of Figure 2.

well-known paintings of Henry VIII. Here in this boy named Henry, the painter seemed to have discovered the spirit and presence of an earlier Henry; young Prince Henry was Protestantism's new *Fidei Restitutor.* This personation of the prince had its own logic: the boy had, after all, been given his Tudor name as a compliment to Queen Elizabeth. Henry VIII had been responsible for beginning the Protestant Reformation in England; Prince Henry, it was hoped, would carry on that Reformation within the Church of England, which many Puritans found still too wedded to the idolatry of Rome. As a popular jingle of the day expressed it,

> Henry the Eighth pulled down monks and their cells,
> Henry the Ninth should pull down Bishops and their bells.

Peake's portrait of Henry gave the country a boy in the brisk garb of the quintessential Protestant hero. He was taking his first steps toward the fulfillment of his destiny, and characteristically those first steps had more to do with personations and symbols than with practicalities or real action.

As it happened, the quintessential Protestant hero portrayed in Peake's painting was all too quickly available for use in the balance against what seemed to be King James's weak attraction for Catholic nations, especially Spain. While Henry was being proclaimed the future conqueror of Spain, James was setting in motion the diplomacy necessary to bring about a peace treaty with that country. This proposed treaty was met with unrelenting scorn from the commonalty. It was known, for example, that several of the powerful lords who sought this unpopular peace were secret Catholics; Henry Howard, Earl of Northampton was prominent among them. The peace party's goal seemed at best craven and at worst treacherous. King James was thought to be nothing more than an unmanly dupe: "It is sayd our King is proclaymed nowe Duke of Gelderland."[5] When the king sent the Earl of Nottingham to Spain with a large retinue in 1604 to ratify the peace treaty, the public streets in London were filled with irreverent, witty, and angry broadsides and ballads which satirized the Spaniards and their friends in England. It was popularly said that "there went sixty fools into Spain" to lead England the way to perdition. By the time the treaty was concluded, a firm anti-Spanish faction had coalesced in Parliament. Whoever the leaders of the war party may have been, Prince Henry became its symbolic head. The

prince at least represented a military dream that would not compromise itself for the sake of a demeaning peace.

II

Portrayed with Prince Henry in Robert Peake's painting had
been John Harington, one of the many young men of good breeding
who were "sent to school" as Henry's noble companions. Another,
the twelve-year-old Earl of Essex, freshly restored to the title which
his vain and rash father had lost to the headsman's axe in the waning
years of Elizabeth's reign, was taken from the company of his mother
(who had disgraced herself in the eyes of the country by marrying for
the third time) by order of the king himself, to be brought up with
Prince Henry.[6] Both John Harington and the young earl subsequently became Henry's bosom friends, his co-conspirators in the
dreams of glory. But there were more noble sons, many more, and
ambassadors from the courts of Spain, France, Holland, and from
the dukedoms of Italy, who paid their respects and presented their
credentials to Prince Henry as second only to his father as a center
of interest in English affairs. And Henry's household grew accordingly. On the 20th of July, 1603, when Oatlands was first established as Henry's residence, the Treasurer of the Household listed a
total of seventy servants—twenty-two above stairs, forty-eight below.
That number was increased twice more before the end of the year to
reach a total of 141 men and women serving the combined needs
and swelling glory of Henry's "collegiate court."[7]

Sir Charles Cornwallis, Prince Henry's Treasurer, has left us a
description of Henry's deportment during those early months as he
gathered about him the vanguard of English youth and nobility.[8]
According to Cornwallis, whose religious piety and official post as
treasurer combined to make him interested in all sorts of economy,
Prince Henry always displayed a most fitting concern for time well
used in the service of God. In the prince's "apting himselfe to the
office he was born unto," a sense of religious duty prevailed, clearly
because his princely role was indistinguishable from the highest service to God. He read histories to learn the manner and form of proper
civil government, but he studied with more keen interest the sciences
thought necessary for military governance and the prosecution of
war—mathematics, cosmography, "the matter and forme of fortifications." Pure bookish theory, however, never displaced the prince's

passion for "necessary exercises and recreations," so that the entire
day was filled with the most intense activity, "as no part of it could
be said to be in vaine bestowed." He loved in particular horses,
"great horses" whose mettle and spirit became inevitably tests of his
own growing strength and resolve. This passion for riding was noted
by the foreign ambassadors who visited Henry, and soon kings and
dukes were sending to England their gifts of Barbary stallions and
other fine specimens. The prince's stables became perhaps the "most
excellently furnished" in England. He and his aristocratic companions kept alive a spirit of chivalrous combat and achievement by
practicing all the popular forms of jousting play, like running at the
ring and tilting. In these forms of mock warfare, Henry excelled, for
he was, in his myth at least, to the manner born. Cornwallis said that
in the military exercises, even in "his first years, he became second
to no prince in Christendome, and to many that practised with him
much superiour." Every man who saw him, every old soldier who
heard of him, every preacher in the pulpit who needed an *exem-
plum* of Christian courage and duty—for these, Prince Henry became a lively and comely symbol of advancing destiny.

Treasurer Cornwallis noted in him what amounted to almost an
avariciousness for testing the limits of his ability: "He loved and did
mightily strive to doe somewhat of every thing, and to excell in the
most excellent." He delighted in rare inventions and in "all kind of
engines belonging to the warres, both by sea and land." He continued his interest "in shooting and levelling of great peeces of ordnance" and in the "ordering and marshalling of arms." So strongly
pronounced in his activities and studies were the themes of warfare,
however, that perhaps even Cornwallis worried that his master might
seem a bit lopsided, even among Renaissance men who had always
emphasized battle as the last and best test of a man's mettle. Cornwallis took pains to introduce into his portrait of Henry the assurance that the prince studied also the gentler arts, like gardening and
building and music and "limning." This last interest, together with
painting, did indeed become an important part of Henry's educational pattern: "he greatly delighted . . . in all sorts of excellent and
rare pictures, which he had brought him from all countries." But his
avid interest in art was not so much a product of his own attempts at
drawing and painting, but rather a quickly developed understanding
of what art could do in personating a man, figuring him forth in the
eyes of beholders as timeless and as almost divine. Peake's hunting
portrait of Henry was perhaps the first lesson the prince had encoun-

tered in the powers of art to translate into visual terms the inner myth by which a man lived. In this, art too was worthy a young man who shared his purposes with the Deity.

Rarely had such a young boy managed to surround himself so with the odor of masculinity. Push of pike and leap of horse—together with all the other trappings of burgeoning manhood—were conventional enough, of course, in the education of any royal prince during the Renaissance. What gave Prince Henry's court in England its extra measure of vitality was the prince's obvious commitment to his own myth. The courtiers of Elizabeth's reign (to draw a convenient comparison) may have postured and declaimed heroically, but always their roles were recognized as just that—roles. Occasionally, the heroic personation undertaken by an Elizabethan courtier, as in the case of Sir Walter Ralegh, came to be indistinguishable from the real man underneath,[9] but generally, symbolic masks were not allowed to become subcutaneous. In the case of Prince Henry, however, it was consistently the case that the boy could not distinguish between the fiction of poetry or paint and the less exalted realities of the adult world. Henry's mind was as mythologized as was his image among the Scots and the English; he believed fervently that the symbols were made flesh in him, that in him the hand of God had made incarnate His truth and justice.

A prince thus aflame was bound to draw comment. Cornwallis could not help making explicit his concern that there was frequently too much intensity in Henry's daily round. The variety of activities suggested some of the intensity: "His other exercises were dancing, leaping, and in times of yeare fit for it learning to swimme, at sometimes walking fast and farre, to accustome and enable himselfe to make a long march when time should require it. . . ." But in some forms of exercise, especially competitive sports, Henry seemed almost dangerously driven. Tennis was Cornwallis's example: "he neither observed moderation, nor what appertained to his dignity and person, continuing his play for the space of three or foure houres, and the same in his shirt. . . ."[10]

Moderation in the affairs of courage, chivalry, manhood, and reformed religion would never characterize this boy. So immoderate was he in the pursuit of his heroic persona that he was distracted not at all by the appetites which made King James a buffoon in the eyes of his subjects and his court a scandal. While the king was capable of childishness and intemperance, much to the distaste of the sober parliamentarians whose sensitive ears burned with each new report of masquerade and outrage at court, Prince Henry continually belied his age and played a role more fitting a mature leader. During that first year in England, an incident was recorded—and doubtless told and retold—that characterized Henry's mastery and spirit. "Being desirous to mount a horse of prodigious mettle" and being denied the assistance of his attendants, who thought this particular stallion too powerful for even Henry, the prince led the horse to uneven ground and got up himself from the side of a bank. He spurred the animal to a full gallop despite the admonishment of those who watched. At last, having thoroughly exercised the horse, he brought him "in a gentle pace back, and dismounting, said to them, 'How long shall I continue to be a child in your opinion?'"[11] He had scarcely ever been a child at all, and at ten years old he was an astonishing embodiment of adult purpose.

III

Henry was full of the *ira per zelum,* the zealous rage; he remarked once to John Harington, "I have a pleasure in over reaching difficult matters,"[12] a statement which revealed much about his self-perception. The theme of overreach appeared quite early in his personation among the English; particularly, it was the English Puritans who first placed Henry in the roles of Alexander the Great, Caesar, Hannibal; the prince responded immediately and favorably to the more obvious implications: Alexander, for example, won his appelation "the Great" by achieving well before his twentieth birthday the full power of manhood embued with divinity. Henry seemed fueled to equal, or to exceed, Alexander's example. The prince was a paradigm for all the young men of the realm, which explained partially why so many of the high-born young men of England were drawn to him. In describing Henry's court, the tutor James Cleland evoked the panoply of personation which had followed the prince since birth: "I recommend in particular the *Academie* of our Noble Prince, where young Nobles may learne the first elements to be a *Privie Counseller,* a *Generall* of an Armie, to rule in peace, & to commande in warre. Here they may obtaine his *Highnes* fauor, as *Hylas* wonne the loue of *Hercules: Patroclus* of *Achilles,* and *Ephestion* of *Alexander* the *Great.* . . ." But Cleland was not content with this praise; saying that Henry was somehow *like* Hercules and Alexander was not enough, was never quite sufficient for those Englishmen who believed as fervently in the myth of conqueror as the Scots did. Henry *was* a god, as Cleland put it, and he gathered other lesser gods around him: "Here is the true *Panthaeon* of Great Britaine, where Vertue her selfe dwelleth by patterne, by practise, by encouragement, admonitions, & precepts of the most rare persons in Vertue and Learning that can be found.... Here dwel al the Gods and Goddesses: They haue bestowed their guifts euerie one vpon this Court...."[13]

Particularly susceptible to the Alexander personation were French Huguenots, many of them resident in England, chafing because their once Protestant King Henry IV had turned Catholic. These Frenchmen took an uncanny delight in Prince Henry's Alexander mask, saying that they were impatient for him to grow to conquering maturity. While they waited for him to take the field against the hated Catholics in their own country, these Frenchmen added their own Gallic flourishes to the myth. With a drawing of a knight in plumes and armor (see Fig. 4), meant to symbolize Henry (*"Le Povrtraict de Monseigneur Le Prince"*), Monsieur D'Esdiguieres grandly identified Henry as England's Alexander: *"Voicy L'Alexandre de la grande Bretaigne.... Le voicy les armes a la main, face et pointe tournees vers L'ennemy de Dieu...."* [Here is the Alexander of Great Britain.... Here he is with arms in hand, face and sword point turned toward the enemy of God....][14] This Christian and strangely medieval Alexander always, it seemed, turned his visor and his lance against "the enemy of God," and there was never any doubt who that might be. Another Frenchman, George Marcelline, first addressed Henry as "MON JEVNE CAESAR ET G. ALEXANDRE" and then described him to all admiring eyes:

> This young Prince is a warrior alreadie, both in gesture and countenance, so that in looking on him, he seemeth vnto vs, that in him we do yet see *Aiax* before *Troy*, crowding among the armed Troops. ... Honour [is] all his nouriture, and Greatnesse his pastime (as it was saide of Alexander) and Triumph the ordinary end of al his Actions.[15]

Henry was often addressed with a cascade of associations, by Frenchmen as well as by less emotional Englishmen: *fortitudino Alexandrum, potentia Craesum, prudentia Solomonem, pietate Josiam,*

Figure 4. Drawing of a mounted knight in armor. Royal MS. 16. E.XXXVIII, fol. 1. Reproduced by permission of the British Library Board.

Figure 5. Peacham emblem of Henry, from *Minerva Britanna or a Garden of Heroical Deuises* (London, 1612). S.T.C. 19511, British Museum Department of Printed Books. Reproduced by permission of the British Library Board.

diuturnitato Hestorem antecellas." [You are surpassing Alexander in
strength, Craesus in power, Solomon in wisdom, Josiah in piety,
Hector in endurance.][16] The shared characteristic of most of these
masks of heroism, whether offered to the prince from the lips of
Frenchmen or Englishmen, was *overreach,* the ability and willingness
to plunge ahead across boundaries, to amaze the world with holy
zeal, but mainly to overcome the world with arms of holiness.
Whether as Alexander or Caesar or Ajax, the personations thrust
upon Henry emphasized barriers broken down, limits crossed, expectations beyond imagining fulfilled. In terms of verbal icon, Henry
was "one figured Caesar, aloft, deposing or treading a Globe vnder
him, holding a book in one hand, and a sword in the other: so that
it may be saide of you, . . . *you are a Caesar."*[17] Henry Peacham, the
English emblem-maker, combined both word and picture in capturing the quality of amalgamation in Henry's personation (see
Fig. 5). Under the drawing of a medieval knight, plumed and bearing a lance, astride a rearing battle horse, Peacham explained:

> THVS, thus young HENRY, like Macedo[n]'s sonne,
> Ought'st thou in armes before thy people shine.
> A prodigie for foes to gaze vpon,
> But still a glorious Load-starre vnto thine:
> > Or second PHOEBVS whose all piercing ray,
> > Shall cheare our heartes, and chase our feares away.[18]

The emblem was further labelled *Par Achillis,* the "equal of Achilles." Such was the manna which sprang up in the morning of Henry's
youth. Feeding on this constant nourishment, his greatness seemed
inevitable to him; he would without doubt tread the globe under his
feet, and soon.

With English and Protestant belligerancy growing in the personation of Prince Henry, foreign governments established not disinterested embassies about the fringes of his youthful court. The French
were especially active in the diplomacy of lavish gifts; the manuscript collection of Prince Henry's correspondence in the British Museum (Harl. 7007) contains many letters between the French king,
Henry IV, and the prince, most of them heavy with congratulation.
Suits of armor, packs of dogs, and stables of horses were sent across
the Channel for "Le Jeune Prince"; the French king even sent a
French riding master to train Henry in the continental styles. "He is
a Prince, who promises very much, and whose friendship cannot but
be one day of advantage "[19] wrote de la Boderie, the French Ambas-

sador in England. De la Boderie was thinking of the contrast, once
again, between King James and his son; James leaned toward the interests of Spain, the ancient enemies of France. Prince Henry, under
the influence of his Puritan myth-makers, hated Spain with a Vatin-
ian hatred, though he was not inclined simultaneously to love Catholic France the more. Prince Henry's young, unsubtle mind was likely
to draw little distinction between two great Catholic states, for both
had been hereditary enemies of England, although for Spain was re-
served his strongest contempt. It was not much of an advantage for
the French, but with Huguenot expatriots in England agitating for
invasion of their own homeland, the French could not afford to
leave off the courtship of the prince. Henry IV in France, it was said,
spoke "ever . . . with great shew of passionate affection towards . . .
the Prince; and at this time he accounted of him as of his own son";
for he was "resolved . . . to cultivate that young plant, since it promised to produce fruits much more favourable to France, than the
stock, from which it was raised."[20] The "stock from which it was
raised" meant King James, of course, whose pro-Spanish sympathies
were well-known; but Queen Anne, as well, had shown herself no
friend of France. As though casting off the last vestiges of that
loathed land of Scotland, with its cold and cheerless Court and Kirk,
she had become—with characteristic unpredictability—a convert to
the Roman Church and a giddy friend of Spain. Being no longer denied her son's presence, she reportedly attempted greater degrees of
influence: "she endeavoured to prejudice him in favour of Spain,
and against France, which, she said, she hoped he would one day
conquer like Henry V. . . ."[21] By this time Prince Henry was very
much a public figure, not the prisoner of some walled nursery, but
he was apparently not totally immune to the apples of discord which
his mother threw into his path; she had learned, with evident skill,
the same siren tune which all the country was piping: "conquer like
Henry V."

The French, meanwhile, discussed granting bribes,—"pensions"
in the sanitized argot of early seventeenth century diplomacy—to
those men closest to the prince and most influential with him; the
Spaniards, as everyone knew, had been thus successful in enlisting
the aid of several powerful English lords at James's court (indeed,
the Spanish had successfully pensioned James himself). But de la
Boderie counselled that such expense would be futile and wasted in
the attempt to bend Prince Henry to the benefit of France. The

prince was of a disposition "to be directed by *his own* understanding," de la Boderie explained, "so that the persuasions of those about him were not likely to biass him towards any thing, but *what he chose himself.*"[22] Ironically, the only course open to those who would tame this young Alexander was actually to encourage the warlike nature with gifts of chivalric hardware. De la Boderie wrote with melancholy resignation to his king: "[You] cannot gratify the Prince more, than by sending him a suit of armour well gilt and enamelled, together with pistols and a sword of the same kind."[23] The Prince of Wales might one day hold that sword to the throat of France, but de la Boderie was right— it was best to cultivate the young plant and hope that its prodigious growth would not choke them all.

IV

In August of 1605 Henry was taken up to Oxford in great estate to be enrolled among the scholars of Magdalen College. King James, Queen Anne, Prince Henry, and all the Court were entertained for three days and nights by Latin plays (one of them, the tragedy of *Ajax flagellifer,* "which was very tedious and wearied all the companie"[24]); by a masque, *The Queen's Arcadia,* written by Samuel Daniel; and by disputations in divinity, civil law, and medicine (among the latter, a debate concerning the harmful effects of tobacco, a subject which so provoked the abstemious king that he found it difficult to let the speakers move ahead without excited interruption). Among those men of medicine who disputed so learnedly was Dr. Gifford, who would later be one of the apprehensive, and disputatious, physicians attending at Henry's deathbed.

The discovery in November 1605 of the Catholic plot to blow up king, prince, lords, and commons assembled at Westminster for the opening of Parliament did much to propel Henry all the more rapidly into his role of Protestant hero. The Gunpowder Plot was taken by many to be evidence enough that Catholicism was infernally dedicated to the destruction of reformed religion and free government, and since King James showed himself squeamish of stern measures and unallied to the warmongering Puritan party, some of the outraged voices in England were directed toward Prince Henry, though he was only eleven years old and still beyond the possibility of real action. "Beware of the Vipers, or, to speak freely, of the Jesuits,"[25] wrote Leonell Sharpe, one of Henry's own chaplains, and indeed there were at work in England priests and seminarians, some of whom obviously divided their evangelism between winning souls and plotting the destruction of powerful heretics; it was not a time conducive for reasoning together. The Reverend Sharpe, among many others, proved that contentiousness and emotion would rule. Francis Herring, for one, published, first in Latin and then in English verse, an enlargement of homilies to Henry on the meaning for Christians to be found in the treachery of Catholics. The book was titled *Popish pietie* and placed its focus squarely on "that Prince of admirable hope," on whom good Protestants must now rely more than ever. Twice now the pope had attempted to lay hands on the prince: first, in Clement's attempt to bribe away the right to educate him, and then in the plot of Guy Fawkes and his confederates "to have put out and quite extinguished the lights of Israel in one day."[26] Every newly uncovered device of Catholic subversion or violence seemed inevitably to bolster Henry's myth as an anointed savior. Why else would the Catholics so exercise themselves?

Many others joined Leonell Sharpe and Francis Herring in pouring out to Prince Henry their roused anger and frustration over the Catholic plot, and their correspondingly exaggerated hopes that religion might be "purified" in England. Sir Alexander Seton, Chancellor of Scotland, wrote Henry and attempted to speak for all the prince's loving Scots subjects: "I wish that your eyes could penetrate into the breasts of your countrymen. You would have seen there not long ago, how great their joy, how sincere their regard and veneration of you was. . . ." Sir Alexander, like so many others, interpreted Henry's delivery from the gunpowder as some sort of individual display of strength and the special visitation of providence: "Go on, most serene Prince, as you have begun, with this greatness of mind and affection to your countrymen. . . . By this means you will procure and establish an everlasting fame and glory to yourself. . . ."[27] The execrations against the Catholics, tied with a nice inevitability to reiteration of Henry's conqueror myth, echoed in the presses for years.

It was a time for shield and sword, those ubiquitous symbols which seemed always at hand when the image of Prince Henry was evoked. Thus Lord Spencer of Althorp sent to the prince from Northamptonshire some new armor, "instruments fit to be about you in these treacherous times,"[28] and Henry, fully aware that the Lord's anointed had been saved from perfidy, acknowledged piously the mysterious working of God: "he would never after suffer himself to be prevented by any business from being present at the sermon appointed to be preached every Tuesday, the day of the week, on which the plot was intended to have been executed."[29] Henry's name and the news of his deliverance from Catholic treachery spread rapidly through Protestant Europe with predictable results: he was now recognized as a promising prince and as a possible future ally by German Protestants. This extension of Henry's "theater" was fateful, for he would thereafter have difficulty thinking of himself as less than an international force. Prince Frederick, the ten-year-old Protestant Count Palatine and future King of Bohemia—a young man who would be no very effectual strategist against the Catholics but nevertheless universally admired among the Protestants for rashly precipitating the Thirty Years War—wrote congratulations to Henry from Germany, a most fateful binding in friendship of two boys both dedicated to the quixotic dream of altering entirely the religion and politics of Europe. The Prince of Wales and the Palatine prince would keep up a warm correspondence for years; Henry would see his sister Elizabeth betrothed to the German Elector and even greater plans laid, but he would see none of it completed.

V

In May of 1606 Sir David Murray, still Prince Henry's loyal servant and Gentleman of the Chamber, was naturalized by special act of Parliament, a compliment both to the knight and to the prince whom he served. The good will which Parliament, especially the heavily Puritan Commons, was willing to extend toward Henry—while parsimoniously turning away in the face of King James's demands for more subsidies—became, in fact, a wedge which James and his ministers could use. Robert Cecil, the Earl of Salisbury and Lord High Treasurer, was strained to the limits of his ingenuity in keeping the government of his indiscreet king afloat and functioning. Lord Salisbury became increasingly Byzantine in manipulating Parliament into granting the king the funds necessary to carry on the affairs of state, while Parliament became progressively tight-fisted. All the good men and true of Commons could see their money squandered on revelry, on a queen who kept priests and danced bare-breasted, on the king's handsome, arrogant favorites. But Salisbury found in Prince Henry an object which softened the hard gaze of Parliamentarians; they would loosen the purse-strings for him. Salisbury, a diligent searcher-out of old precedents, resurrected the statute of the twenty-fifth year of Edward III which established the feudal "aid" which could legally be extracted from every landowner in the realm to honor the "knighting" of the king's heir.[30] The Protestants of England could hardly protest since it was for their future champion that the aid was being raised, though they knew well enough that the revenue would disappear in the sieve-like cracks of James's court.

By 1607 Henry had become one of the leading literary patrons in England. In April of that year Lord Lumley died without issue and the prince purchased his entire library, the most valuable and extensive private collection in the country, next to Robert Cotton's.[31] Henry's generosity to the whole company of English poets, including Ben Jonson, George Chapman, Samuel Daniel, Joshua Sylvester, and many others, signaled a stampede of writers who rushed forward to dedicate their books to the honor of the prince.[32] Henry gave many of them gratuities and subsidies and took some of them into his official household (George Chapman, for example, as Sewer-in-Ordinary). Significantly, the larger majority of the books dedicated to Henry continued to be written by bellicose Protestants; they either spoke pietistically of putting on the whole armor of God or they showed Henry the world laid out beneath him. He was their "eagle."

But he was no scholar. By the time he had entered his teens, Henry was interested in one thing only: the manly "exercises." It was King James who was studious and scholarly; Prince Henry came to shun those pursuits as soft, feminine, and unbecoming the future conqueror of Catholicism. Queen Anne, who hardly can be faulted with consistency of intent, played no small part, apparently, in seeing to it that Henry left his books for the tilt-yard. After the years in Scotland when her motherly influence was barred, Anne might have attempted, one would think, to smother her son or at least divert him from the masculine pursuits; this sort of diversion she would attempt later, but for now she evidently, and according to rumor, had other motives which were far from wholesome: "she used all her efforts to corrupt the mind of the Prince by flattering his passions, diverting him from his studies and exercises, representing to him, out of contempt of his father, that learning was inconsistent with the character of a great General and Conqueror."[33] Whether scholarship and broad learning were out of keeping with the role of a "great General and Conqueror" was a debatable question (and it *was* con-

stantly debated in the many books which were dedicated to the attention of Henry and to his preparation for rulership), but what was
not debatable was that the prince had become a quite visible opposite of his father. This contrast between father and son became one
of the chief topics of conversation and gossip, and apparently a constant source of pleasure to those who wished James no good will.
(One of those latter was possibly Queen Anne.) In 1607 the Venetian ambassador wrote back to his government a detailed account of
the growing friction. The prince, though only thirteen years old, "is
marked by a gravity most certainly beyond his years" (a key trait repeatedly noted by many). He studies, the ambassador reported, "but
not with much delight, and chiefly under his father's spur, not of his
own desire." For his stiff-necked resistance to the interests of learning, which more often than not displayed itself as a curt arrogance,
"he is often admonished and set down" by the king. Indeed, according to the ambassador, King James became so exasperated on one occasion with his son that he first gave him a stern lecture and then
added that if Henry did not attend more earnestly to his lessons the
crown would be left to his brother, the Duke of York, "who was far
quicker at learning and studied more earnestly." Henry made no immediate reply, but it was clear that he was unimpressed by the ex-
travagance of the king's threat. The prince's own self-fulfilling myth
seemed far stronger than the threats of his father. Later, however,
when Henry was further lectured by his tutor Adam Newton on his
dilatory attention to his books, he said, "I know what becomes a
Prince. It is not necessary for me to be a professor, but a soldier and
a man of the world. If my brother is as learned as they say, we'll
make him Archbishop of Canterbury." The king, according to the
ambassador, "took this answer in no good part" when he heard it,
and the Venetian added rather darkly, "nor is he overpleased to see
his son so beloved and of such promise that his subjects place all
their hopes in him; and it would almost seem, to speak quite frankly,
that the King was growing jealous. . . ."[34] That the king was growing
jealous was perhaps the easy conclusion for an outsider to make but
perhaps not the correct one. Prince Henry's arrogance obviously did
concern the king, but jealousy in James seems a diagnosis slightly off
the mark. A boy so self-assured, so ambitious, and so much the center of other men's hopes—and a boy who stood next in line to inherit the seat of power from which he could logically put into execution those ambitions and hopes, not to mention exercise unchecked

the full arrogance of his spirit—such a boy was enough to make King James frown and fret. Jealousy was not the logical emotion for the father.

James was clearly aware of the motivating forces which were fashioning Prince Henry's personation, and he knew what men and what opinions entertained his son's ear. While the prince and his admirers could narcotize themselves in the sweet unrealities of their myth, King James had left to him the much less appetizing realities and practicalities of rule. He was determined to offend no other country, to stay clear of contention, and to provoke no contests.[35] Part of his motive may have been the product of cowardice—certainly, his subjects imputed all of his peacefulness to fear—but he had good strategic reasons for shuffling his country away from war. England was ready to fight in one way only—in the swaggering, alehouse talk of its old veterans and in the fiery zeal of Puritan preachers. But there was no army, trained and lean for the rigors of campaigning; the navy was decaying and full of graft; no money existed for raising and maintaining a military force.

And yet, the figure and image of young Prince Henry attracted unfailingly the sad, frantic moths who wished for nothing more fervently than to incinerate themselves in some grand and holy war on the Continent. They ransacked not only classical history and mythology for comparisons suitable to describe what Henry was and could be; they also recalled England's greatest heroes as examples for the prince (as Queen Anne had done in urging her son to conquer France as Henry V had). These voices cried for Henry to pluck up drowned chivalry by the locks:

> ... your Grace's name begins already to be spread through the whole world. I hope in God, that you shall follow the footsteps of the Prince of Wales, King Edward the third's son [Edward the Black Prince, who defeated the French at the Battle of Poitiers], who not only did subdue France, but also reduced the proud Spaniards in their own country.[36]

It was inevitable—and this was the thing James had perhaps feared most—that Henry would, on the basis of such mythologizing, attempt some overt action toward the fulfillment of these Christian hopes.

VI

In May of 1607 the French Prince de Joinville visited the court of King James, and when he returned to France in June, Prince Henry took the opportunity to send with him a personal ambassador who was actually a spy. This man, an "engineer," surreptitiously "took the opportunity of examining all the fortifications of [Calais]. . . . The French Ambassador discovered this by means of a friend, . . . who drew this secret out of the Engineer himself, after entertaining him in their return to London, the latter confessing, that he was employed by Prince Henry, who had long waited for such an opportunity."[37] It was a provocative act, at once subversive and aggressive, but it presented a difficult diplomatic problem for the French. If the spying out of the defenses of Calais had been ordered by King James or by one of his senior ministers, the motives of the English would have been unambiguously clear. The French could have responded immediately and with heat to such a breach. But here the culprit was a thirteen-year-old boy who had been lavishly courted with gifts and praise; what, after all, were his motives in sending a spy into France? To raise a hue and cry over the incident might serve only to show how weak and nervous France was, that she should shriek in alarm at the natural curiosity of a mere boy. But was Henry still only a mere boy and was his curiosity purely natural? And another consideration was also at work. The Gallic pride would find it unendurable to admit to the whole world that French security had been so easily subverted by a beardless lad. How the Spanish would chuckle at that! How the lynx-eyed princes of Italy would laugh at that! So the French found it convenient to pass off the incident, seeing that Henry "was not of an age nor in a condition to think seriously of such things; nor was England in a situation to undertake any design of that kind."[38]

And King James was determined that Henry should remain incapable of further actions which might threaten the peace of Europe. James had determination enough, but he was also rather ineffectual, so that his efforts at quelling the coltish impertinence of Henry seemed to many observers no other thing than the common jealousy and petulance which the Venetian ambassador had first mentioned. "The King despises his son because the people love him," buzzed the gossip, but the observation of French ambassador de la Boderie was closer to the truth: King James "often shewed, that he was not pleased to see [Henry] *advance* so fast."[39] James knew Henry's disposition and warned his Privy Councillors to turn aside the boy's schemes and requests. But those ministers designated by the king to help rein in young Henry also suffered the censure of jealousy.

Particularly susceptible to this charge was the Earl of Salisbury, certainly the most powerful—and hence the most feared and hated— man in James's government. He was a small, dark little man with a hunchback and a lame leg. (Queen Elizabeth dubbed him her "pigmy.") He was also an unusually effective politician, so it was perhaps inevitable that his physical condition and his administrative skill should coalesce for the popular imagination into some devilish, charmed deformity. To many Englishmen he was almost a tiring-house Machiavel; he reminded some Londoners of Richard Burbage in the role of Richard III; like Prince Henry, who more readily took to the national role prepared for him, the Earl of Salisbury was trapped in the garb which the people tailored for him. If the English people needed a hero in Henry, they also needed villains. Spain and Catholic Europe would do as distant monsters, while the Earl of Salisbury would also serve nicely as Satan's familiar, a sort of door-yard variety of villain, but one who was feared and hated nevertheless. Young, brazen Henry and the powerful earl—like Everyman and the Vice—sometimes squared off against each other, or rather, observers at court frequently insisted on seeing the coming struggle for power as a mythic contest between the Son of Light and a child-devouring Titan. Thus the Frenchman de la Boderie wrote to his government: "For besides [Henry's] exerting his whole strength to compass what he desires, he is already feared by those, who have the management of affairs, and especially the Earl of Salisbury, who appears to be greatly apprehensive of the Prince's ascendant; as the Prince, on the other hand, shews little esteem for his Lordship."[40] The earl was the center of power in James's government; the king had laid by to Salisbury's management most of his administrative reins, and now the king's son was showing a premature interest in that centralization of power. The earl was too practical and harried a man to waste his strength on jealousy (indeed, where there was jealousy it likely flowed in the opposite direction, originating in Henry), but he may well have been "greatly apprehensive," in de la Boderie's phrase, for he saw that the young tiger had ceased to doze in the sun.

Notes to Chapter 2

1. Thomas Birch, *The Life of Henry, Prince of Wales* (London, 1760), 32.

2. *Calendar of State Papers, Venetian,* X (1603-1607), par. 104.

3. See Marcelle Thiébaux, *The Stag of Love* (Ithaca and London, 1974), 17-58; Terence Hanbury White, *The Book of Beasts* (London, 1954); Tom Artin, *The Allegory of Adventure: Reading Chretien's "Erec" and "Yvain"* (Lewisburg, Pa., 1974), 61; Roy Strong, *The English Icon: Elizabethan and Jacobean Portraiture* (New York, 1969), 55-56.

4. See Edmund Spenser, *Works,* variorum ed., I, 377, 418, 430, 477-478.

5. *The Diary of John Manningham,* ed. John Bruce (London: Camden Society, 1868), 155. Cf. Sir Anthony Weldon, "The Character of King James," in *The Secret History of the Court of James the First,* II (Edinburgh, 1811), 11: "He was infinitely inclined to peace, but more out of feare then conscience, and this was the greatest blemish this king had through all his reign, otherwise might have been ranked with the very best of our kings." On popular reaction to the Spanish Peace, see Edward Phillips Statham, *A Jacobean Letter Writer* (London, n.d.), 62, and C.V. Wedgwood, *Poetry and Politics under the Stuarts* (Cambridge, 1960), 16-17. On the effect of the Spanish Peace on the English Royal Navy, in which Prince Henry was to take a mighty interest, see William Laird Clowes, *et al., The Royal Navy* (Boston and London, 1887-1903), II, 46: "Whether the conclusion of the treaty with Spain was bought by Spanish gold scattered freely in the English court, or whether James would have braved the opposition of his advisors for the sake of his desire for peace are questions that have no place here. The effect of the peace is certain. It gave to Spain breathing space in which to recover his strength, and thus robbed the Navy of the well-deserved right of bringing the quarrel to an honourable close. It also opened the door to that gross mismanagement which allowed our seas to become infested with pirates of all nations."

6. Chamberlain to Carleton: "Wherewith many that wisht her well are nothing pleased, and the speach goes that the King hath taken order and sent her word that her sonne shalbe brought up with the younge prince," *Letters of John Chamberlain,* I, 194. It should be noted that a close copy of Peake's hunting portrait of the Prince hangs at Hampton Court, with the young Earl of Essex substituted for the young Lord Harington.

7. See Birch, 35.

8. The following quotations and paraphrases in the text, all

from Cornwallis, *A discourse of the most illustrious prince, Henry* (London, 1641), sigs. C 4^V-D 1^V, quoted and discussed by Max Molyneux in his introduction to James Cleland's *Institutes of a Young Noble Man* (New York, 1948), xxiii-xxiv. See also, William Harris, *An Historical and Critical Account of the Life and Writings of James I*, 2d ed. (London, 1772), 249-250. On the matter of Henry's great delight in military trappings: "The Prince de Joinville, who . . . had been at the court of England in May and June, 1607, and returned to that of France about the end of November . . . having sent a present of arms and horses to the Prince, his Highness returned him thanks for them in a letter dated Feb. 11, 1607-8. 'I perceive, my cousin, that, during your stay in England, you discovered my humour; since you have sent me a present of the two things, which I most delight in, arms and horses'" (Birch, 100).

9. This is a primary argument in Stephen Greenblatt's recent *Sir Walter Ralegh: The Renaissance Man and His Roles* (New Haven, 1973), a most interesting and provocative book. There are obvious similarities to be remarked behind Ralegh's shaping of himself to match a variety of roles and Prince Henry's shaping of himself to the pattern of a single myth.

10. Cornwallis, quoted by Molyneux, xxiii.

11. Birch, 385.

12. Sir John Harington, *Nugae Antiquae* (London, 1804), I, 390. See also Blaikie Murdoch, *The Royal Stuarts in their Connection with Art and Letters* (Edinburgh, 1908), 144.

13. James Cleland, *Institutes of a young Noble Man*, ed. Max Molyneux, fols. 35, 36.

14. Royal MS.16.E.XXXVIII, fol. 4^V.

15. George Marcelline, *Les Trophees du Roi Jacques I* (London, 1609), sig. aij^V, and Marcelline's own translation of the same in the following year, *The Triumphs of King James the First*, fol. 66.

16. R. Barker, Bodleian MS.Jones.44, fol. I^V.

17. George Marcelline, *The Triumphs of King James the First*, 1610, fol. 73.

18. Henry Peacham, *Minerva Britanna or a garden of heroical deuises* (London, 1612), fol. 17. This important English emblem book is available in facsimile, ed. John Horden (Scholar Press, 1969).

19. Birch, 69.

20. Sir George Carew to Salisbury, 26 Aug. 1607; de Puisieux to de la Boderie, 20 July 1607. Birch, 89.

21. Birch, 45.

22. *Ibid.*, 90.

23. *Ibid.*, 70.

24. John Chamberlain to Ralph Winwood, *Letters of John*

Chamberlain, I, 208.

25. Birch, 63.

26. Francis Herring, *Pietas pontificia* (London, 1606), trans. and pub. as *Popish pietie* in 1610, from which the quotations are taken: sig. A 4^V.

27. Birch, 80. For further expressions of rage against the Catholics, coupled with the myth of Henry, see William Hubbard, *Great Brittaines resurrection* (London, 1606 ?), sig. G 3; Thomas Cooper, *Nonae Novembris in memoriam liberationis à proditione sulphurea* (Oxford, 1607), sig. ¶ ¶ ¶1^V; John Rhodes, *A briefe summe of the treason intended against the king and state* (London, 1606), sigs. B 3, B 4^V; William Smyth, *The black-smith* (London, 1606), sig. E 1; William Leigh, *Great Britains, great deliuerance, from the great danger of popish powder* (London, 1606). Recent researches into the Gunpowder Plot reveal a possible irony: Prince Henry had possibly changed his mind about attending the opening of Parliament and may never have been in real danger. See Paul Durst, *Intended Treason* (South Brunswick and London, 1970), 91.

28. Birch, 65.

29. *Ibid.*, 61-62.

30. Chamberlain to Carleton, 28 Oct. 1608: "Here is a speach likewise, that there is a subsidie or somwhat els due upon every knights fee thoroughout England in February next when the Prince comes to fifteen yeares old toward making of him knight," *Letters of John Chamberlain*, I, 267. On the continuing scandal of Queen Anne's deportment, see, for example, *The Diary of Lady Anne Clifford*, ed. V. Sackville-West (London, 1923), 16-17: "Now there was much talk of a masque which the Queen had at *Winchester* and how all the ladies about the Court had gotten such ill names that it was grown a scandalous place, and the Queen herself was much fallen from her former greatness and reputation she had in the world."

31. See Edward Edwards, *The Lives of the Founders of the British Museum* (London, 1870), I, 162.

32. This aspect of Henry's impact is most thoroughly covered by Elkin Calhoun Wilson, *Prince Henry and English Literature* (Ithaca, 1946). For supplementary information, see Franklin Burleigh Williams, *Index of Dedications and Commendatory Verses in English Books Before 1641* (London, 1962), 93. For some aspects of Henry as literary patron, see Mary Bradford Whiting, "Henry, Prince of Wales: 'A Scarce Blown Rose,'" *Contemporary Review*, 137 (1930), 492-500.

33. Birch, 46.

34. *C.S.P., Venetian*, X (1603-1607), par. 739.

35. For a very revealing discussion of James in this light, see

Maurice Lee, Jr., *James I and Henri IV* (Chicago, 1970).

36. Colonel Clement Edmondes, writing to Henry out of Holland. Birch, 43.

37. Birch, 86-87.

38. *Ibid.*, 87.

39. *Ibid.*, 77.

40. *Ibid.*, 76. Cf. 109-110: Salisbury attained the Lord Treasurer's post on May 6, 1608, and de la Boderie wrote that although Salisbury had the whole administration of the government in his hands, his power would no doubt be lessened by Prince Henry, "who already shewed some jealousy of him," but it would be a long time before this came to pass, for the King and Queen were not ignorant of their son's disposition, and they would try to keep him low and surrounded by persons dependent on themselves, so that it would not be easy for Henry to emancipate himself.

Prince of Wales:
"He Delights to Go upon the Deep"

I

Both Henry's consuming interest in the Royal Navy and his famous friendship with Sir Walter Ralegh commenced soon after his arrival in England; indeed, the two enthusiasms were related and fed each other. Even before he had met Ralegh in the Tower, Prince Henry had realized that English conquest and empire were tied irremediably to the strength and size of the navy; Ralegh added first-hand knowledge and practical advice to Henry's naval education. Sir Walter showed the boy prince theoretically how the sea might be a road to glory and conquest, unwittingly teaching a youthful arrogance the means to fulfill itself.

The prince's first relationship with ships and sailing began in 1604 as just another piece of complimentary "theater." The Earl of Nottingham, Lord High Admiral, responded to Henry's obvious delight in sailing ships by ordering master shipwright Phineas Pett to build a little launch for the prince for both instruction and entertainment upon the Thames. The ship which Pett built was more a stage prop in the drama of Prince Henry's personation than a sea-worthy vessel: it was twenty-five feet long at the keel, twelve feet in breadth, and was "garnished with painting and carving both within board and without very curiously" and "furnished at all points with ensigns and pendants." The little boat was launched on March 6 to the sounds of Henry's favorite music, trumpets and drums, and on March 22 Henry christened the ship *Disdain* and took Pett into his official service.[1] Thus Pett came within the circle of Henry's "friends," for whom the young boy could summon up the fiercest loyalty. In Pett's case, the prince's loyalty to him would have great ramifications, for Phineas Pett was more an embellisher of ships than

a good designer of them, yet his ineptness—and what later was revealed as dishonesty and embezzlement as well—was under the protection of young Prince Henry, so the English navy could really do
nothing to free itself of a "master shipwright" who could not build
good ships.

But under Henry's patronage, Pett rose rapidly in the service.
For the state visit of the King of Denmark, Queen Anne's brother,
during the summer of 1606 Pett was given orders to make the Royal
Navy ready for inspection, and later he was given two of the premier
ships in the fleet, the *Ark Royal* and the *Victory*, for dry-docking,
"by reason the Victory was given by the King to the Prince, whose
servant I being," said Pett, "it was held fit to be most proper to
me."[2] Prince Henry's own little navy was growing. But being given
his own miniature ship, the *Disdain*, and the full-sized *Victory*,
which had seen heroic duty in 1588 against the Spanish, was not
enough for Prince Henry. Grander schemes were taking shape in his
head which involved building greater ships to carry his banner.

The Royal Navy had been in steady decay since the death of
Queen Elizabeth,[3] who had also realized the necessity of a powerful
navy, so it was decided to strengthen the rotting fleet with a mighty
new ship, the *Prince Royal*, the first three-decker in the royal navy.
Phineas Pett got the commission, and he responded first by carving
out a stunning model of what he proposed to build, "most fairly garnished with carving and painting, and placed in a frame arched, covered, and curtained with crimson taffety."[4] This he presented to
Prince Henry's awed inspection on November 11, 1607. It was going
to be a spectacular ship, for it fitted Henry's notion of the sort of
flagship that should carry a conquering prince. Everyone was so
taken by the gingerbread of Pett's carving that no one thought to
ask if such a ship was well-proportioned and seaworthy; it was spectacle which engaged all eyes, not practical realities.

Order was given to lay the keel for the *Prince Royal* the next
summer. The prince's friendship with Walter Ralegh was well under
way by that time, for Henry told him of the plans for building the
great new ship and asked him for his advice. Ralegh did not like
what he heard of Pett's design. A ship so built would be too heavy
and sluggish, overcharged and too long at the keel—"fitter for the
narrow seas in summer than for the ocean, or long voyages." Ralegh
recommended a ship of 600-800 tons, 100 feet at the keel, thirty-

five feet broad at its widest; "two decks and a half is enough," he said.[5] But Pett proceeded to lay down a frame 115 feet long, forty-three feet wide, and to add a towering super-structure which would make the *Prince Royal* squat in the water like a bloated toad. The ship would weigh 1187 tons when complete. So Ralegh's advice to the Prince would be completely ignored,[6] from which Sir Walter should have learned that Henry was already showing at least one of the family traits—the inability to distinguish good advice from poor. Henry looked at Master Pett's carved model of the *Prince Royal, his* ship, and knew that anything less grand would be less serviceable for his destiny.

II

And his destiny seemed to beckon from several directions at once. The Virginia Company had been organized in April 1606, and Henry had followed its fortunes with keen interest, partially because of his friendship with the old colonizer Ralegh, but largely because the Virginia plantation was the first real English challenge to Spanish domination of the New World. Henry sent his gunner, Robert Tindall, to the colony, much as he had sent his "engineer" to France, to send back a report on the land, its inhabitants, and its fortifications. Tindall sent back in June 1607 a sketch of the James River and a journal for Henry's edification.[7] Henry was soon insinuating himself further into the Virginia adventure; he invested part of his own revenue to become an official shareholder in the Virginia Company and he was called the Patron of the Virginia Plantation, which was not entirely an empty compliment. When lack of discipline threatened to break the colony apart, Henry saw to it that Sir Thomas Dale, an old soldier and former servant during his days as prince in Scotland, was appointed governor. Dale went to Virginia as a harsh disciplinarian and soon the colony was thriving under his admittedly stern measures. And thriving also was Prince Henry's reputation; the Virginia headland was soon sprouting with landmarks named for him: Cape Henry, Fort Henry, Henricopolis, and Henrico College, the first chartered college in America which was intended to train savages in the true religion. Henry's name among the good, stern Puritans who would populate the new world was associated with the spread of the Gospel. The empire over which Henry was to reign would be the Kingdom of

God on earth, from which the idols of both heathens and Catholics
would be expunged.[8]

Several books published between 1607 and 1610 extolled this
notion of empire and Henry's part in it. William Crashaw in preaching a sermon before the Virginia Company in London mentioned
both the monetary profit of the plantation ("XX. in the C.") and
the profit in human souls won to God. "I hold euery man bound to
assist," said the very Puritan Mr. Crashaw, "either with his *Countenance, Power,* and *Authoritie* (as doe our gracious Soueraigne and
noble Prince) or with their *persons,* as some; or with their *purses,*
as others." Crashaw summed up the roles of both James and Henry
by invoking the usual mythology:

> . . . our mighty King & noble Prince, [in making] them-
> selues *fathers and founders* of this plantation and protec-
> tors of this royall enterprize, thereby [show] themselues
> *new Constantines or Charles the great:* for by the attempt-
> ing and atchieuing of this great worke of the heathens
> conuersion, let their highnesses bee assured, the ages to
> come will stile them by the glorious names of *Iames the
> great,* and *Great Henry.* . . .[9]

Pierre Erondelle, a Frenchman whose Protestant religion made the
growth of English colonies in the New World more desirable than
the success of French enterprises there, also recognized in Prince
Henry a great promoter of righteous empire:

> Christian charitie inuiteth you to be cheife worker in the
> sauing of millions of soules: The necessitie of your Coun-
> trie of Great BRITAINE, (ouer populous) doth require
> it: And lastly your poore Virginians doe seeme to implore
> your Princely aide, to helpe them to shake off the yoke
> of the diuel, who hath hitherto made them liue worse
> then beasts.[10]

In preparing the third edition of *Certain Errors in Nauigation,* Edward Wright found a new patron in Prince Henry; he offered the re-
vised and enlarged edition of his book to the prince because of his
association with "the discouerie of strange and forraine lands and
nations yet vnknowne, whereby the poore people there liuing in
darkness and in the shadow of death . . . may in short time grow to
some acquaintance with this our Christian world. . . ."[11]

The "discouerie of strange and forraine lands" which Wright
alluded to in 1610 likely had reference to the search for the North-
west Passage, which had been going on with renewed energy since
1607, much of it drawing the avid interest and participation of the
prince. Henry Hudson's four voyages between 1607 and 1611 were
undertaken for a number of English trading companies, but they had
the much more powerful blessing and interest of Prince Henry. On
his last voyage in 1610, when Hudson met his mysterious fate, he did
not perish before naming yet another landmark in honor of his patron, Prince Henry's Foreland, one of the capes in Hudson's Straits.
Following that tragic voyage—during which many ambitious Englishmen fervently believed Hudson had discovered the Passage to the
Orient—the Northwest Passage Company was chartered with the
Prince of Wales as its head and "Supreme Protector." "In regarde it
is an enterprise tending to soe worthie an end," read King James's
order granting the charter,

> and wch now at last after manie proofes hath obtayned
> so happie and likely a begininge, Wee have thought of
> some extraordinarie meanes to grace and honor the same.
> And, therefore, conceiving hope that both the accion it
> selfe willbe the more fortunate, and the undertakers
> thereof the more encouraged, if it shalbe countenaunced
> by o^r most deare and welbeloved sonne, *Henry, Prince of
> Wales:* KNOWE yee that wee doe first of all constitute
> and ordaine that o^r said deare sonne . . . shalbe . . . called
> Supreme Protector of the said Discovery and Company.[12]

The king also gave to the Company the motto, *Iuuat ire per altum*
("He delights to go upon the deep"), which Prince Henry also adopted
personally as a phrase best describing his own goal and destiny. For
the great voyage of discovery undertaken by Admiral Thomas Button soon after the formation of the Company, the captain carried
with him "Certaine Orders and Instruccons, set downe by the most
noble Prince, Henry." To demonstrate the seriousness with which he
regarded Admiral Button's holy cause, Prince Henry's first two orders governing the voyage commanded daily prayers and religious
observance and the punishment of "prophane speeches"—"noe
swearing or blaspheming of his Holie name, noe drunkennes or lewde
behaviour."[13]

III

Though the Virginia and Northwest Passage Companies were important in establishing Henry's image and aura beyond the seas, these were primarily commercial undertakings which piously claimed the salvation of souls as a valuable by-product of trade. Although he was much interested in these enterprises as extensions of English power, it was still on the Royal Navy and the building of the *Prince Royal* that he bestowed his greatest attention, especially in 1608 and 1609 when the officers of the navy—Phineas Pett among them—were subjected to an investigation which not only slowed down the construction of Henry's three-decker but also threatened to halt entirely the rebuilding of what Henry had come to regard as *his* navy. Pett was guilty of a whole catalogue of petty crimes and grander larceny, showing himself the typical public servant during James's reign by lining his pockets well against the day some eruption in the state might cast him on the shoals. Among other embezzlements, he built himself a fine house from materials requisitioned for the constructing and fitting out of the king's ships. He also estimated that the *Prince Royal* would require for her construction 775 loads of timber, whereas 1627 loads were actually requested. No one knew the disposition of those 852 extra loads of good English wood, but it seemed likely that they did not become part of the ship's planking or even part of Pett's favorite "garnishment" of the super-structure. But even such blatant graft was fairly typical for the day, and besides, Prince Henry, once sworn to a man's protection, would hear no wrong spoken of him. Henry went so far as to lead Pett by the hand through the park at Whitehall "in the public view and hearing of many people" near the time of the trial and then to stand by the shipwright at Woolwich and loudly proclaim his honesty and innocence both to the king's commissioners and finally to the king himself. By defending Pett and some others from the royal investigation, the prince was not only protecting his servants; he was also insuring himself loyal agents within the Royal Navy against the time he should wish it responsive to his commands. Prince Henry quite commandeered the naval inquiry and completely blunted its well-intentioned purpose; he further thoroughly surprised his father with what seemed an expert knowledge of ships and the sufficiency of their building; more than that, he fairly crowed in triumph when the investigation fizzled: "Where be now these perjured fellows that dare thus abuse his Majesty with these false informations, do they not worthily deserve hanging?"[14]

Henry became a constant visitor at the shipyards of Woolwich, watching the progress of his *Prince Royal.* On one occasion Master Pett had arranged by secret signal for the sudden discharge of thirty-one brass cannon, which mightily surprised and pleased the prince. Then on September 24, 1610, the grand ship was ready for launching. Prince Henry and scores of gentlemen arrived and climbed aboard the towering ship to ride it triumphantly down its tracings into the Thames. Henry and Lord Admiral Nottingham stood "where the great standing gilt cup was ready filled with wine to name the ship, so soon as she had been on float, according to ancient custom and ceremony performed at such times, by drinking part of the wine, giving the ship her name, and heaving the standing cup overboard." The order was given to cut the ropes. As she slid down, the great *Prince Royal,* being over-weighted with so many people, stuck fast at her widest in the dock gates. All the great gentlemen of the realm climbed down off the ship and went home; only Prince Henry lingered to see what could be done to get his ship free of the dock, but as high-tide would not arrive until after 2 A.M., the prince posted to Greenwich, promising to return after midnight. He did so, with a few loyal companions, through a driving rain and wind storm, but he arrived in good time to board the ship before the tide lifted her out of the dock gates and floated her into mid-channel. There, with a handful of his most intimate friends around him, he christened the ship and claimed her as his own. Together he and his friends drank off the rest of the wine and then went below to the ship's stores and began drinking long toasts to the future out of the ship's beer. The rising sun found them next morning drifting triumphantly drunk in the grandest white elephant in the English navy; the prince was unusually pleased with himself, with his fantastic new ship, and with his all-night exploit. He ordered the firing of cannon to proclaim his arrival to the sleepy inhabitants of Woolwich.[15]

IV

The year 1610 marked the launching of the *Prince Royal,* Henry's formal investiture as Prince of Wales, his sixteenth birthday, and his most intense efforts to realize his full princely power, of which his activities in and about the royal shipyards were only a part. For two or three years the friendship with Sir Walter Ralegh had been growing stronger and more intimate; Ralegh was perhaps flattered by the attentions of the young heir, but more than that, Sir Walter found it convenient to cultivate a friendship with the young man who could some day, as king, set him at liberty from the cruel confinement of the Tower—where, indeed, Henry's own father had sent him soon after his accession. Not only was Ralegh's friendship with Henry a hedge against an uncertain future of living at the king's mercy, it was also a means of exercising still a bit of influence in the state and of needling the king simultaneously. From approximately 1608 to 1610 Ralegh wrote voluminously for Henry; he turned his letter of advice concerning the building of the *Prince Royal* into *Observations Concerning the Royal Navy*, wherein he lay down full plans for reforming the old service, and he wrote besides *A Discourse of the Invention of Ships, Anchor, Compass, etc.* He wrote for Henry *Maxims of State* and *The Cabinet Council*, works of mature cynicism, with a sinewy thread of Machiavellian bitterness running through them; and he had found that although Henry was not always able to appreciate his good advice on shipbuilding, the young prince listened attentively to all Ralegh's opinions about Spain and the advisability of decisive war with that treacherous kingdom.

Ralegh could not say enough against that ancient enemy. King James had only just concluded his peace treaty with Spain in 1604, despite the grumbling of old English veterans both in and out of the Tower, and James understandably took a dim view of Ralegh's diehard belligerency. Sir Walter had known from the beginning King James's desire for peace with Spain, yet with characteristic impertinence, Ralegh had presented the peace-loving king with "A Discourse Touching War with Spain" soon after James's entry into his English inheritance. In his "Discourse Touching War," Ralegh continued the argument he had begun in 1596, that now was the time to launch a decisive attack against the weakened Spaniards. Queen Elizabeth had not listened to such talk in 1596, but King James was listening in 1604 with a keen ear to Ralegh's offensive arguments. I have heard that the Spanish want a peace treaty, Ralegh wrote, "and I know they have good cause to desire it: but . . . from whence comes this great moderation and compliance, but only from the knowledge of our strength, and their own weakness?"[16] Peace, Ralegh reasoned, would only serve the Spanish to prepare covertly for another, perhaps fatal, attack on England: "But after the Spaniard shall have repaired his losses, I know not how your majesty may be assured of his amity: for the kings of Spain were not wont to keep either promises or oaths longer than they may prove profitable to themselves."[17] Ralegh's final argument against a Spanish peace treaty was based on the kind of religious bigotry which James particularly disliked: "The [Spanish] king being a catholic, and a child of the pope's, he can never in any respect affect you, or any other prince or state of the reformed religion."[18]

King James had not welcomed Ralegh's remarks, as Sir Walter had well realized before he sent them, but Prince Henry did. The prince took the diminished empire of Spain seriously. He had been told repeatedly by the religious controversialists of Scotland and England that Spain must be rooted out, its Catholicism sown with salt. It was only logical that Henry should ask Sir Walter, whose quarrel with Spain had been so public, whose experience in fighting the Spaniards so carefully chronicled, what strategy might be best in fulfilling the Great Mission. "It is the Spaniard that is to be feared," Ralegh wrote to the prince: "the Spaniard, who layeth his pretences and practices with a long hand. . . . it were an horrible dishonour to be overreached by any of those dry and subtle-headed Spaniards."[19] Along with such admonitions Ralegh tantalized Henry with his opinion that Spain's possessions in the New World were "subject to invasion, expulsion, and destruction; so as . . . an easy force will cast them out. . . ."[20] Such talk was all too pleasing to the would-be conqueror.

Ralegh's own combative spirit had grown explosive during the long years of his imprisonment, so that images of aggression, conquest, and invasion controlled the tone and content of many of the shorter pamphlets which he wrote for Henry. "The art military is of all other qualities most necessary for princes," he wrote, quoting the weariest cliché of the Renaissance, and he added: "Invasion is lawful against barbarians, whose religion and impiety ought to be abhorred, chiefly if they be potent, and apt to offend; for the cause of such war is compulsion and suppression of evil."[21] (Walter Ralegh perhaps did not consider all Catholics barbarians, but Prince Henry likely did.) If, on the one hand, King James wanted peace with Spain and neutrality toward the Catholic-Protestant troubles which were brewing on the Continent (the religiously motivated Thirty Years

War was just then fermenting in Germany), Ralegh pugnaciously told
Henry, "Neutrality is always a thing dangerous and disallowable."[22]
It was the purging fury of the fight which Ralegh longed for, and he
carried Prince Henry's youth with him toward that flame. Eighteen
was the "age most apt" for a young man to go to war,[23] he told
Henry, as though the boy could become vicariously his arm to work
a revenge on a world which now shunned him. The boy was a responsive pupil: he remembered the legacy which his eighteenth year
was to bring to him, to England, and—if he had his will—to all of
Europe.

But in 1610, while Henry was still sixteen, he had occasion to
exercise in Ralegh's behalf the sort of political influence which the
knight had vaguely hoped for. A contest erupted over Ralegh's Dorsetshire estate of Sherborne, and Henry was able to succeed where
Ralegh's other friends failed.

V

Ralegh, a full year before Queen Elizabeth's reign was over and
perhaps sensing that his life and fortune would not flourish under
the new Scottish King, had legally transferred the ownership of his
beloved Sherborne estate to his son, young Wat Ralegh. In practical
terms, this transference of deed simply meant that the property
could not be seized should Sir Walter find himself *persona non grata*
in the new regime of King James. As it turned out, Ralegh had acted
with the most fortuitous of instincts, for all too quickly after James
became king, Ralegh was indicted, tried, and convicted of treason.
The taint of treason meant automatic confiscation by the government of all lands, titles, and privileges held by the traitor. Ralegh's
few remaining friends sighed with relief that Sherborne had been
safely bestowed before that taint of treason fell, however unjustly.
Sherborne would at least shelter and provide for Ralegh's family, despite what the king's mercy planned for Sir Walter himself. But his
enemies—and they were aplenty and multiplying fast, now that a
royal and judicial mandate existed to strip him of everything port-
able—thought it strangely more than coincidental that Ralegh had so
cleverly transferred his property just prior to being charged with
high treason. This circumstance, his enemies thought, condemned
Ralegh with a certainty. The hairbreadth escape of the valuable Sherborne estate also prompted the power- and land-hungry hangers-on

of the court—those blind mouths who gobbled up the remains of the disgraced and the once favored—to look again at the document by which the transference of Sherborne was completed. There someone noticed a secretary's omission of a handful of words—"shall and will henceforth stand and be thereof seized"—which invalidated the deed and overthrew all. Ralegh fought the inevitable in the law courts: early in 1609 the case was terminated against him, Sherborne reverted to the Crown, and James found himself with a rich plum to bestow on whichever butterfly fluttered into his affection.

Robert Carr, a handsome young Scotsman who had followed the fortunes of his king into England with hopes for advancement, fell from his horse during a court tilt and broke his leg in full view of the king. By breaking his leg, young Carr also broke the king's heart. His Majesty called for his surgeons, his chaplains, his servants all; he had Carr borne into the royal chambers where the wound could be nursed. Carr was soon appointed Gentleman of the Bedchamber, then rose rapidly as Viscount Rochester, Knight of the Garter, and finally, Earl of Somerset. Thus the court was accustomed to the spectacle of a young minion rising into the highest offices. A suitable estate had to be found for so suitable a young lord, and Sherborne had come conveniently within grasp. Ralegh was doubly stricken with the cruelty of his fate: to lose Sherborne because of nine or ten words and to lose it to the likes of Robert Carr! Ralegh boldly wrote to the young Scottish upstart, maintaining civility but communicating with grace the pain and outrage he felt:

> It is come to my knowledge that yourself (whom I know not, but by an honourable fame) have been persuaded to give me and mine our last fatal blow, by obtaining from his Majesty the inheritance of my children, lost in law for want of words. . . . Sir, seeing your day is but now in the dawn, and mine come to the evening . . . I beseech you not to begin your first buildings upon the ruins of the innocent, and that their griefs and sorrows do not attend your first plantation.[24]

The letter had no effect, nor did any of Ralegh's entreaties by way of Queen Anne or his wife Bess. "I mun have it for Carr," James insisted. Sir Walter turned to Prince Henry, and Henry went, a crusader for righteousness, "with some anger to his father."[25]

Prince Henry's youthful indignation had been building over the entire question of Ralegh's imprisonment, and now the matter of

Sherborne and Carr had turned him into a potent force. The prince had been heard to remark, even before the crisis of Sherborne and the embarrassment of his father's infatuation for Robert Carr, that only his father would keep "such a bird" as Ralegh in a cage. King James had now to face what grown men for centuries have considered the most awesome of forces: a young man full of himself and redolent with righteousness, a young man possessed with a singleness of purpose that older men—certainly his father among them—found difficult to maintain in a world ruled by multiplicity and ambiguity. But Henry knew his cause was right, and he had much of his training in aggressive manliness from the very master he now sought to defend.

We have no record of the actual meeting between Prince Henry and King James, but we do know for a certainty the outcome. After the conference the gift of Sherborne was cancelled (a lesson in fate which failed to teach young Carr, that "mushroom of yesterday," the dangers of lying too long in the glorious sun), but a more than generous sop of 20,000 pounds was handed over to him. The money seemed to blanch Carr's wound at losing the property, but if Ralegh had not lost Sherborne utterly to one of the king's creatures, neither had he won it back for his family. Everyone assumed that Prince Henry would also eventually accomplish that feat, as well as Ralegh's freedom from the Tower. (After Prince Henry's sudden death, Sherborne was indeed signed over to Robert Carr, who lost it almost immediately in his spectacular fall from power in 1614. The Dorsetshire estate was subsequently passed about from one ill-fated owner to another. It was forever lost to Ralegh, but it seemed to carry a curse for those who attempted to benefit from Sir Walter's bad fortune.)

VI

Henry had been displaying his power in other ways and to other people. For example, as far back as the Christmas festivities of 1608 Henry had exhibited a rash arrogance which amused those who wished to turn him loose on Spain and the other Catholic nations. During that Christmas season of 1608 Henry chose to test his will and authority against two of the most powerful and respected peers of the realm, the Earls of Southampton and Pembroke. The two earls had come to Whitehall for the Christmas plays and masques—both were great literary patrons—but Henry took a fancy to the lodgings which the two noblemen had occupied within the rambling palace. He commanded them preemptorily to move their households and horses to make way for the Prince of Wales. When they refused, "the Prince had them removed by his people to the indignation of these gentlemen. . . . This is a great proof of spirit on the part of the Prince, who, though only [fourteen] years of age, gives the highest promise in all he does."[26]

Soon after, a group of old military hands drew up for the prince a manuscript entitled "Arguments for War." By arms was laid the foundation of this state and by arms will it be preserved, the authors told Henry by way of preface, and then proceeded to list reasons for foreign wars: (1) preservation of our own peace; (2) venting of factious spirits ("when people have no enemies abroad they'll find some at home"); (3) instructing our people in arms; (4) wealth from spoils; (5) additional revenues from subjected territories; (6) additional honor and title for our king; and (7) increased dominion. The prince hardly needed this new inducement; his mind was already well set, but the rain of prophecy fell almost daily and King James could not prevent most of it falling on the young crop, though the king was by now trying actively to reverse the trend in his son. He commissioned the bibliophile Robert Cotton to write "An Answer to Propositions of War,"[27] though Sir Robert's admirable scholarship was wasted on Henry.

Though Henry had long been a fully realized and highly symbolic Prince of Wales in England, and had lately begun to take action on the strength of that symbology, he was still not formally—and legally—invested with his principality and with the lands and revenues connected to it. Early in 1609 the Venetian ambassador reported the following: "The Prince of Wales, who is now old enough, shows a wish to enter on his estates, from which are derived various emoluments at present enjoyed by some of these great Lords. The Council, however, have pointed out to the King that it would be greatly to his service that the Prince should leave him the revenues for another two years in order to facilitate the payment of Crown debts. The Prince has been persuaded by the Earl of Salisbury, who took him a jewel worth six thousand crowns."[28] But such bribery was clearly ineffective for keeping Henry indefinitely off the scent; he wished his Principality of Wales for the completion it would give his youthful authority and for the ambiance which the expected income would give his plans for war. For the same reasons, King James and the Earl of Salisbury wished to keep him from the prize, but the king's own worsening financial condition necessitated a complete shift of policy. Salisbury had used young Henry once before in squeezing out aid from Parliament; he would do so again in 1610 by calling a new Parliament and by tying together the king's fiscal well being and the symbolic investiture of Henry. The prince would be allowed to enter the full glory of his title, but not without serving the ends of Salisbury's political schemes.

At the opening of the Parliament of 1610 King James addressed the Lords and Commons on the pressing need for subsidy, and prominent among the reasons was the coming investiture of Henry: "the time of creation of my Sonne doeth now draw neere, which I chuse for the greater honour to be done in this time of Parliament. As for him I say no more; the sight of himselfe here speakes for him."[29] Six days later, in a conference between the leaders of Commons and Lords, Lord Treasurer Salisbury reiterated the two reasons for convening the session: (1) the Creation of Henry, Prince of Wales, and (2) the granting of subsidy to the King: "Now, as it is an exceeding greate comforte for us to see a king and a prince live together, so it must needs be a greate perell and danger if either of theyme should want meanes sufficient for theyre maintenance. For the branche cannot prosper and florish except the roote be fedd."[30] The Commons' affection for Henry and their pride in what he represented for the future were strong inducements; they would grant a subsidy, but they balked at the full amount requested by Salisbury.

First, there was the matter of long-standing grievances, prince or no prince. Parliament wished, among other things, for the abolition of purveyance and wardships. Purveyance was one of the oldest prerogatives of the monarchy, and one of its greatest abuses, for by the right of purveyance the king could command for his royal use victuals, horses, carts, even laborers, as he moved his household about the countryside. For a king as strapped for revenue as James was, purveyance was an absolute and practical necessity; by it he could, and did, live—like Becky Sharp—on "nothing a year."

The Court of Wards was equally ancient but even more profitable; by feudal law every landowner in the realm owed the king some service or duty. When a landowner died and left his inheritance to a child not yet of age, that child with his inheritance was automatically a ward of the king, placed under the "guardianship" of the throne, which understandably meant to see its rights and interests protected. Until that child came of age—fourteen for girls, twenty-one for boys—the wardship was administered absolutely by the king or by his designated officers who had control of lands, revenues, even the rights to approve or deny marriage. The income from the Court of Wards was enormous, its abuses a heavy and infuriating burden to the people; and that old popular villain, the Earl of Salisbury, was the Master of the Court of Wards.

On March 18, 1610, the Venetian ambassador reported how the contest over wardship was taking shape:

> Parliament stands firm . . . in demanding abolition of wardship, otherwise it will vote nothing beyond the ordinary subsidy. . . . The King temporises. . . . He says that as to the profits he places himself in their hands, but that he has to consider whether it becomes his conscience and his honour to renounce the wardship of minors. . . .[31]

But into the complicated maneuvering came Prince Henry himself, and his interest was for anything but reform. He argued strenuously with his father against giving up the royal prerogative, for he himself had his eye on the added power and wealth which the Mastership of Wards would give him. Everywhere, it seemed, Lord Salisbury was feeling the grasp of this impertinent young Prince:

> The Prince also [shows] a desire for the guardianship of wards at present held by Lord Salisbury to his incredible benefit and influence; for by law not only is he not bound at any time to render account of income, but after supplying the necessary and suitable aliment all the rest of the income is at his disposal; he also has the right to give both males and females in marriage to whomsoever he pleases. For these reasons the Prince urges that an office of such weight should not lie outside the Royal House.[32]

Walter Yonge recorded in his diary in February, 1610, that "the Prince is persuaded that that office doth belong unto him, but the King will not give way thereunto."[33] No indeed. James, unwilling to give up either purveyance or wardship to the demands of Parliament, was equally unwilling to see the latter fall within the insatiable grasp of his son.

VII

Prince Henry approached his investiture with a growing momentum. His full mythology was unrolled for the people:

> Such occasions of ioy to vs, of happinesse for vs, such tri-
> umphes, applauses, Iubilees as these, do draw from vs
> gratulation and acclamation, in that *God hath not onely*
> *giuen his iudgements vnto the King, but his righteous-*
> *nesse to the Kings sonne,* leauing such a hope for the
> young, such a comfort for the old, such happiness for
> all; such a young *Ptolomey* for studies and Libraries;
> such a young *Alexander* for affecting martialisme and
> chiualrie, such a young *Iosiah* for religion & piety. . . .
> we should desire the benefit of this spirituall *Creation*
> to put on the roabes of righteousnesse, the sword of the
> spirit, to receiue the staffe of protection, to be placed as
> signets on Gods hand.[34]

Henry began the year of investiture appropriately, with a spectacular
tournament held on the Feast of Epiphany. Henry had come up to
London in mid-December of 1609 to make all ready for his appearance in the lists of chivalry. The Venetian ambassador wrote:

> It will be the first time he has appeared in public in the
> lists. He found some difficulty in obtaining the King's
> consent, but his Majesty did not wish to cross him. At
> the next meeting of Parliament which is summoned for
> the 9th of February next, they intend to confer on him,
> with all the ancient ceremony, the Principality of Wales
> which he greatly desires. . . . In virtue of this title the
> Prince will enjoy the revenues of the Principality and will
> have a seat in the Council of State.[35]

As much as the title and the money, Henry desired that seat on the
Privy Council, where he could indeed begin to sway events to his
design.

All the pomp and romantic medievalism of the high years of
Queen Elizabeth were resurrected for Henry's tournament. Ben
Jonson was commissioned to write the speeches and the masque, in
which Prince Henry was shown in "St. George's Portico," arising out
of the ruins of "Old Chivalry":

> Do's he not sit like MARS, or one that had
> The better of him, in his armor clad?
>   .   .   .   .   .   .
>
> Or like APOLLO, raisd to the worlds view,
> The minute after he the *Python* slew.[36]

Jonson dramatized the spirit of King Arthur presenting a magic shield to the prince, and then Henry awakened from her sleep an allegorized figure of Chivalry. On the face of it, Jonson's devices may seem merely complimentary and purely conventional, following with docility the dominant myth of the conqueror laid down many years before. But Jonson by this time was pulling away slightly from the military metaphor which the prince seemed to demand of those who used their art to celebrate him and interpret him for the masses. I shall discuss more fully the evolution of Jonson's attitude toward Henry—together with the changing attitudes of many poets and writers of temperate political and religious views—in the next chapter. It is perhaps sufficient here to note that in Jonson's speeches for Henry's "Barriers," unlike the entertainment at Althorp when the prince first entered England, the royal figure ceased to be onlooker and the *object* of praise. Rather, Prince Henry took part in the masque at his "Barriers"; he was, in fact, the center of the stage—he had become, quite literally, dramatic *subject*. He was a prince playing a prince, the symbolic role-player who moved simultaneously through three worlds—the actual, the poet's fiction, and the combined mythologized image in the eye of the beholders.[37] At the opening of 1610 Prince Henry had indeed arrived at a kind of apotheosis in his personation.

After Jonson's formal masque, the actual tournament "at barriers" was fought, but for Henry it was all continuous pageant, for all his being was mask:

> . . . in the great banqueting-house, all . . . were assembled;
> at the vpper end whereof was the Kings Chayre of State,
> and on the right hand thereof, was a sumptuous pauilien
> for the Prince and his associats, from whence with great
> brauery and ingenious deuices, they descended into the
> middle of the Roome, and there the Prince performed
> his first feates of armes, that is to say, at Barriers against
> all commers, beeing assisted only with six others, . . .
> Euery Challenger fought with eight seuerall defendants,
> two seuerall combats at the two seuerall weapons, viz.
> at push of pike, and with single sword, the Prince per-
> formed this challenge with wonderous skill, and courage,
> to the great ioy and admiration of all the beholders. . . .
> These feates of armes with their triumphant shewes be-
> gan before ten a clocke at night, and continued there vn-
> till the next morning being Sunday: and that day the

Prince feasted all the combatants, at Saint Iames, and
then gaue rich prizes vnto three of the best deseruers
defendants.[38]

That warlike, chivalric persona which Henry had displayed at his
barriers was well captured in an engraving of Henry done by Simon
van de Passe (see Fig. 6) which was copied and printed repeatedly.
Michael Drayton used it with the dedication of his *Poly-Olbion*,
with the following descriptive verses (for which compliment Henry
granted him an annuity of ten pounds, no small sum in those days):

> BRITAINE, *behold here portrayd, to thy sight,*
> Henry, *thy best hope, and the world's delight;*
> *Ordain'd to make thy eight Great* Henries, *nine:*
> *Who, by that vertue in the trebble Trine,*
> *To his owne goodnesse (in his Being) brings*
> *These severall Glories of th'eight English Kings;*
> *Deep Knowledge, Greatnes, long Life, Policy,*
> *Courage, Zeale, Fortune, awfull Majestie.*
> *He like great* Neptune *on three Seas shall rove,*
> *And rule three Realms, with triple power like* Jove;
> *Thus in soft Peace, thus in tempestuous Warres,*
> *Till from his foote, his Fame shall strike the starres.*[39]

Van de Passe's engraving was interesting enough for the medievalism
of its programme—the plumed helmet and the jousting knights in the
background—as though Prince Henry were an embodiment of a past
vitality (this strength dramatically emphasized, of course, by the
thrusting lance, the prince's legs muscular and braced for the lunge),
but more interesting ultimately was the prince's face, seen in rigid
profile. This was a face certainly older than sixteen, but a face difficult to place in time, the timeless quality much enhanced by the profile angle. The mighty Roman nose, the strong chin, and the serious
eye all combined to render Prince Henry out of time and beyond it.
Figures seen in profile traditionally transcended time, for there was
no eye contact with the viewer which might localize the subject and
identify him along with the viewer in the here and now. No, van de
Passe's prince was well beyond the strictures of the sort of time which
pressed on those who might have gazed on this engraving with admir-
ation; here was a prince thrusting his lance of reenergized chivalry
into the future where he would ever be the master, not the subject,
of mutability.

Other evidence that Henry had reached a high level of symbolic

Si Pass sculp A° 1612.

Are to be soulde by Compton Holland . ouer
gainst the Exchange at the signe of the Globe .

ILLUSTRISSIMI GENEROSISSIMIQUE PRI. HENRICI
MAGNÆ BRITANNIÆ ET HYBERNIÆ PRINCIPIS,
Vera Effigies.

Figure 6. Van de Passe's engraving of Henry. Catalogue of Engraved
British Portraits, Vol. II, no. 14, p. 507. British Museum Department
of Drawings. Reproduced by courtesy of the Trustees of the British
Museum.

Figure 7. Miniature portrait of Henry, framed in shell, from the studio of Isaac Oliver. National Portrait Gallery (London), No. 1572. Reproduced by permission.

immutability among his people showed itself in a miniature painted by Isaac Oliver (see Fig. 7). Oliver used a similar romanesque profile to show a Prince Henry who had receded even beyond the medieval in his legendary presence: Oliver painted Henry in the draped toga of classical antiquity. The framing scallop shell niche, with its usual associations with divinity and immortality, completed the impression: this was Prince Henry as Roman general, if not as Roman god.

These stunning personations of Henry testified to his myth during the year of his investiture. Furthermore, there proceeded a steady heaping up of symbols right through the actual investiture ceremonies in June. Henry came up to London by barge from Richmond for the ceremony, and he was met on the Thames with a great water pageant wherein his patronage of England's ocean kingdom was both acknowledged and encouraged. (It seemed natural and fitting that Henry should enter London by water, but the Venetian ambassador observed at the time that "The King would not allow him on this occasion, nor yet on his going to Parliament, to be seen on horseback. The reason is the question of expense or, as some say, because they did not desire to exalt him too high."[40]) Nothing good can befall England, said the actor Richard Burbage, portraying Amphion, except Neptune show his favor, and on Henry's "sacred self" all of heaven had smiled. The prince was Jove's eagle, spreading his mighty wings and lifting his gaze on high: "Sunne of true-born Majestie shines in your bright eye."[41]

The two days before the investiture were filled with feasts and masques and the creation of new Knights of the Bath. Though King James may have wished not "to exalt him too high," Henry had arrived at the finest hour of his young life. On that Monday morning, June 5, 1610, Parliament met and awaited the arrival of Henry. They sat in state according to their rank, with the archbishop having precedence, followed by the Marquis of Winchester, all the earls, seventeen bishops, and the barons of the kingdom who formed the upper house. "Lower down" were all the members for the constituencies who formed the lower house of Parliament, with their Speaker situated on a raised chair with the arms of England above him. Special places had been provided for the Lord Mayor of London and twenty of his aldermen, for the ambassadors of Spain, France, the United Provinces, and other nations, and "a litell beneth them sate the litell sonnes of the nobilitie, I thinke to the number of xxiiij which was a verie goodlye sight to beholde so manie litell infants of

suche noble parentage, about the age of nine or tenne yeares apeece,
some more and some lesse."[42] Henry's brother and sister were there,
the Duke of York and the Lady Elizabeth; but Queen Anne was conspicuously absent. Dominating the whole of the assemblage was the
king, seated under a sumptuous canopy at the upper end of the
chamber.

Everyone, except the sober parliamentarians from the lower
house, were dressed in their bravest finery for this event. The reds and
crimsons and scarlets of the earls, bishops, and judges dominated the
hall, adding the symbolism of color to the symbolism of rite. At
least one of the members of Commons was put off by this display.
John Noies, the Member of Parliament representing Calne, wrote
home to his wife afterward a detailed account of the ceremony, with
a few pointed criticisms: "Yf I shoulde take in hand to write of the
apparell and facions of the ladies and maydes of honor I shoulde be
as foolishe as they were vaine, and therefore I saye no more then this
that they were unspeakable brave, and intollerable curious." Master Noies might modulate his puritan disdain enough to allow for
such show on the occasion of the elevation of Prince Henry, the
champion of Christianity, but the pious M.P. could not help feeling
that he at least was out of place in such a setting: "The whole howse
beinge thus furnished with sumptous and shininge apparrell I thought
my selfe to be like a crowe in the middes of a great manie of golden
feathered doves."[43] But John Noies and those others from Commons
who shared his unease amidst the pageantry and show were Prince
Henry's most ardent constituents; though they came to watch him
invested among the trappings of a court they disliked, they somehow assumed him not really a part of it. This was merely an odd
station on his march to the battlefield, they thought, not realizing
how thoroughly their conqueror prince was a child of such theater.
Without the art, the glitter, the illusion, he was nothing on which to
found the unrealistic hopes of an entire ambitious nation.

The assembled Lords and Commons were kept waiting for more
than two hours as Henry made himself ready. He finally entered accompanied by twenty-five newly created Knights of the Bath ("so
termed," wrote John Noies, "as some thinke, because they were
bathed and washed with sweete waters"), and at his appearance "all
the trumpeters and drumme players did sound out theyer instruments, with others which played uppon cornets and flutes with such
an acclamation and exultation as if the heavens and the earthe would

Figure 8. Portrait of Henry, attributed to Isaac Oliver. From the collection at Parham Park, Sussex. Reprinted by permission.

Figure 9. Detail of Figure 8.

have come togeather."[44] Henry strode to the center of the chamber, where he stopped and bowed three times to the king. The Earls of Nottingham and Northampton came down from the king's dais and escorted the prince forward, while the Earls of Sussex and Huntingdon bore the heavy train. Henry knelt before his father for more than fifteen minutes while his several titles were read in Latin and his letters patent were presented by the Earl of Salisbury. Henry was created Prince of Wales, Duke of Cornwall, Earl of Chester, Duke of Rothsay, and Baron Renfrew. He was ceremoniously robed in a mantle of purple velvet, and King James girded him with a sword of office, placed a coronet on his head, a ring on his finger, and a long golden wand in his hand. Henry was characteristically solemn, the king unusually jovial, considering what this symbolic investiture would do to the prince's already considerable pride. It was said that James "displayed great affection, now saying that the Prince must not mind humbling himself to his father, now playfully patting his cheek and giving him other tokens of love."[45] The "great affection" of the king was purely in character, but his joking admonition "that the Prince must not mind humbling himself" was reminiscent of what the king had said to his son on receiving the news of his accession to the English throne: "Be not insolent. . . . Be not willful."

In honor of his own elevation to the Principality of Wales, Henry commissioned a magnificent equestrian portrait of himself—another revolutionary first in the history of English royal portraiture (it was amazing how this one royal prince consistently called on the artists of England to transcend the traditional limits of their art to find new idioms to express his princely glory). In this very large portrait (see Fig. 8), Henry sat astride an unusually large and powerful horse. The prince seemed delicately fragile in contrast to the solid weight of the horse, so that the portrait communicated both overwhelming power and a sense of airy grace. In the distance the rising sun shed her symbolic rays of truth upon the gloomy world into which the prince rode with such smiling confidence. Worked into the skirts of Henry's armor and along the edges of the horse's saddle was a repeated *impresa* (see Fig. 9, detail), a highly symbolic emblem which was supposed to communicate a royal or heroic figure's private vision of himself and of his role in this world. Henry's *impresa* depicted human arms issuing from the ground and holding aloft anchors, while the sun rose over mountains in the distance. Anchors were the usual symbols for faith, while the rising sun was conventionally associated with

hope and the coming of truth. Here then was Henry, not as others
wished him to be so much as he himself perceived his role in the sixteenth year of his life: a sure anchor for his country and his religion,
the crusader for righteousness.

In conversations Henry had with Sir John Hayward, during which
the Prince encouraged Hayward in writing his *History of the III. Norman Kings of England,* the prince showed that he was fully aware of
the process and usefulness of personation as it applied to royalty.
History, Henry told Hayward, was as much a contribution to the
royal persona as the more obvious means of paint and poetry. "And
is not this," he said to Hayward,

> an errour in vs, to permit euery man to be a writer of His-
> torie? Is it not an errour to be so curious in other matters,
> and so carelesse in this? We make choise of the most skil-
> full workemen to draw or carue the portraiture of our
> faces, and shall euery artlesse Pensell delineate the dispo-
> sition of our minds? Our apparell must be wrought by
> the best Artificers, and no soile must be suffered to fall
> vpon it: and shall our actions, shall our conditions be de-
> scribed by euery bungling hand? Shall euery filthie fin-
> ger defile our reputation? Shall our Honour be basely
> buried in the drosse of rude and absurd writings? Wee
> are carefull to prouide costly Sepulchers, to preserue our
> dead liues, to preserue some memorie that wee haue
> bene: but there is no monument, either so durable, or so
> largely extending, or so liuely and faire, as that which is
> framed by a fortunate penne; . . .[46]

This was a remarkable speech, for Henry showed himself dissatisfied
with the arts alone for mythologizing his role; history also, that apparently unmanipulatable handmaiden of truth, must be made to
serve the myth. Henry did indeed know the uses of personation. What
was left for him to discover were the harsh, unexpected limits. He
was, in fact, quite vulnerable.

Notes to Chapter 3

1. *The Autobiography of Phineas Pett,* ed. W. G. Perrin, *Publications of the Navy Records Society,* vol. 51 (London, 1918), 20-22.
Edward Edwards thinks it possible that it was on the occasion of the
launching of the *Disdain* in the spring of 1604 that Prince Henry

could have met Ralegh for the first time. The ceremony took place on Tower Wharf and Ralegh was then resident in the Tower. See *Lives of the Founders of the British Museum* (London, 1870), I, 160.

2. Pett's *Autobiography*, 29.

3. Amply demonstrated by Michael Oppenheim, *A History of the Administration of the Royal Navy* (London, 1896; reprt. Hamden, Conn., 1961), *passim*.

4. Pett's *Autobiography*, 31.

5. The letter was reprinted from *Remains of Sir Walter Ralegh*, 1656-1657, in Edward Edwards, *The Life of Sir Walter Ralegh* (London, 1868), II, 330-332.

6. Unaccountably, many of Ralegh's biographers have perpetuated the mistaken opinion that Prince Henry and shipbuilder Pett were guided by Sir Walter's design. Edward Thompson (*Sir Walter Ralegh*, 1936) follows this line, as do Donald Barr Chidsey (*Sir Walter Ralegh: That Damned Upstart*, 1931), Hugh Ross Williamson (*Sir Walter Raleigh*, 1951), and Willard M. Wallace (*Sir Walter Raleigh*, 1959). These writers and others who persist in labeling Phineas Pett as that "good and honest shipbuilder" should beware that they have only Master Pett's word on it. He was, as his *Autobiography* clearly shows, an egregious Uriah Heep. He most certainly did not make himself Sir Walter Ralegh's pupil in the design of sailing ships.

7. Alexander Brown, *The Genesis of the United States* (London, 1890), I, 108-109.

8. See *C.S.P., Venetian*, XI (1607-1610), par. 449: "The Prince has put some money in [the Virginia Plantation], so that he may, some day, when he comes to the Crown, have a claim over the Colony." Sir Thomas Dale's appointment to the Colony and Henry's part in it are detailed in Brown's *Genesis of the United States*, II, 870-872; and in Robert Hunt Land's "Henrico and Its College," *William and Mary College Quarterly Historical Magazine*, 18, n.s. (October, 1938), 453-498; see particularly 460-464. See also, Ralph Hamor, *A true discourse of the present estate of Virginia* (London, 1615). About the general spirit of exploration which associated itself with Henry, William Laird Clowes had this to say: "The impetus given to maritime enterprise by the encouragement of the government of Queen Elizabeth did not lose its force at her death, but continued in full vigour, . . . due partly to that love of adventure which had been so thoroughly aroused, . . . but also to the warm and active support which the great Queen's policy received from her young godson, Prince Henry," *The Royal Navy* (London, 1898), II, 82. That there should have been and was great Puritan interest in Virginia and in Henry's role in that enterprise is obvious enough. See, for

example, H. R. Trevor-Roper, *Archbishop Laud* (London, 1940), 99: "James I had complained that the Virginia Company 'was but a seminary to a seditious Parliament,' and that, in spite of the time and money absorbed by it, 'yet it hath not produced any other effects than that smoky weed of tobacco.'"

9. William Crashaw, *A Sermon preached in London* (London, 1610), sigs. C 2, D, I, I 2. See also Brown, *Genesis of the United States*, I, 367.

10. Erondelle's dedication to Henry of Marc Lescarbot's *Nova Francia* (London, 1609), sig. ¶ ¶^{V}.

11. Edward Wright, *Certain errors in nauigation*, 3d ed. (London, 1610), sig. *4.

12. Printed in *The Voyages of Captain Luke Foxe and Captain Thomas James in Search of a North-West Passage,* ed. Miller Christy (London: Hakluyt Soc., 1894), II, 644.

13. *Ibid.,* II, 636; see also I, xvi-xvii, xix-xx, 125, 241; II, 635. For more information concerning Henry's interest and involvment in the Northwest Passage enterprises, see *Narratives of Voyages toward the North-West,* ed. Thomas Rundall (London: Hakluyt Soc., 1849), pp. 81-85; Samuel Purchas, *Purchas His Pilgrimage,* 4th ed. (London, 1626), fol. 819; *Henry Hudson the Navigator,* ed. G. M. Asher (London: Hakluyt Soc., 1860), 104; George T. Clark, *Some Account of Sir Robert Mansel and of Admiral Thomas Button* (Dowlais, 1883); Brown, *Genesis of the United States,* II, 556, 574; Clowes, *The Royal Navy,* II, 86; Pett's *Autobiography,* 95; *Letters of John Chamberlain,* I, 321-322.

14. Quotations from Pett's *Autobiography,* 50, 62. On the miscalculation in building the *Prince Royal,* see both Oppenheim, *A History of the Administration of the Royal Navy,* 186, and Clowes, *The Royal Navy,* II, 3-5.

15. Pett's *Autobiography,* 35, 76-86.

16. *The Works of Sir Walter Ralegh* (Oxford, 1829), VIII, 307.

17. *Ibid.,* VIII, 307.

18. *Ibid.,* VIII, 310.

19. *Ibid.,* VIII, 239.

20. *Ibid.,* II, 328; see also VIII, 389.

21. *Ibid.,* VIII, 68, 69; see also VIII, 102.

22. *Ibid.,* VIII, 95.

23. *Ibid.,* VIII, 72.

24. Quoted by A. L. Rowse, *Sir Walter Ralegh* (New York, 1962), 256.

25. *The Works of Sir Walter Ralegh,* VIII, 788.

26. *C.S.P., Venetian,* XI (1607-1610), par. 393.

27. Cotton's "Answer" published with the original "Arguments

for War" in *An Answer Made to Certain Propositions of War and Peace, Delivered to his Highness by some of his military servants* (London, 1655); discussed by Thomas Birch, *The Life of Henry, Prince of Wales* (London, 1760), 186-187.

28. *C.S.P., Venetian,* XI (1607-1610), par. 430.

29. *The Kings Majesties Speech to the Lords and Commons, xxj. March 1609* (London, 1609), sig. F 3ᵛ.

30. *Parliamentary Debates in 1610,* ed. S. R. Gardiner (London: Camden Soc., 1862), 3; see also 1-2, 48-49.

31. *C.S.P., Venetian,* XI (1607-1610), par. 826. For illuminating discussions of the Court of Wards, see H. E. Bell, *An Introduction to the History and Records of the Court of Wards and Liveries* (Cambridge, 1953) and Joel Hurstfield, *The Queen's Wards* (London, 1958). Also for general help in sorting out many of the issues between Crown and Parliament, including wardship and purveyance, see David Harris Willson, "The Earl of Salisbury and the 'Court' Party in Parliament, 1604-1610," *American Historical Review,* 36 (January, 1931), 274-294.

32. *C.S.P., Venetian,* XI (1607-1610), par. 430; see also par. 837.

33. *The Diary of Walter Yonge, Esq.,* ed. George Roberts (London: Camden Soc., 1848), 19.

34. Daniel Price, *The creation of the Prince* (London, 1610), sigs. D 2 - D 2ᵛ.

35. *C.S.P., Venetian,* XI (1607-1610), par. 738.

36. *Ben Jonson,* ed. Herford and Simpson, VII, 327.

37. I am indebted here to Stephen Orgel, *The Jonsonian Masque* (Cambridge, Mass., 1965).

38. John Stow, *Annales* (London, 1631), sig. Ffff4ᵛ. Quoted by E. C. Wilson, *Prince Henry and English Literature,* 79.

39. *The Works of Michael Drayton,* ed. J.W. Hebel (Oxford, 1933), IV, iv*.

40. *C.S.P., Venetian,* XI (1607-1610), par. 945.

41. *London's love to the royal Prince Henry* (London, 1610), reprinted in John Nichols, *The Progresses, Processions and Magnificent Festivities of King James the First* (New York, 1828), II, 322.

42. From the ms. account of the investiture written by John Noies (in the private collection of W. Cleverly Alexander), *Report on Manuscripts in Various Collections,* vol. III, Historical Manuscripts Commission (London, 1904), 259. This account has been supplemented by *C.S.P., Venetian,* XI (1607-1610), par. 945. See also *The order and solemnitie of the creation of Prince Henrie* (London, 1610).

43. Hist. MSS. Comm. *Var. Collect.,* III, 260.

44. *Ibid.*

45. *C.S.P., Venetian,* XI (1607-1610), par. 945.

46. John Hayward, *The Lives of the III. Normans, Kings of England* (London, 1613), sig. A 2ᵛ.

4

The Rival Myth:
Warfare vs. Fertility

I

Henry was by the year of his investiture reformed religion's most dazzling work of art, sculpted in flesh and blood. What the Protestants—especially the Puritans—could do to shape him they had done, in tract, sermon, and essay, but also occasionally in poem and song. In turn, the royal portraiture which depicted the growing prince for the nation's eyes reflected the stunning success of the mythologizing process.

Though Henry had been from birth wrapped in the robes of a belligerent Protestantism, there was, in England at least, a counter force represented by moderate Protestants (and, one is assured, by some secret Catholics), whose devotion to the *via media* made religious controversy and war-mongering repugnant. This group of writers—largely poets—had by Henry's investiture in 1610 lost any hope of shaping him to a more temperate national role. They did not see the dangers of the radical Protestant mythologizing process until the prince was incontrovertibly the possession of the Puritans—or, seeing early the danger of a prince made the center of a Puritan cosmography, the moderates lost the initiative by developing too slowly a counter-personation of their own to offer Henry. Either way, the prince was lost from the civilizing influence of the moderate view. This battle of alternative personations—though the outcome was never in doubt—goes directly to the heart of what Henry had symbolically become by the year of his investiture, so it seems worthwhile to delay the narration of the years 1610-1612 in order to account for this literary struggle between rival myths.

The Puritan/Protestant personation (to recapitulate briefly) began with the mask of Hercules in Scotland, developed a mystique of masculine chastity and a disdain for the feminine, and became most forcefully associated in England with the overreach of Alexander the Great. This persona was driven by a need to cross boundaries, to burst outward through what the radical Protestants considered the suffocating ring of Catholicism, but for all the phallic thrust of sword and lance, this conqueror personation was rather noticeably sterile:

> God will strengthen your arme, and giue edge to your sword to strike through the loins of all them that are the supporters of that Antichristian and wicked state.
>
> Robert Abbot[1]

> Go forward, Princely Solomon, . . . give the Whore of Babylon that foil, & fall, from which she shall neuer rise, euen that deadly blow whereof she shall neuer recouer.
>
> William Crashaw[2]

This conquering prince, whether compared to Alexander, Caesar, Hannibal, or a more pious Josiah, was a slayer, not a life-bringer:

> Renowmed [sic] Prince, . . . giue me leaue, . . . to wish . . . that I may liue to march ouer the Alpes, and to trayle a pike before the walls of Rome, vnder your Highnesse Standard.
>
> Samson Lennard[3]

> You are learned enough for a Prince. . . . Do not therefore mold any longer among your bookes. . . . To horse, to horse, the quarter is broken, the bloody Trumpet hath sounded; true & mortall warre is open.
>
> Edmond Richer[4]

Or, as Daniel Price expressed it, Henry as conqueror was a cure for the disease of popery, but a cure that killed the body to save the soul:

> The *infection* of Popery spreads too farre: . . . The eies, the harts, and hopes of all the Protestant world, be fixed vpon your *Highnesse,* all expecting your Gracious faithfulnes, & readines in the extirpation of that man of sinne. March valiantly herein . . . and the God of Princes shall protect you.[5]

In perhaps the most characteristic set of metaphors used to de-

scribe Henry—comet, bright star, new sun (with the inevitable pun)
of the western hemisphere—the prince was given those qualities which
knew no limits or boundaries: he shined above the earth and the rays
of his light/truth fell on all nations. But that light sparking from
Henry's eyes could be more like the gaze of a basilisk than the benevolent warmth of a heavenly body, simply because Henry was so often
a "COMMET of dreadfull terrour."[6] William Leigh described "the
blaze" of honor which he saw in the "Princely countenance" and
Gervase Markham spoke of "the glorie of your countenance."[7]

As the myth developed, that which Henry looked upon with favor would flourish. One writer observed that the ancient art of horsemanship had been given new life because Henry had bestowed his attention upon it, and another writer professed that Henry's divine
sense of sight could animate dumb granite: "by your fauorable looks,
giue [my words] a speaking-power, as the Sunnes reflection did on
the Image of *Memnon.*"[8]

If the prince could be called upon to look with favor on a poet's
song or preacher's harangue, by extension those self-same mystical
beams would strike terror into the hearts of the unworthy, the wicked,
and the pagan. Indeed, for the Puritans Henry was the center of all
lines of sight: he was a colossus, seemingly all eye, piercing into every
corner and revealing the godly—who gloried in his light—and the un-
godly—who hid their eyes. "The eyes of all Christendom are now cast
vpon you, to see you begin,"[9] said one pamphleteer in an outright
call for war, for what mattered above all else in Henry's Puritan myth—
what had mattered from the beginning—was appearance. Sight was by
ancient and common assumption the most powerful of the senses,
much feared as the easy tool of Satan in seducing the faithful Christian. How many patriarchs, heroes, and saints had been tempted to
sin by the waywardness of the eye? Yet for England's Puritans, Henry
was God's own vision of the future, so those who should have dis-
trusted mere appearance indulged in an orgy of sight. Henry was sight
purified; when he looked on the world he was not deceived by appear-
ances (though he himself was primarily show), and by his light others
could see with intensified and purified sight. Those dwelling in the
sub-lunar world, surrounded on every side by the corruptible, seeing
as in a glass darkly, suddenly found in Henry a celestial light, an inti-
mation of divinity, a revelation of God's promise for a new heaven
and a new earth. For those who believed in young Prince Henry and

in his myth, his light-filled countenance seemed to lead them upwards
—and outwards—toward the new Jerusalem. There was, of course,
nothing revolutionary in using a semi-divine figure as intermediary
between the world of despair and mutability and the world of perma-
nence and glory. This represented, after all, the platonic doctrine of
correspondences and the possibility of ascent through contemplation,
though the Puritans had replaced the beautiful women of the poets—
Beatrice, Laura, Julia, etc.—with an equally mythic young prince.

Something like a psychology of perception developed among
the partisan Protestants of England: Prince Henry was, as the anonymous author of a sonnet ("To My Lord the Prince") put it, "Centre
where lines of all hearts loues do meete."[10] As Henry was seen in one
of his royal portraits, or in a masque at court, or in the imagery of
complimentary verse, he was a center which defined perimeters; all
other things were secondary and took their position and function
from their relationship to him. But it was not only the features of
each work of art in which Henry was depicted that arranged themselves according to his ascendancy; the nation itself formed God's
greatest work of art, with Prince Henry the focal point. All lines of
sight met in Henry. This exercise of a national Protestant perception
meant that all of Catholic Europe could shrink to an insignificant bit
of background detail—like the deer park in Peake's hunting portrait
of Henry—for the prince, representative of God's blessing, commanded and overwhelmed the foreground.

This myth of Henry allowed ambitious Protestants to see the
geography of Europe from a self-flattering angle: the Channel was a
mere pond, easily stepped across, and Catholic Europe, a theater
where Henry's appearance would be enough to frighten Spaniard,
Frenchman, and Turk alike. With the godly Prince Henry as the center of every picture, both those on canvas and those in the mind, the
lines of perspective could stretch into infinity. In fact, the further
off the enemy, the smaller he seemed, so that from the vantage point
of Protestant England—beguiled by this trick of heroic illusion and
perspective—no wall or limit or boundary looked strong enough or
high enough to contain their conquering prince. It was only a matter
of time. He was, as Peacham had already written, "A prodigie for
foes to gaze vpon, / But still a glorious Load-starre" for England.[11]

There was in this Puritan myth of Henry a massive irony: it was
surely paradoxical that those left-wing religious forces in England,

which generally favored the republican inclinations of Parliament against the prerogative of monarchs, should construct an image of a prince who was, by the working of his myth, illimitable. Part of that paradox dissolves, however, when we remember that Prince Henry was from his birth programmed to be a conqueror of other countries more than a ruler of his own. His face was turned carefully away from Great Britain toward the bastions of Catholicism. Beyond the irony that the Puritans helped shape for themselves a prince who, had he become king, would surely have been repugnant to them, there is perhaps the more compelling psychology of martyrdom. Pride, ordinarily, was as much a cardinal sin for Puritans as for Catholics; yet the sort of pride—arrogance, really—which went into the Henry myth was fuel for self-immolation. (One recalls Patrick Galloway expounding upon the story of Isaac at the time of Henry's baptism.) Those Protestant minds which saw Henry in the robes of some conquering hero had also been fed on the blood and fire of John Fox's martyrology. Those two mythologies combined to produce an even greater paradox: England's hero must bear a flashing sword and ride over his enemies unscathed, but he must also shed his blood courageously in desperate sacrifice. That he could not do both did not bother the otherwise logical minds of England's Puritans, and we need not spend reams of paper exploring their psychology to understand that Prince Henry was ceremoniously dressed in the robes of the conqueror while he was being led to the slaughtering stone of martyrdom. Catholic legend was full of immolated saints, from whose blood the ground of faith was replenished; Protestantism had warriors enough but very few heroic sacrificial lambs, those types of Christ who could revitalize the nation by the example of their wounds. But as we have seen, Prince Henry was the Puritans' great work of art, unrealistic and impractical to the core. By his immolation he could rally the nation to a fervor of faith and reform. But that a national transformation depended more upon the sacrifice of Henry than upon his triumph was probably not understood clearly by the men who impelled the prince toward his fiery destiny. They wished the boy only goodwill, godspeed, and the ministering protection of heaven—or so they likely would have replied had they been asked—yet the myth by which they made Henry live speaks differently. Henry, in the heavy robes of his honor, stood uncomprehending before the abyss into which his ambitious subjects would hurl him.

II

But not all his subjects. There were those who found the Protestant myth of conqueror repugnant, and they began to speak against it only after it had taken firm hold of Henry's mind and had infused most of the country with the promise of fulfilled ambitions. The first warnings came from those who in a general sense saw ruination in Henry's growing pride. A thoughtful man and scholar like Robert Cotton, for example, in writing his "Answer to Propositions of War" spoke directly to Prince Henry from the precedents of history: "It is manifest by warrant of our own examples, that the Kings of England . . . preferred unjust peace before the justest war: none enthralling their minds with ambitious desires of extending territories. . . ."[12] Henry's mind, trained as it was to shun soft and feminine peace, might find Cotton's arguments laughably unheroic, but that military turn of mind, said Sir Robert, was exactly the force which was so dangerous:

> The last mischief is the disposition that military education leaueth in the minds of many; for it is not born with them that they so much distaste peace, but proceeds from that custom that hath made in them another nature. It is rarely found that euer Ciuil troubles of this State were dangerously undertaken, but where the plot and pursuit was made by a spirit so infused (fols. 20-21).

The war-mongering party had hailed Henry as a "prodigie," but Cotton warned of the second meaning of that *prodigy:*

> . . . euery age breeds some exorbitant spirits, who turn the edge of their own sufficiency upon whatsoeuer they can deuour in their ambitious apprehensions, seeking rather a great then a good fame; and holding it the chiefest Honour to be thought the wonder of their times: which if they attain to, it is but the condition of monsters, that are generally much admired but more abhored (fol. 22).

Bishop Hall, who had himself once called on Henry to defend the faith against the fiendish *Peace of Rome* in 1609, changed his tone when he began to see that in the prince's mind defense of England meant aggression against Europe. No friend of the Puritans, Bishop Hall could speak very bluntly at times and he knew the myth which

needed pricking; he addressed the "Gentlemen of his Highnesse Court"
sharply: "I speake boldly, the Court is as nigh to heauen as the Cell,"[13]
and in an "Epistle" to Adam Newton, the prince's life-long tutor and
part of the company which had flattered his ambitions, Hall warned
against flattery as the greatest of dangers to princes: "It had beene
better for many great ones not to haue been, than to haue beene in
their conceits more than men."[14] *Conceit* for the early seventeenth
century was primarily an imaginary picture, a poetic vision, and
Henry had been to a remarkable extent the product of religious and
military *tropes.* Hall understood well enough the dangers which lay
ahead, not in the boy himself so much as in the collective imagination which was shaping him:

> Who can but wonder, that reads of some not unwise
> Princes, so bewitched with the inchantments of their Par-
> asites, that they haue thought themselues Gods immortal,
> and haue suffered themselues so styled, so adored? Nei-
> ther Temples nor Statues, nor Sacrifices haue seemed
> too much glory to the greatnesse of their selfe-loue
> (fol. 280).

Hall had seen, undoubtedly, the portraiture which Henry inspired,
had read and heard the prevailing metaphors, for his characterization
was all too accurate. He let Adam Newton know that such *art* was
the culprit and called on the tutor to break its false hold on Henry:

> How happy a seruice shall you do to this whole world of
> ours, if you shall still settle in that princely minde a true
> apprehension of himselfe . . .; To break those false glasses,
> that would present him a face, not his owne (fol. 280).

This theme that Prince Henry knew not his own face, had become the captive, not the author, of his military persona, appeared
in other places. In the remarkably ecumenical and tolerant *Catholique traditions,* translated from French and published in 1609 by
Lewis Owen, the role of peace-maker was praised for Henry's benefit.
"Princes and Soueraigne Magistrates should beare sole authority,"
Owen conceded, but

> not so much to dispute and winne the victory, as to con-
> ferre, and amiably to agree: The God of peace will giue
> the fruit of peace, to his glory and our good. But I know
> not by what Inchantment or destinie, Kings for the most
> part know not their forces, and willingly do dispoyle

> themselues of a greate part of their owne Authoritie,
> and many times perceiue it too late.[15]

Owen suggested that within any prince's personation lay great powers, but all of Prince Henry's masks seemed to wear the grim face of
war. Owen called on Henry to be a "great Reconciler" (sig. A 2^v),
but that particular mask must have seemed too small and ignomin-
ious for a boy who had been raised on irreconcilable controversy. The
arguments in *Catholique traditions* were well in advance of their
times; had Henry been molded in the personation of the Prince as
Healer—and had he lived to fulfill it—the history of England's religious
and political strife might have been far different. But it was mighty
deeds which had captured the prince's imagination and fervor. Countering that aura, Owen wrote of an even more glorious undertaking
than conquest—the reconciliation of differing religions:

> Great Attempts become great Princes. And is there a
> greater or a more worthy enterprise, more holy in itselfe,
> and more comfortable to the world, then the re-establish-
> ing of peace in the Church, and the refreshing of Chris-
> tendome, through the reconcilement of the differences,
> which ignorance, auarice and ambition haue hatched, and
> which passion and stomacke doe as yet maintaine? (sig.
> A 2)

But reconcilement, the binding of religious wounds, was not part of
the Puritan programme for Henry.

It was a considerable commonplace to dedicate a history or
tragedy to the edification of a great man—in some general sense almost everything written had its educational value, quite apart from
the special genre of "courtesy books." Samuel Daniel, in dedicating
his tragedy of *Philotas* to Henry, warned against ambition:

> To you most hopefull Prince, not as you are,
> But as you may be, doe I giue these lines:
> That when your iudgement snall arriue so farre,
> As t'ouer-looke th'intricate designes
> Of vncontented man: you may beholde
> With what encounters greatest fortunes close,
> What dangers, what attempts, what manifolde
> Incumbrances ambition vndergoes:
> How hardly men digest felicitie;
> How to th'intemprate, to the prodigall,
> To wantonnesse, and vnto luxurie,

> Many things want, but to ambition all.
> And you shall finde the greatest enemie
> That man can haue, is his prosperitie.[16]

Samuel Daniel was in the service of Queen Anne, herself violently solicitous of Catholicism, especially of Spanish Catholicism. Daniel introduced into his masque, *Tethys' Festival; Or, The Queen's Wake* (written at Anne's instigation for performance in honor of Henry's investiture on June 5, 1610) another blunt plea to the newly enrobed Henry to change his warlike mask for one more beneficial to England. I shall not tarry to examine the entire masque, for it was only in an opening presentation of a sword, scabbard, and scarf that the focus of the dramatization lighted on Henry.

It was a simple matter in the presentation of a court masque to bring a royal spectator suddenly and symbolically onto the stage, merely by addressing that spectator and by making him the recipient of the focusing power of the poetry and spectacle. Thus Henry was made briefly a non-speaking actor in *Tethys' Festival*. Tethys, Queen of the Ocean and wife of Neptune (the part was played by Anne herself, an avid masquer, to the chagrin of many Puritans), presented a richly ornamented sword to Henry as an additional honor to her newly invested son. Zephirus (enacted by Charles, Duke of York, a young and wobbly understudy to the magnificence of his elder brother) was commanded by Tethys to bear the sword to Henry, while she pronounced the requisite lecture on its significance. Daniel, apparently eager for any opportunity to challenge the Puritan myth of the prince or merely willing to serve Queen Anne's own dislike of the anti-Catholic party, made much of the scabbard in which the sword was enclosed and of the scarf, which was a binding force. The Queen/Tethys spoke of the prince as life-force, bounded by England's natural borders:

> greete the Lord
> And Prince of th'Iles (the hope and the delight,
> Of all the Northerne Nations) with this sword
> That she vnto Astraea sacred found,
> And not to be vnsheath'd but on iust ground.
> Herewith, says [Tethys], deliuer him from mee
> This skarffe, the zone of loue and Amitie,
> T'ingird the same; wherein he may suruay,
> Infigur'd all the spacious Emperie
> That he is borne vnto another day.

> Which, tell him, will be world enough to yeeld
> All / workes of glory euer can be wrought.
> Let him not passe the circle of that field,
> But thinke Alcides pillars are the knot;
> For there will be within the large extent
> Of these my waues, and watry Gouernment
> More treasure, and more certaine riches got
> Than all the Indies to Iberus brought. . . .[17]

Almost like a conjurer, the Queen tried to weave with a magic phrase a restraining net about the ambitions of her son: "Let him not passe the circle of that field."

Henry attracted enough of the sort of warnings contained in Daniel's dedicatory sonnet attached to *Philotas* and in *Tethys Festival* for us to know that something other than a vague sense of his general welfare was drawing the comments. Pointed warnings appeared repeatedly, aimed at Henry's proud, ambitious personation. Since Henry had early been pictured as a Protestant Alexander, that role was frequently given new and quite harsh scrutiny by those moderate in both their religion and their politics.

III

One of those who reinterpreted the mask of Alexander for Henry was Sir George More, in his *Principles for yong princes.* With commendable directness More served up a stringent antidote both to the Stuart understanding of Divine Right and to the prince's particular persona which relied so heavily on God's special favor. Sir George made it quite clear that kings and princes were nothing more than men, more subject to divine, ecclesiastical, and the common laws than master of them or coequal with them. More mentioned Alexander the Great, first as an example of a just prince, but Sir George was at pains to remove any aura of incarnation; in fact, More's Alexander was shown later to be too proud, ambitious, disdainful of his subjects and unfaithful to his word. More took special care to divest Alexander of "the Great-" ness and of the mystique of rulership, quite in contrast to the Puritan authors who, ironically, had been all too ready to find in Henry a godhead and in Alexander the Great a pattern for Prince Henry. A prince must not be proud, wrote More; Caesar was murdered because of pride; a prince should be humble. The only metaphorical heightening which More allowed to the role of the prince involved his notion of the Commonwealth: "your High-nesse must labour, and spend the fruits of your haruest, for the hon-our of your selfe, and good of the commonwealth."[18] More spoke of Henry, not as the harvest itself, not quite as the fertility of land and people, but as the Lord of the Harvest, and as such, quite crucial to the well-being of the nation. Henry, or any other prince, might repre-sent in his person a force for fertility, but the life-giving property was fragile. The lord absent from his land was unthinkable; how could the commodity and felicity of his people be nurtured if the prince had pursued triumph to foreign lands? That had been one of Alexan-der the Great's mistakes; the false face of the appellation "Great" had led him away from land and people to fulfill the conceited linea-ments of base flattery: "A Prince therfore, to the end he may be strong at home, and need no forren force, should alwaies respect his owne subiects" (fols. 67^V-68). Implicit in that "respect" which a prince should show "his owne subiects" was an understanding that it was his roots in home soil which needed nurturing. This notion of domestic fertility as a function worthy of Henry's attention—contin-gent always on the prince's actual presence as an in-dwelling force—would eventually develop as a literary persona and rival myth. It was as though the royalist-conservative-Anglican voices in England, sens-ing Henry's determination to leap the Channel into a sure, consuming fire, thought they could restrain him by suggesting that the very fe-cundity of the soil was dependent upon his constant residence.

The suggestion of confinement, then—albeit a confinement rich with symbols of plenty and happiness—became one of the key images of the alternate myth. George Chapman, for example, long in Prince Henry's debt for his royal generosity, chose not to repay his young patron by adding to the approved personation. Rather, Chapman consistently contributed to the alternate myth of a prince within close bounds, serving the spiritual and physical well-being of his own small country. In *Euthymiae Raptus; or the Teares of Peace* (1609), Chapman, with an ironic eye on the Henry myth as it had developed, praised for the prince's benefit King James for out-laboring Hercules in stretching a universal peace across Europe. King James as Peace-Maker had cast nets over "th'impious lust of *Mars* ";[19] Chapman hoped other kings would follow James's example and limit the fractious spirits of war: "See, All; and imitate his goodnesse still" (l. 7). In the poem, Chapman as "the Interlocutor" declares himself the servant of Peace for the remainder of his life (ll. 1014-1021), and Peace replies

that the poet should write all he has discovered so that it might edify
others (l. 1048). The allegorical figure of Peace continues:

> But might it touch vpon
> Your gratious Princes liking; hee might doe
> Good to himselfe, and all his kingdomes too:
> So virtuous, a great Example is;
> .   .   .   .   .   .
> tell him you know me; and that I,
> That am the Crowne of Principalitie,
> (Though thus cast off by Princes) euer vow
> Attendance at his foote; . . . (ll. 1050-53; 1059-62)

Chapman, as an official member of Henry's household (Sewer-in-
Ordinary), could observe at close quarters the effect on the young
man of the mythologizing force which had been at work on him since
birth. Chapman must have stood by and listened to the boy talk of
his ultimate conquest of Europe. Though there were those who
beamed with approval on such talk and incited him to further boasts
—or to the real action symbolized by Henry's involvement with the
Royal Navy—Chapman would not join the intoxication of that myth.

In his dedication to Henry of the first twelve books of his translation of the *Iliad,* Chapman returned to the theme of confinement
in a long verse epistle. A prince's perfect happiness, Chapman wrote,
is not born with him, nor can it be purchased with gold; only he who
"gouernes inward" is blessed with happiness.[20] A prince's mind is a
microcosm in which "traitrous passions"—like overweening ambition
and pride—must be sent to the "Towre" (ll. 7-8):

> and in his minde [he]
> Holds such a scepter, as can keepe confinde
> His whole lifes actions in the royall bounds
> Of Vertue and Religion; . . . (ll. 9-12)

Thus a royal mind virtuously at peace with itself produces mysteriously the "complete empire" (l. 14). If Henry could tune his mind
to the virtues of "Princely presidents" (l. 15) found in Homer, he
would no longer think seriously of leading his nation in violent aggression against Catholic Europe. Homer's work was so sagacious,
Chapman advised, that Alexander the Great could have saved himself
much torment of spirit had he benefited from its instruction. Alexander, like Agamemnon, puffed by pride and committed to sacrilege
in the name of piety, broke the bonds within which royalty should

confine itself and led his people into a war which destroyed other nations as well as his own. To the prince who had been repeatedly called the English Alexander, Chapman ominously said: Alexander thought himself "sent from heauen . . . so diuine a creature" (ll. 22-23), but the end result of his pride proved him a singularly vulnerable mortal. God's divinity among men, the poet told the young, would-be demigod, is represented by Learning (ll. 73 ff) and Poesie (ll. 92 ff), not by the flashing brilliance of kings (ll. 80-81). These were all stern words, but Henry, seeing only with those mythic eyes which "flashed terrour to the East," could not comprehend the snares at his feet.

IV

One of the strongest voices to join this warning chorus was, ironically, Sir Walter Ralegh's. Ralegh, who had written so many pamphlets for Henry which were cynically bellicose and anti-Spanish, took a much modulated tone in his great masterpiece, *The History of the World*, written, as Ralegh said, for the instruction and benefit of his prince and benefactor. Despite how much Henry may have applauded Ralegh's shorter writings, which disclosed for his youthful eyes the secrets of ships and warfare and the weaknesses of Spanish fortresses in America, the *History of the World* could not have been so congenial. The *History* was animated by a not uncheerful pessimism regarding the abilities of any man—prince or yeoman—to seize initiatives and to control events; additionally, Ralegh's portraits of the great men of the past—heroes for whom Prince Henry had demonstrated a self-flattering curiosity—seemed shaped from one single and mighty theme—ambition begets cruelty and cruelty destroys itself.[21] But perhaps most unsatisfactory to the ego of a proud young prince would have been Ralegh's sense of the claustrophobia of men trapped by their pride; for all its massive sweep and the immensity of its stage, the *History of the World* was controlled by the cramped metaphors which Ralegh had learned from his Tower confinement.

The counterpoint in the *History* was between those whose ambitions drove them to cross boundaries and transgress limits in search of their destinies, and those who found a measure of grace by learning to walk the circumference of their tethers without despair. By far, those of the former group predominated in the *History* and the lesson should have been clear enough to Henry. Yet Ralegh knew well how self-flattery and self-mythology worked: "We behold other men's

tragedies played before us, we hear what is promised and threatened:
but the world's bright glory hath put out the eyes of our minds...."[22]
Perhaps Prince Henry was simply too much the thrall of "those be-
traying lights," but Ralegh attempted nonetheless to open his eyes.
The unflattering portraits of ambition multiplied in the *History*:

> The wars which David had made were just, and the blood
> therein shed was of the enemies of God and his church;
> yet for this cause it was not permitted that his hands
> should lay the foundation of that holy temple. Hereby it
> appears how greatly those princes deceive themselves,
> who think by bloodshed, and terror of their wars, to
> make themselves in greatness like to the Almighty, which
> is a damnable pride; not caring to imitate his mercy and
> goodness, or seek the blessedness promised by our Sav-
> iour unto the peacemakers (IV, 506).

> A valiant man he [Romulus] was, very strong of body,
> patient of travel, and temperate in diet, as forbearing the
> use of wine and delicacies: but his raging ambition he
> knew not how to temper, which caused him to slay his
> brother, and neglect to revenge the death of Tatius his
> companion in the kingdom, that he himself might be
> lord alone in those narrow territories (IV, 712).

> But of all this, and other [Nebuchadnezzar's] magnifi-
> cence, we find little else recorded, than that (which in-
> deed is most profitable for us to consider) his overvalu-
> ing of his own greatness abased him unto a condition in-
> ferior to the poorest of men. And not undeservedly fell
> these judgments of God upon him (V, 36-37).

> But as it is hard to discern and withstand the flatteries of
> our own appetites, so did Philip's ambitious desire to in-
> vade Persia abuse his judgment so far, that the death
> wherewith himself was threatened, he understood to be
> delivered of his enemy, whom he intended to invade (V,
> 296).

> In this sort did this glorious king [Darius], confident in
> the glittering, but heartless multitude which he com-
> manded, dispose of the already vanquished Macedonians:
> but the ill destinies of men bear them to the ground, by
> what strong confidence soever armed (V, 305).

The symbol of cruel ambition in the *History* was invasion, the willful crossing of boundaries, whether physical or imaginary, to impose one man's will upon hundreds, whether for the sake of lust, profit, or religion. All such ambitious spirits, though they triumphed initially and drank from golden goblets, ended badly. Nebuchadnezzar was but one paradigm among many: for his sins of pride he grew long of hair and nail and roamed the fields with beasts.

But the most powerful example for Henry should have been Ralegh's thorough portrait of Alexander the Great, since he was one of the Puritans' favorite masks of greatness for Henry. Ralegh joined George More and Chapman in denigrating Alexander's reputation, and interestingly enough, it was the transgression of limits which most condemned Alexander in Ralegh's eyes. The metaphor which Ralegh twice applied to Alexander evoked not only a power illimitable but also a power unnatural: "like the breaking in [upon land] of the ocean-sea" and "an overflow of waters, drowning all the level" (V, 303, 381). Alexander "ran over so large a portion of the world in so short a space, . . . limited by no greater opposition than desert places, . . . like the Colossus of Rhodes, not so much to be admired for the workmanship . . . as for the huge bulk" (V, 311). This was power and glory disproportionate, ugly and chaotic to the Greek mind, a sure product of vaulting ambition to Ralegh. Some of Alexander's counselors advised him to cease his conquering, Parmenio chief among them, but Alexander would hear nothing which suggested a limit to his grasp. The inability to see the freedom in confinement or the ironic imprisonment which the limitless horizon imposes was fatal for Alexander. Ralegh commented: "it is probable, that if he had followed [Parmenio's] advice, and bounded his ambition within those limits, he might have lived as famous for virtue as for fortune . . ." (V, 335). Soon every man, from wisest counsellor to lowest foot soldier, could see Alexander for what he was. By exalting himself—as Ralegh's steel-clad irony invariably worked—he debased himself. The army grumbled against him:

> . . . for the ambition of one man, a man that disdained Philip for his father, and would needs be called the son of Jupiter, they should all perish; for he not only enforced them to make war against worlds of enemies, but against rivers, mountains, and the heavens themselves (V, 333).

Since "the bounded earth sufficed not his boundless ambition" (V, 348), it was left to heaven to teach him humility. His death was as ignoble and unheroic—proportionate, in short—as his life had been a study in giantism.

For quietude and some small measure of blessing, Prince Henry must give up the large geographies of the imagination, wherein he saw his banner riding ever ahead of the wind. Ralegh had shown him poison in those ambitions. Only in small places did the heart and soul learn to bear their fruits:

> For while the law of nature was the rule of man's life, they then sought for no larger territory than themselves could compass and manure; they erected no other magnificent buildings, than sufficient to defend them from cold and tempest; they cared for no other delicacy of fare, or curiosity of diet, than to maintain life; nor for any other apparel than to cover them from the cold, the rain, and the sun (II, 347).

This is not the totality of Ralegh's message in the *History,* but it represents the heart of it. Ralegh could not be sanguine about ambition which led to over-extension and invasion—precisely the course of action Prince Henry was set upon—although Sir Walter continued to excoriate the Spanish in digressions and asides. To metaphors of boundlessness were attached ironic defeat and debasement; peace and fruitfulness, where they were a possibility at all in the *History,* were attached to images of confinement and limit.

V

Whereas Ralegh's contribution to the dialogue of rival mythologies was largely a negative one—showing mainly the defects inherent in the conqueror myth rather than positively portraying an alternate image which might engage Henry's imagination—the poet Ben Jonson manufactured a complete mythology in which Henry could exercise his need for distinct destiny without feeling compelled to lead his nation into war. Though Jonson had more than once expressed his contempt for the Arthurian romances, he employed those materials (apparently at the urging of Henry, who liked to style himself "Meliadus Lord of the Isles" and in other ways to affect the chivalric trappings of mythic knighthood) in his "Speeches at Prince Henry's Barriers" in 1610. But however Jonson may have disdained the Arthurian

legends as sources for poetic invention, the old tales did provide a
vehicle for turning the prince's attention away from the sterile power
motif found in the Puritan renderings of classical and foreign heroes
(Alexander, Caesar, etc.) to the more fertile themes of domestic English demigods. Uppermost in Jonson's programme for the Barriers
masque was a personation which emphasized domestic fertility above
military exploit.

The Jonson's task was complicated immeasurably by the highly military nature of the Barriers: how do you offer an alternative to aggression on an occasion designed to praise aggression and the exercise of
power? Prince Henry recognized in the Barriers an opportunity for
culminating theater; the sport at barriers was, after all, a tournament
in the grand chivalric manner which hovered on the edge between fic-
titious game and actual battle. Of course, for Henry fiction *was* actual, so he was determined to observe to the last detail the chivalric
formulas, from formal challenge delivered in open court to the tro-
phies of battle. That Jonson found himself servant to these old, romantic formulas must have seemed a mixed blessing indeed. But Jonson was evidently determined to balance the myth of military glory
with a sober lesson in history and an alternate myth of fertility.

In Jonson's programme, a thoroughly mythologized King Arthur
(now a translated star, Arcturus, "once thy king, and now thy starre")
was awakened in the firmament by the earth-bound Lady of the Lake
who bewailed the long ruin of British chivalry.[23] Since in Arthurian
legend it was the Lady of the Lake who gave King Arthur the magical
sword Excalibur and helped rescue him from various dangers while
he lived, Jonson's prologue would seem to have demanded that a
now canonized Arthur return the symbolic sword to the Lady who
could then bestow it on the new Knight of Chivalry, Prince Henry.
This would have seemed the obvious course for the masque to take,
especially since it celebrated Henry's symbolic arrival at chivalric
manhood. But Jonson chose instead a quite surprising symbol—a
shield—to come down out of heaven from the hands of the sainted
Arthur. So Jonson's presentation see-sawed between an acknowledgment that the arts of warfare were necessary adjuncts of kingship
and an insistence that the civil virtues of peace and fertility should,
nevertheless, come first. In using a shield rather than a sword as his
primary image, Jonson was taking the slightly daring course of sym-
bolizing *defense* when officially *offense* was the occasion for celebration. The tension was introduced in the verse which King Arthur

spoke as he prepared to present the shield to the Lady of the Lake;
Prince Henry was first acknowledged in the guise that he had adopted,
the boundless conqueror imagined by the Puritans:

> Let him be famous, as was TRISTRAM, TOR,
> LAVNC'LOT, . . .
> .   .   .   .
>   His name
> Strike vpon heauen, . . .
> Beyond the paths, and searches of the sunne
> Let him tempt fate; and when a world is wunne,
> Submit it duely to this state, and throne,
> Till time, and vtmost stay make that his owne
>   (ll. 86-7; 88-93).

But this vision of Henry as aggressive conquering knight was strangely
sabotaged in Arthur's next six lines (the shift signaled by the initial,
contradictory *but*), the undercutting further strengthened by the
physical presence of the symbolic shield:

> But first receiue this shield; wherein is wrought
> The truth that he must follow; and (being taught
> The wayes from heauen) ought not be despisd.
> It is a piece, was by the fates deuisd
> To arme his maiden valure; and to show
> Defensiue armes th'offensiue should fore-goe
>   (ll. 94-99).

The push-pull effect of hearing first the offensive young prince characterized and then of hearing *and* seeing the much more domestic
value of defense symbolically praised has even today an ironic effect.
And having once introduced the shield, rather than the conventional
Excalibur, as his principal symbol, Jonson was determined to empha-
size the difference. Rather than let the Lady of the Lake immediately
present the shield to Henry, with appropriate complimentary verses
so that the tournament could commence, Jonson introduced the figure of Merlin, awakened from his long, slumbering imprisonment to
deliver a sententious lecture on the meaning of Arthur's shield to
Prince Henry, who was revealed as Meliadus Lord of the Isles, sitting
in "St. GEORGE'S *Portico*," unruined miraculously "or but late
built" (ll. 135-136).

   Framed by Inigo Jones's architectural design, Prince Henry was
made unconsciously part of a visual symbol which would be repeated

in Merlin's lecture: the Prince was the informing life-force *within* the designer's scenery which made St. George's portico arise out of the "ruins of Chivalry," just as the prince was the fount which fed the springs of his nation. His function as fertility force only worked when he found his proper "frame" and remained within it. To fly out to prosecute foreign wars would mean the collapse of the design. It seems doubtful that Prince Henry could have appreciated the full meaning of the visual symbol of which he was the central part. When the scenery opened to reveal him seated in costumed state to the unctuous praise of the court, Henry would have known only that once again the workings of artistic perspective had brought him to the center of all eyes. He could not sense, perhaps, that the poetic perspective of Jonson and Jones not only showcased him for admiring eyes but also controlled him and limited him symbolically. The prince was, after all, held in place while Merlin read him a lecture which warned against war and praised the fruits of peace.

As Merlin read and elucidated the shield for Meliadus, Jonson seemed to be de-mythologizing the myth of conqueror-knight, or at least reducing it to a more proper place in the scheme of a healthy nation: "No gyants, dwarfes, or monsters here, but men" (l. 174). The knight who receives this shield, said Merlin,

> His arts must be to gouerne, and giue lawes
> To peace no lesse then armes (ll. 175-6).

But while the conqueror-motif was being questioned as myth, a fertility motif was taking its place. The Lady of the Lake who called forth Prince Henry had been in Arthurian romance Meliadus' lover; she was obviously added to the masque by the scholarly Jonson to reinforce subtly the fertility theme. The shield, explained a no less scholarly Merlin, "describes each state / Preceding there, that he should imitate" (ll. 177-8). What ensued was a short course in the history of English monarchs, as the defensive metaphor of the shield was extended to describe the good policies of Edward I, Edward III, Henry VII (whose "golden fleece" was England's own wool industry, l. 197), Henry VIII (who built forts and girded the coast, ll. 204-05), and Elizabeth (who built a "wall of shipping," l. 209), while a submerged but powerful metaphor of fertility also ran through the lecture on English history and implied the domestic virtues already implicit in the meeting of Meliadus/Henry and the Lady of the Lake: "trades and tillage" (l. 188), "the fatnesse of his land" (l. 192), "The

trade of clothing, by which arte were nurst / Whole millions . . ."
(ll. 194-5). "Ciuill arts the martiall must precede" (l. 212), Merlin
concluded, then moved into the next set of exempla: those who had
used invasion and had prosecuted war into foreign lands.

Some were granted hero status, but cautiously, for the justness
of their cause: Edward the Black Prince, Henry V, and Elizabeth. But
others, who began well, tempted "their starres beyond their light"
(l. 236), like Richard the Lion-Hearted. Merlin finally pronounced a
cautionary summation over the war-like rulers of England's past:

> . . . t'inuite
> Your valure vpon need, but not t'incite
> Your neighbour Princes, giue them all their due,
> And be prepar'd if they will trouble you.
> He doth but scourge him selfe, his sword that drawes
> Without a purse, a counsaile and a cause (ll. 329-34).

But once again, the symbolic undercurrents in Jonson's verse told a
more forceful mythic tale: just as fertility and domestic calm had
characterized the imagery of those monarchs who girded the English
coast and remained within bounds, so images of death and blighted
fertility undercut the portraits of England's warrior kings. No few
lines better sum up the horrid chill which the power-motif could produce for a nation than those describing Edward I's "holy" crusade
(significantly, in 1270, while he was still Prince of Wales):

> Whilst vpright EDWARD shines no lesse than he,
> Vnder the wings of golden victorie,
> Nor lets out no lesse riuers of the bloud
> Of *Infidels*, but makes the field a floud,
> And marches through it, with S. GEORGES crosse,
> Like *Israels* host to the *Ægyptians* losse,
> Through the *red sea*: the earth beneath him cold . . .
>   (ll. 237-43).

Despite the glittering gold trappings and the heightened allusions,
the fertile tilled ground, once fat with life and health, which had
characterized England's peaceful kings, has been replaced by a perver-
sion of the sown seed, by a river of blood from which only crops of
hatred will grow. Images of death continue to follow the march of
conquerors through Merlin's speech: Edward the Black Prince (again,
as Prince of Wales) was like a young lion invading the household
herds of France (ll. 262-63); at Poitiers he was like the salt-sea flow-

ing across the land or "like a fire carryed with high windes" burning
all the landscape (ll. 269-71). The young lion, the sea, and the fire
are all images of power, but here they bring death, sterility, and implied starvation.

After Merlin's dissertation on the shield, Chivalry was wakened
by the pronouncement of Meliadus' name three times, and the barriers were fought at her insistence. Henry acquited himself creditably;
he fought sixteen bouts with the pike and thirty bouts with the sword,
winning for himself honors in both endeavors. But even with his
blood up and his pride soaring, the prince was made to listen to one
last speech which Jonson had prepared for Merlin:

> Nay, stay your valure, 'tis a wisdome high
> In Princes to vse fortune reuerently.
> He that in deeds of *Armes* obeyes his blood
> Doth often tempt his destinie beyond good (ll. 405-08).

Though Jonson could not control the military occasion for his
"Speeches at Prince Henry's Barriers," he could control the tone and
imagery through which emerged a quite different emphasis from the
one Henry's ears were most accustomed to hearing from his Puritan
followers.

The next time Jonson was called upon to honor the Prince of
Wales in a court masque, in *Oberon, the Faery Prince,* performed on
New Year's Day, 1611, the vocabulary and imagery of militarism was
quite thoroughly eliminated. Jonson was not bound by occasion to
flatter or even acknowledge the prevailing myth, as he had been at
the time he wrote the speeches for the Barriers, so his programme for
Oberon offered an alternative and positive personation for Henry
which was untainted by the hateful belligerency of Puritan militarism. Jonson was certainly willing to allow Henry a transforming mythology—as the following discussion of the masque will show—though it
was of quite a different order from the aggressive boundary-crossing
which the left-wing Protestants emphasized. In *Oberon* native vitalities and the odor of fertility engulfed the figure of Henry and made
him the center toward which other English life-forces were drawn,
and out of which they seemed to flow refreshed. But though an actual heightening of the mythic presence was extended to Henry in
Oberon, whereas it had been stinted in the Barriers masque, once
again the programme of the personation insisted that the prince's
power was localized and by definition rooted in English soil.

Oberon opened on a waste bathed in moonlight, a setting natural enough for the antics of the antimasque, in this case ten Satyrs with their "prefect" Silenus. The Satyrs were ready for their usual routs of shaggy drunkenness, and Jonson appeared to be opening with the conventional antimasque—figures as disorderly and lewd as one could desire—against which he characteristically arrayed the characters and symbols of the masque proper, the radiance and superior moral power of the latter invariably banishing the chaotic rout of the former. But in *Oberon* the traditional pattern was altered to accommodate the more complicated personation Jonson was fashioning for Prince Henry: rather than allow aggression of any kind to be associated with Henry (the usual banishment of the humours of ill-will represented by the personages of the antimasque), Jonson allowed his Satyrs—energies and passions redirected rather than banished—to join the blessed entourage of Oberon, the Fairy Prince. Rather than conflict, the masque dramatized a pervasive love which replaced the virtue of triumph with the superior virtue of magnanimity.

Within the context of this plotting, the moon-lit waste of the masque's opening scene was symbolic of the transitory, lust-filled world of animality. In human terms, this was Jonson's symbol for the world where man's power/aggression motive reigned, here characterized comically in the way its life-force is squandered in gratuitous obscenity and drunkenness. The moon conventionally suggested the deforming powers of Circe or Hecate—that force that could read a man's impulses and give them hideous form by changing him into goat or pig—but the moon also suggested the very transitoriness of a world defined by lust and aggressiveness: "Times be short. . . . The . . . Moone too will not stay."[24] The Satyrs, because they were slaves of time, could experience their power only by exercising it feverishly. It was against this frantic theme of an evaporating life-force that Jonson played his personation of Henry.

Silenus began to anticipate Oberon/Henry quite early in the first scene. He first called for "Chaster language" (l. 50) among the Satyrs, for "These are nights / Solemne, to the shining rites / Of the *Fayrie* Prince, and Knights: . . ." (ll. 50-2). Then Silenus used the word which summed up much of Henry's personation in Oberon: "he doth fill with grace, / Euery season, eu'ry place" (ll. 61-2). *Grace* was, of course, the word indicating the Christian's transformation by God's love, but even outside the Christian context, *grace* implied an embracing and benevolent love. Grace suggested a motive quite opposite to the lust motive or the aggression motive; it suggested a love which could be expressed without being squandered and lost (unlike the Puritan motif of power which raced headlong toward self-immolation). On the day sacred to Oberon, Silenus continued,

> Our PAN'S father, god of tongue,
>   BACCHVS, though he still be yong,
>   PHOEBVS, when he crowned sung,
>   Nor MARS, when first his armor rung,
> Might with him be nam'd, that day.
>   He is louelier, then in May
>   Is the Spring, and there can stay,
>   As little, as he can decay (ll. 66-73).

Oberon, then, was also master of time, rather than its puppet, and master also of the vernal world which only set the Satyrs on fire and consumed them in their passion. But the reason the Satyrs would be able to join Oberon's retinue, rather than be summarily banished, was that they represented a force essentially related to Oberon's; but whereas their vitality was dependent on and symbolized by moon, wine, and May, Oberon's power was saved, calmed, and extended by a grace which admitted no decay.

But it takes some time for the Satyrs to understand the nature of Oberon's power. Characteristically they can think of his beneficence only in terms of aggression and in terms of power exercised conspicuously. They speculate on what gifts and rewards they might expect if they went to serve Oberon. What followed was an increasingly lavish series of images suggesting utter transitoriness; the Satyrs, until Oberon actually arrived, remained prisoners of graceless lust:

> *Satyre 4.* Will he giue vs prettie toyes,
>   To beguile the girles withall?
> *Satyre 3.* And to make 'hem quickly fall?
> *Silenus.*   Peace, my wantons: he will doe
>   More, then you can ayme vnto.
> *Satyre 4.* Will he build vs larger caues?
> *Silenus.*   Yes, and giue you yuorie staues,
>   When you hunt; and better wine:
> *Satyre 1.* Then the master of the Vine?
> *Satyre 2.* And rich prizes, to be wunne,
>   When we leape, or when we runne?
> *Satyre 1.* I, and gild our clouen feet?
> *Satyre 3.* Strew our heads with poulders sweet?

Satyre 1. Bind our crooked legges in hoopes
             Made of shells, with siluer loopes?
Satyre 2. Tie about our tawnie wrists
             Bracelets of the *Fairie* twists?
Satyre 4. And, to spight the coy Nymphes scornes,
             Hang vpon our stubbed hornes,
             Garlands, ribbands, and fine poesies;
Satyre 3. Fresh, as when the flower discloses?
Satyre 1. Yes, and stick our pricking eares
             With the pearle that *Tethys* weares.
Satyre 2. And to answere all things els,
             Trap our shaggie thighs with bels;
             That as we do strike a time,
             In our daunce, shall make a chime
Satyre 3. Lowder, then the rattling pipes
             Of the wood-gods;
Satyre 1.   Or the stripes
             Of the *Taber;* when we carrie
             BACCHVS vp, his pompe to varie (ll. 84-131).

Though still imprisoned by the wrong love motive, the Satyrs
had taken the first steps toward the superior service of Oberon, and
as if in answer to this willingness,

> . . . *the whole* Scene *opened, and within was discouer'd
> the* Frontispice *of a bright and glorious* Palace, *whose
> gates and walls were transparent* (ll. 138-140).

But before the palace could be opened in the last climactic moment
of the masque, there were still symbolic steps to be taken by the Satyrs and further energies to be gathered in preparation for the revelation of the masked prince. To further heighten the fertility personation—and to demonstrate dramatically that passionate fires were not
to be banned this night but only redirected—Jonson introduced two
"Syluanes" before the gates of the palace, "armed with their clubs,
and drest in leaues, asleepe." These were the traditional wildmen of
English superstition and folklore, their fertility functions testified to
by their garments of green leaves and by their herculean clubs. The
Satyrs had great fun at the expense of the greenmen, thinking them
clownishly ineffective guards and finally awakening them with the
song of blue fly and bee (ll. 210 ff.). The Sylvans were ridiculed for
falling asleep at their posts:

>   Is this your guise
> To haue both your eares, and eyes
> Seal'd so fast; as these mine *Elues*
> Might haue stolne you, from your selues? (ll. 222-25).

But the ridicule proved misdirected, for the palace and those within, the Sylvans explained, dwelt on a plane removed from common pursuits and from stealth by night. Oberon and his knights had been (and, again, the overtone of Christian salvation is remarkable) "Quick-'ned by a second birth":

> Looke! Do's not his *Palace* show
> Like another *Skie* of lights?
> Yonder, with him, liue the knights,
> Once, the noblest of the earth,
> Quick'ned by a second birth;
> Who for prowesse, and for truth,
> There are crownd with lasting youth:
> And do hold, by *Fates* command,
> Seats of blisse in *Fairie* land (ll. 143-151).

Oberon/Henry symbolized an almost divine transcendence, a moral perfection transformed into living myth and free from the clutches of impermanence. One might have expected the inharmonious souls of the Satyrs to perceive their own unworthiness before Oberon's perfection and to flee from this vision in terror or in resentment (one thinks of Milton and how he would have resolved the antimasque), but they gazed on rapt and longed for the morning light which, one of the Sylvans told them, must break before the palace gates would open. The Satyrs sang a lewd song to the moon, encouraging her to give up her love for Endymion ("This is not the proper way / Of your palenesse to be rid," ll. 266-67) and to retire so that day might come and Oberon might appear; it was characteristic of Jonson's programme that the earth forces, which were to be associated with Prince Henry's function as native fertility god, redirect their passionate vitalities toward a higher love rather than lose them altogether in favor of some pallid and ineffectual otherworldliness. So the Satyrs retained their essential characters as rough, shaggy figures of sexuality; but now their sexual energies were flowing toward the source of creativity and love—national harmony, if you will. They no longer thought of "prettie toyes," "wine," and "siluer loopes." They were quite weary of transitoriness and of a world ruled by the moon, which they characterized tauntingly as a whore:

> Come, your changes ouerthrow
> What your looke would carry so;
> Moone, confesse then, what you are (ll. 272-74).

The masque had opened in moonlight, symbolic of flying time and of humanity deformed; the Satyrs had seen the fairy palace, the far-off vision of immutability, of sexual thriftlessness transformed into a never-dying state of grace, and to make that vision assume reality they had first to banish the moon. They finished their chiding song to the moon and *"fell sodainely into an antique dance, full of gesture, and swift motion."* This was the fully Dionysian moment of the anti-masque, when the frenzy of brain and soul was transformed into physical movement, but Jonson was careful not to suggest that this state of heightened vitality need be chastely banished; rather, these energies would surround and bear up the prince in his appearance.

As a cock crowed announcing the breaking of day, Silenus interrupted the Satyrs' dance with

> See, the gates alreadie spread!
> Euery *Satyre* bow his head, (ll. 289-90)

thus dramatizing and completing the unusual union of an almost Christian reverence with the greenworld's passion, a union in which the life-denying capabilities of both the former and the latter (the subservience of the one and the aggression of the other) were balanced and harmonized by grace. The entrance of Oberon/Henry was itself a spectacle of timelessness (the prince and his fellow masquers were dressed *á l'antique*), borne on a tide of primitive energies:

> *There the whole palace opend, and the nation of* Faies
> *were discouer'd, some with instruments, some bearing
> lights; others singing; and within a farre off in perspectiue,
> the knights masquers sitting in their seuerall sieges: At the
> further end of all,* OBERON, *in a chariot, which to a lowd
> triumphant musique began to moue forward, drawne by
> two white beares, and on either side guarded by three*
> Syluanes, *with one going in front* (ll. 291-8).

Prince Henry understood well enough the symbolic import of his entrance, of all stately entrances, for that matter, though he seemed crudely untuned to the fineness of Jonson's personation. Prince

Henry, though he was here subject and object of the highest level of
art tricked out for political purposes, was so thoroughly the child of
the Puritan myth—far less graceful and subtle artistically—that he had
proposed to the king and to Ben Jonson that he make this particular
entrance on horseback.[25] A masque played cavalierly on horseback
appealed to Henry's other image of the overpowering prince, filling
court and chamber with his thunder, but such a presentation obviously crossed Jonson's purposes. King James refused Henry's request
—much to the poet's relief—and Jonson went on with his original programme of soothing the passions of youth while directing them toward fruitfulness free of debilitating rancor or lust. Not only was
military conflict banished, along with aggressive displays of lust, or
power, or lust for power; conflict was made symbolically impossible
by the subsuming love which Prince Henry was made to represent:

> Melt earth to sea, sea flow to ayre,
>   And ayre flie into fire,
> Whilst we, in tunes, to ARTHVRS chayre
>   Beare OBERONS desire;. . (ll. 300-03).

Although Henry was thus granted in *Oberon* a fair measure of
mythic power, he was nevertheless subtly subordinated in the masque
to a higher authority. In the Barriers masque, Jonson had used English history as the subordinating and controlling force, but in *Oberon*
King James—who sat in state and observed the performance—was
drawn into the play symbolically as the very light which dawned to
allow Oberon's appearance. Thus at the moment when Henry might
have been prepared to assume the full glory of his dramatic personation, Jonson changed the focus abruptly to suggest that Oberon's
power and magnificence depended for its being on a higher source.
As the masquers played to the king enthroned, Silenus indicated
James and spoke to the entire court, including those transformed by
masks:

> 'Tis he, that stayes the time from turning old,
> And keepes the age vp in a head of gold.
> That in his owne true circle, still doth runne;
> And holds his course, as certayne as the sunne.
> He makes it euer day, and euer spring,
> Where he doth shine, and quickens euery thing
> Like a new nature: so, that true to call
> Him, by his title, is to say, Hee's all (ll. 350-57).

That *Oberon* was the fullest expression we have seen of the prince's alternate personation should be clear enough. In full artistic control of his materials, Jonson was able to awaken the new year of 1611—Henry's first full year as Prince of Wales—with a complex programme in *Oberon* which both recognized the bubbling ambitions of high-born youth—the ambitions which the Puritans had successfully attempted to turn into pure aggression—and maintained that such potentially destructive vitalities and energies must be redirected inward toward national fertility, rather than outward toward conquest and death. And anyway, Jonson said in *Oberon,* the prince is son of man, not father of his own fate; he must take his light from the king and learn to wait. It is perhaps melancholy to point out that, although Henry allowed himself to become an actor in these fictions of national fertility, his mind was never free of the Puritan myth of conqueror, in which strength and growth could have but one utilitarian object—conquest.

VI

I shall end this lengthy survey of the formation of Henry's alternate personation as native fertility god by examining a curious and little-known example of folk drama, and though the step down from the high gloss of Jonson must seem a precipitous one, *Chester's triumph in honor of her prince* will be highly useful in concluding this particular part of our discussion, for it employed to a remarkable extent the fertility persona and demonstrated—no less remarkably—the successful spread of that personation of Henry outside the circle of Court and City.

It is important to note that although any myth labeled "Puritan" would have been shared or held in common by an enormous number of Englishmen in 1610, by no means was the countryside monolithic in its opinions or in its vision of the future. And those who did not share the aims of radical Protestantism's programme for Henry were not necessarily recusant Catholics (though tenacious or secret Romans might not be expected to look sanguinely on the prospect of their own Prince of Wales slaughtering fellow brothers in the faith); rather, those tied to the bountifulness of the earth, the vast yeoman class of England, needed no separate identities as Catholic or Protestant to know that a holy war in either religion's name meant that men left their sheltering soil to become the human waste of foreign

fields. The bitter irony in that alone might mean that a fair portion of
parishioners all over England would turn a deaf ear when their left-
ward leaning preachers exhorted them to take up arms against Catholic Europe. To tear the Whore of Babylon to shreads in a sermon was
one thing—it was colorful and entertaining—but to suggest that a
young prince waited in the south of England to lead them in a crusade across the Channel was another thing altogether.

Chester had long been an official concern in London for the
numbers of its recusants; in London the bishops and the Lords of
Council did not know the small fee-holders and merchants who dwelt
around them, but in Chester the sheriffs and petty officials did: fines
against Catholics went uncollected or even unlevied. Property was not
confiscated; proclamations or edicts could go largely ignored. People
lived, for all the contentiousness of national politics, in a relatively
calm insularity, where folklore was more powerful than classical personations.

In the case of the rise of Prince Henry, as both a real force in the
affairs of England and as a symbolic presence, Chester occupied a
unique position, for she was a "Palatine County." The Earl of Chester
could exercise within his domain certain sovereign rights, particularly
judicial rights, and by dint of ancient annexation, the Earldom of Chester belonged to the Prince of Wales. With Henry's investiture came
revenues and privileges, none more far-reaching than in Chester. As
June of 1610 approached, the people of that county must have known
Henry's eye was upon them; their *Triumph in honor of the prince*
says much about their preoccupations as they symbolically greeted
their new lord.

Chester's triumph is a surprising mixture of country carnival and
court masque, of pageant and folk festival. It is alternately self-con-
scious—when its author, "Her ill Townsmen, RI. DAVIES," attempts
pretentious rhymed couplets—and joyously uninhibited:

> A man, by strange devises, clyming to the toppe of a
> very high spire steeple, standing at the Market-crosse,
> called S. Peter's steeple, carrying an auncient of our col-
> ours of S. George, displaying the same upon the said stee-
> ple, and fixing the same to the barre of iron that the vane
> hangeth upon; likewise sounding a drumme, shooting off
> a peece, and flourishing a sword, and standing upon the
> crosse of the said barre of iron, stood upon his hands
> with his feete into the ayre, very dangerously and won-

derfully to the view of the beholders, with casting fire-
workes very delightfull.[26]

Throughout all of the *Triumph* there was enough evident and latent
Catholicism to have given the Star Chamber cause for concern, but
the use of bells and what the Puritans would have called "heathenish
idols" paraded through the streets were metamorphosed by a much
more generalized folklore which amalgamated and reduced everything—church, state, and certainly the new Prince of Wales and Earl
of Chester—into an essential doctrine of fertility. Seemingly discon-
nected vignettes were performed, but all were linked by the same
sympathy for the soil. For example, the following mimed show was
an obvious blending of two or more legends, their common properties
being rites enacted to ensure fertility:

> Two disguised, called Greene-men, their habit embroydred
> and stiched on with ivie-leaves, with blacke sides, having
> hanging to their shoulders a huge blacke shaggie hayre,
> savage-like, with ivie-garlands upon their heads, bearing
> Herculian clubbes in their hands. An artificiall dragon,
> very lively to behold, pursuing the savages entring their
> denne, casting fire from his mouth, which afterwards was
> slaine, to the great pleasure of the spectators, bleeding,
> fainting, and staggering, as though hee endured a feeling
> paine, even at the last gasp and farewell (p. 293).

Though the execution of the dragon was carried out with riotous
burlesque (given unction, no doubt, by good palatine ale), the symbolic meaning of such a charade is venerable and potent. Like the
burning of the Witch of Winter in parts of Italy, the slaying of the
dragon allows the spring to return; the buried allusion to St. George
in the Greenmen's conquest is doubly significant, for in the old legends, St. George slew a dragon which had devoured all the crops
(the dragon winter) and which had brought pestilence on a city; and
Chester held its Triumph in honor of Henry on St. George's Day,
April 23. In this case, St. George carried none of the associations with
militant Protestantism, Chester's St. George was descended from a
much older folk belief which associated him with the vernal god—he
slew the ravaging dragon winter at the opening of spring. By a logic
informed by this symbology, Prince Henry became for the inhabitants
of Chester a new St. George, the bringer of fertility.

In one way or another, Prince Henry and St. George were linked, were pronounced interchangeable in role and function for the people; the heraldic arms of Prince Henry were paraded with the scutcheon of St. George. A man "representing S.GEORGE, accoutred and armed at all points" (p. 294) rode in procession, as did a painted portrait of Prince Henry, as though both the prince and St. George shared a mythic being which could be summoned by paint or costume. Interspersed through it all were more obvious symbols:

> Another, on horsebacke, representing PLENTIE ... a wreath of wheat-eares upon her head, with a garland of the same athwart her body, casting and strewing wheate abroade amongst the multitude as shee roade along (pp. 294-95).

The speeches were commenced by Fame and Mercury, who announced the occasion for such universal joy and characterized the prince whom all honored. Chester, Britain, and Cambria were next given speeches wherein they promised service to the Prince or described their joy, the last of the three promising to fight valiantly "in his just cause." But the real culmination of the *Triumph* was given to the parts of Peace, Plenty, Love, and Joy, who contributed the controlling imagery:

Peace. Brother with brother, nay, the foe with friend
For 'mine' and 'thine' shall never more contend.
No massacre nor bloody strategeme
Shall stirre. . . .

. . . .

For, like to olive branches, they shall beare
Fruit that gives Love an appetite to beare;

. . . .

Plentie. I'll stuffe your barnes up to the throat with graine,

. . . .

I'll fructifie the Earth with rarest fruites

. . . .

So as the soile, that beares seed timely sowne,
Under the burthen of their waight shall groane.

. . . .

As long as I with Nature till your ground.
What shall I say? your life-supporting staffe,
The staffe of bread, I'll throw abroad like chaffe

(pp. 301-02).

Love and Joy in consort banished a wolfishly blood-thirsty Envy ("To see an army, when their foode is scant, / Eate their own excrements; O! this is sport," p. 303), and the quartet of domestic virtues reigned in the name of Henry. With the fractious spirit that loves war overcome by the love motive, Chester greeted her prince and earl in the full glow of the fertility myth.

It is jarring to note that soon after his investiture, Prince Henry applied to the king for increased privileges to levy fines on recusants. Despite how widely and deeply the alternate personation of Henry had spread, he had put on the mailed glove of the conqueror and he was determined—mere boy that he was—to bring his fist down on enemies of the faith both in England and, of course, on the Continent.

Notes to Chapter 4

1. *The true ancient Roman Catholike* (London, 1611), sig. ¶5ᵛ.

2. *The Sermon preached at the crosse, Feb. xiiij. 1607,* 2d ed. (London, 1609), sig. ¶3.

3. Dedication to his trans. of Philippe de Mornay's *The Mysterie of iniquitie: that is to say, the historie of the papacie* (London, 1612), sig. ¶iiijᵛ.

4. *The French herald summoning all true Christian princes to a general croisade for a holy warre against the great enemy of Christendom, and all his slaues* (London, 1611), fols. 39, 41.

5. Daniel Price, *The defence of truth against a booke falsely called the triumph of truth* (London, 1610), sig. *2ᵛ.

6. George Marcelline, *The Triumphs of King James the First* (London, 1610), sig. A 2.

7. William Leigh, *Great Britaines, great deliuerance, from the great danger of popish powder,* 2d ed., pub. with *First Step towards heauen* (London, 1609), fol. 158; Gervase Markham, *Cauelarice, the English horseman* (London, 1607), sig. ¶2.

8. Markham. *Cauelarice,* sig. ¶2; Marcelline, *Triumphs of King James,* sig. A 2ᵛ.

9. Edmond Richer, *A treatise of ecclesiasticall and politike power* (London, 1612), sig. A 4ᵛ.

10. *A Poetical Rhapsody, 1602-1621,* ed. H. E. Rollins (Cambridge, 1931), I, 305.

11. Henry Peacham, *Minerva Britanna* (London, 1612), fol. 17.

12. Robert Bruce Cotton, *An Answer made to certain propositions of war and peace* (London, 1655), fol. 6.

13. Joseph Hall, *Epistles. The Second Volume* in *The Works of Joseph Hall* (London, 1625), fol. 332.

14. *Epistles in Six Decades*, in *The Works of Joseph Hall*, fol. 280.

15. In the dedication of his trans. of Morton Eudes, *Catholique traditions* (London, 1609), sig. A 3[V].

16. *The Complete Works in Verse and Prose of Samuel Daniel*, ed. Alexander B. Grosart (New York, 1963), III, 99.

17. *Ibid.*, III, 314-315.

18. George More, *Principles for yong princes* (London, 1611), sigs. A 3[V]-A 4. See also, fol. 1[V], 5[V], 7[V]. Alexander and Caesar are discussed as bad examples of rulership primarily in Chaps. 14 and 15.

19. *The Poems of George Chapman*, ed. Phyllis Brooks Bartlett (New York, 1941), 173.

20. *Ibid.*, 385.

21. I am here much indebted to J. H. Adamson and H. F. Folland's interpretation of the *History*, and to their study of Ralegh generally: *The Shepherd of the Ocean* (Boston, 1969).

22. *The Works of Sir Walter Ralegh* (Oxford, 1829), II, 55.

23. *Ben Jonson*, ed. Herford and Simpson (Oxford, 1941), VII, 325.

24. *Ibid.*, VII, 341.

25. *C.S.P., Venetian*, XII (1610-1613), par. 115.

26. *Chesters triumphe*, 1610, reprinted in John Nichols, *The Progresses of King James the First* (London, 1828), II, 292. See David M. Bergeron's *English Civic Pageantry* (London: Edward Arnold, 1971), 92-94, and the same author's article, "Prince Henry and English Civic Pageantry," *Tennessee Studies in Literature*, 13 (1968), 109-16.

Lord of the Ascendant

I

Though singers of the *via media,* like George Chapman and Ben Jonson, and those good burghers of Chester, invested Henry in their poetry as future god of domesticity and fertile soil, he itched to cross the Channel for those fields where his more radical subjects saw him as great conquering knight of the Reformed Religion. Convenient to those warlike ambitions, the religious and territorial struggles which would lead inevitably to the Thirty Years War were beginning to bubble on the Continent, and Henry watched the building passions with interest. He let everyone know that he intended to interpose himself in Europe in the fullness of time.

As far back as 1606, when the prince was still prepubescent but precociously running at the ring and reining in powerful horses, a dispute had erupted between Venice and the Papacy which threatened, if the Holy Father had his way, effectively to end the freedom of the Venetian republic. But the Doge and Senate had refused to bend, to the utter delight of England's Protestants, who, on the simple grounds that Venice was defying the pope, chose to see bonds of spiritual kinship between their own non-Catholic monarchy and the very Catholic Republic of Venice. The enthusiasm in England for the Venetians had risen even higher when the Doge and the Senate expelled all Jesuits from the state as treacherous subversives. The Gunpowder Plot had been uncovered only in the previous year, and the wound of terror and effrontery in England was still red with religious fever; the English knew well enough the utter perfidy of the Jesuits, and they had crowed with delight that even in a Catholic state the odious brood of Loyola could be correctly recognized as *genus monstruosum.* King James, ever perceived by his countrymen as phlegmatic in the interests of his professed religion, knew well enough that Jesuits (as well as Puritans) were threats to stable government, and he had exclaimed on the bravery of the Venetians, "Oh, this will very soon completely confound the Pope. . . . O blessed and wise Republic!"[1]

Twelve-year-old Henry was also stirred by the spectacle of the Venetians facing bravely the Goliath of Rome, and he longed to find for himself the five smooth stones with which, with God's help, he would fell the giant. But he was not old enough nor strong enough in 1606, and with a self-consciousness that revealed an understanding of his destiny, he told the Venetian ambassador in London to convey his regrets to the Doge and Senate: had I been "bigger," he said, I would have joined the Republic. The pluckiness of the boy seemed to have amused the Venetians, though they went to elaborate pains to acknowledge the prince's offer and thank him for his love,[2] and in the English court, as well, some appeared to be smiling indulgently at the boy's ardor, though James surely realized that such ambition would not be put aside along with the pastimes of childhood. Indeed, Henry's pastimes had never been childish; they had savored from the very earliest days of a man's exercise in preparation for some mighty, culminating task. James would see the need to hold an increasingly firm grasp on his son; where absolute control proved futile, the king would fall increasingly into the frown.

Coinciding with Henry's approaching investiture three years after the conflict between Venice and the Papacy, another crisis, far more serious in its implications for the peace of Europe, was precipitated by the disputed succession in the Duchy of Cleves. Duke William (aptly called "William the Simple") had, by dying without issue there, belied his nickname and thrown northern Europe into a struggle of incredible complication and subtlety. Numerous claimants to the Duchy of Cleves grew like mushrooms in the very twilight of the unfortunate duke's funeral, but the two with the strongest claims—John Sigismund, Elector of Brandenburg, and Wolfgang Wilhelm, son of the Count of Neuberg—were both Protestants, and instantly the contest became an issue of religious interest in England.[3]

The stakes were perceived in England as high, but the Holy Roman Empire, Spain, and France alike saw that what glistered was gold. The Empire moved to take Cleves for the Catholic side by installing the Emperor's brother, the Archduke Leopold, in the walled city of Julich, the principal seat of the Duchy. Spain stood ready to aid the Empire against encroachments of Protestants from either the

United Provinces or from the German petty states. King Henry IV of
France, nominally a Catholic, had a more complicated game to play,
one which would end with his bloody assassination. Through the
mounting crisis, Prince Henry Stuart would feel a growing bond of
comradeship with the French king and with his ambitions, so that it
would appear that King Henry's earlier courtship of the prince, by
way of French horses, dogs, armor, and even a French riding master,
had indeed won over a young man whose affection for the interests
of France against the interests of Spain had finally overcome his dislike for all Catholics everywhere.

France, though a Catholic state and little disposed to aid the be-
leaguered Protestants of Germany, was also an ancient enemy of Spain
and a rival of the Austrian Empire. Henry IV, who had, as Henry of
Navarre, been a great champion of French Protestants (though he
found it convenient to convert to Catholicism after he had united all
of France under his rule), saw an opportunity, if he aided the German
Protestants in Cleves, to drive a French wedge into the Empire while
opening a way to surprise and take the Spanish Netherlands for France.
It was a dangerous situation, and King Henry was able, amazingly, to
persuade the peace-loving James of England to commit 4,000 English
troops to the strangely polyglot union of France, the German Protestants, and the United Provinces. But perhaps James's acquiescence in
Henry's scheme was not so amazing after all, for after making his
commitment to join the action in Cleves, King James could of course
turn instantly and with some righteousness to Parliament, whose
many Puritans had frequently urged just such an intervention in Europe, and claim irritably that his subsidy must now be increased: "But
in case it might bee obiected by some, that it is onely vpon occasions of
warre, that Kings obtaine great Supplies from their Subiects: notwith-
standing my interne Peace, I am yet in a kinde of warre, which if it
bee without, the more is your safetie."[4]

The French King Henry was not an easy man for the English to
trust; some saw him as a traitor to his original Protestant faith, now
only too willing to drag England into his scheme of self-aggrandisement, while others thought they saw a noble heart working out of
love for the Reformed Religion which he had never totally lost,
though politic circumstances had forced him to embrace Catholicism.
Prince Henry was one of the latter; though the prince felt he had
some claims to France himself, he was captivated by the image of
another man of the name of Henry—and "Most Christian King"!—

rallying Europe against the might of Spain and the Empire. This was what the boy prince had longed to do himself. So Prince Henry played no small part in urging his father to ally himself with the French in the battle over Cleves, and while the 4,000 English troops were mobilized out of veterans already in service in the Low Countries, Prince Henry approached his investiture in June 1610 with a secret plan.

Henry IV intended to march on Cleves toward the end of May 1610, and Prince Henry determined to don his robes of investiture only long enough to receive his titles and the symbolic blessing of his nation before dashing off to ride with the French king at the head of his nascent crusade. Englishmen far in excess of the 4,000 cynical professionals would be sure to follow, and thus, thought Prince Henry, would begin his long-prophesied career. Protestants on the Continent had conceived of the same grand scheme—Prince Henry of England was that well known to them by 1610—and they talked of Great Henry of England uniting their interests, rather than the self-serving, philandering Great Henri of France. In an April 24, 1610 dispatch, the Venetian Resident in Milan passed along the news that "though the Protestant Princes of Germany wish to lower the House of Austria they have no desire to aggrandise France." They would, however, the Venetian Resident continued, "be inclined to the Prince of England" as their leader, "though his Father is not much disposed towards that."[5] It was not alone Prince Henry's great destiny that had become a reliable currency throughout Europe; King James's own unheroic determination to block his son's rise to glory, for whatever reasons, had also become every petty diplomat's small change.

But events swift and bloody would do more than James could hope to alter Prince Henry's scheme to ride out onto the field of gold with King Henry. The assassin's knife struck Henry IV on May 14, 1610, and ended that monarch's life, as well as Prince Henry's immediate plans. The assassin proved to be a Catholic zealot named Ravaillac, and to Prince Henry the symbolic lesson of the French king's intended service to the Reformed Religion seemed all the more obvious, if infinitely more bitter. The prince went thoughtfully to his investiture, the determination to strike decisively at murderous European Catholicism growing harder within him, while the king his father, who had never harbored a fugitive affection for the French Henry, went into a kind of mourning peculiar to his nature: he doubled the guard about his person, wore thicker quilting over his chest against the bared bodkins which he now imagined were poised all about him, and to his subjects looked so much more the coward.

Prince Henry, meanwhile, observed the marshalling of forces against Julich, and received reports from the English commander there as though he were at the head of an English War Department in ways more palpable than his symbolic role might indicate. The English general at the siege of Julich, Sir Edward Cecil, wrote full reports on the battle to Henry, sent drawings and diagrams of the fortifications and of the ordering of the siege, and appealed to the prince when his command was challenged by a fractious and trouble-making Scotsman.[6] Henry followed it all from England, whether content this time to allow the Protestant allies to reduce Julich without his physical presence (which they did by August 22, 1610) though with his symbolic blessing, or whether actually prevented by the king from setting sail to join the fight. No matter. He had made up his mind that when fire broke out again in Europe, he would ride to meet it. He carried in his head a clock which ticked louder as he neared his eighteenth birthday, when it would, he was assured, chime forth the hour of God's wrath for the wicked pope, for Spain, and for all their minions. Sir Walter Ralegh had once remarked to Henry, while he was still an adolescent without the threat of imminent action in his eyes, that "the age most apt for the war was anciently observed to be about eighteen years, and so the Romans used: *Facilius est ad virtutem instruere novos milites, quam revocare praeteritos* [It is easier to teach courage to raw recruits than to call back veterans.] "[7] How those words might haunt Ralegh now, for like every other image advanced to the dressing of Henry's persona, this prophecy the prince found a brother to his heart.

II

The last six months of 1610 and the opening of 1611 were largely occupied with Henry's persistent struggle with his father and with the chief ministers of the state—primarily with the Earl of Salisbury —to obtain the full rights, tenures, and income of his titles. Though the king and Salisbury were partially successful in blocking occasionally his too rapid rise, Henry had behind him the potent force of the nation's good will, not to mention his own assurance of his proper role; he was not to be denied what was his by right and by strength of symbology. He was showing himself fully worthy of the characterizations which separate men, writing at the commencement of 1610, had created for him:

> *Sir Thomas Edmondes:* . . . the Prince . . . now beginneth to take a great authority upon him. . . . He maketh himself already very much respected and even by our greatest men in authority, and many men out of the pregnancy of his spirit do make many descants of many things that may hereafter ensue.

> *John More to William Trumbull:* You will have heard of the Christmas triumphs of our pregnant Prince, whose princely towardliness gives daily hopes of his future worthiness. . . .[8]

That both writers should unconsciously have evoked the same image of fertility—"our pregnant prince"—was ironic; certainly not all thought Henry's pregnancy was bound to spawn a blessed generation, and indeed it would not. On the issue of recusants alone—the matter over which the hard-working tenure-holders of Henry's Earldom of Chester had cause to be concerned—the prince would prove himself a most dear husband. Theoretically, with his Principality of Wales, his Dukedom of Cornwall, his earldom, and with his other titles came both revenues and also certain administrative powers. The power to identify, arrest, and fine recusants—those who found it difficult or impossible to let go of the Catholic religion—was a particularly cruel way to polish up one's Protestant credentials.

However determined Prince Henry might have been to root the last Catholic out of England, King James had always favored leniency, at least toward the Catholic laity although events between 1605 and 1610 made such toleration politically difficult. First, the Gunpowder Plot had inflamed the Protestant majority and robbed them of the powers of discretion in distinguishing fanatic Catholic plotters from good English citizens who saw no inherent conflict between their loyalty to their Catholic faith and their loyalty to the state. The Puritans, whose viewpoint became Prince Henry's, professed themselves unable to distinguish between a traitorous Catholic of Guy Fawkes's ilk and a Catholic merchant or farmer living in Gloucestershire or Hereford; both were traitors to God for serving a heathen idolatry, and analogously, they must also be traitors to the state. That King James did not quite see it this way mattered little; he was willing enough to hunt down "Jesuited Catholics," for they had shown themselves alchemically inclined toward gunpowder and deeds done by moon-light, but Parliament forced him to go further. In the months follow-ing the discovery of the Fawkes conspirators, Parliament passed a harsh bill against recusants which included an oath of allegiance.[9] By that instrument, known recusants were commanded to acknowl-edge James as lawful king and to deny—and this was the crucial clause in the oath—the pope's power to depose him, for by the power of ex-communication arose the damnable and impious doctrine that a good Catholic could seek the murder of his heretic lord. Despite James's reluctance to tighten the noose on England's Catholics, who were in the vast majority utterly loyal to the throne, he was somewhat frus-trated by the oath of allegiance, but its administration soon turned, or so it seemed, to the benefit of the king's policy of toleration, for loyal Catholics apparently did not shun the taking of the oath. Those who refused to sign, however, were considered "Jesuited," and on them—few though they were—the heavy thumb of London was laid. This administration of religious conformity slowly drifted away from rigorousness as time took some of the shock away from the Gunpow-der Treason.

But then came Henry IV's assassination in France, the second event in five years to hurl the English Protestants into a frenzy of anti-Catholicism, and unluckily this second act of violence coincided with Prince Henry's arrival on the first rung of power. If his father had proven weak of heart in staining his hands, Prince Henry had a basilisk's gaze. For a time, though, even James himself was touched with the general hysteria, as Arthur Wilson described him:

> But now being startled with this poysoned knife, he ven-tures upon a *Proclamation,* strictly commanding all *Jesu-its* and *Priests* out of the Kingdom, and all *Recusants* to their own Houses, not to come within ten miles of the *Court.* . . .[10]

And rumors of foreign assassins, of the same breed as Ravaillac, in-creased; Walter Yonge wrote in his diary on June 13, 1610:

> About the beginning of this month the King kept himself very private by reason that he had very perfect intelli-gence that there were four seminaries or Jesuits which lately did arrive in England to destroy both his Majesty and the Prince.[11]

But most significant for the course which Prince Henry would choose—and attempt to follow—was the flood of Puritan literature which swept out of the small presses in the months following King Henry's assassination, much of it dedicated or otherwise addressed to England's prince and the populace's Defender of the Faith (though the actual title still belonged to his father).

As always during his life, Henry once again found his identity and the prescription for action in the imagery of left-wing Protestantism. Two tracts in particular, both bearing feverish dedications to the prince, offered for his edification woodcuts which depicted the general enemy against which the fretful king had shut his door. *Pluto his Trauailes, Or, The Diuels Pilgrimage to the Colledge of Iesuites* bore on its title page a woodcut (see Fig. 10) of a bearded figure blessing a kneeling seminarian and giving him the injunction, "Murder the King," while the Devil himself stood by in monk's habit and seconded the commission with "I will helpe thee." Observing this laying on of hands—and waiting as it were in the wings—were several more seminarians who, presumably, would take their turns kneeling before the Archfiend before going off on their deadly missions. The *Fiery Trial of Gods Saints* offered an even more imaginative picture of Catholicism (see Fig. 11), basing its woodcut on the creature of Revelations 13:

> 1. And I sawe a beast rise out of the sea, hauing seuen heads, and ten hornes, and vpon his hornes *were* ten crownes, and vpon his heads the name of blasphemie.
> 2. And the beast which I sawe, was like a leopard, and his fete like a beares, and his mouth as the mouth of a lion: and the dragon gaue him his power and his throne, & great autoritie. (Geneva Bible, 1560)

There could be no doubt who rode astride the beast and out of whose mouth the three froglike demons leaped (*"Estote proditores* [Traitors, stand forth]. Goe kill your Prince," the Pope hissed, cartoon-like), to enter the three figures. Only one—the figure in the recognizable garb of the seminarian—bore a visible dagger; the implication seemed to be that in the England of 1610-1611, the agents of the pope would not always be easily detected; some, like the last of the three "proditores," looked suspiciously like an ordinary English courtier.

Fueled with such apocalyptic visions, Henry busied himself with the pious work of persecuting the Catholics who dwelt within the lands newly invested to him. He was, for example, strongly urged to

Figure 10. Title page engraving from Fennor's *Pluto his trauailes*. S.T.C. 10785, British Museum Department of Printed Books. Reproduced by permission of the British Library Board.

Figure 11. Engraving facing title page of *Fierie Tryall of Gods Saints*. S.T.C. 24269, British Museum Department of Printed Books. Reproduced by permission of the British Library Board.

petition James for the right to collect penalties from all recusants, whether or not they had signed the oath of allegiance; according to Lucy Aiken he was fully intent on following this "odious course," which would have meant a whole network of spies and informers, but Lord Chief Justice Coke was enlisted to find in the law prohibitions against such grants for penal forfeitures.[12] Henry dropped that scheme, but there were other men, who out of genuine religious heat or out of greed, were able to guide the prince's actions against the recusants.

One of these was Sir Arthur Gorges who during King James's first year in England had been disgraced and blocked from preferment because of his friendship with Sir Walter Ralegh. Sir Arthur had after the Gunpowder Plot shown himself an ardent hunter-out of papists; "the fyre is not yet owte of theyr fyngers," he said, and complained that the very scaffold on which the mutilated bodies of the conspirators were displayed "defiles the fairest gate of Paul's Church." (His complaint was evidently not an aesthetic one.)[13] His vehemence won him little advantage, however, until the prince, who also happened to be the friend and protector of Ralegh, showed himself receptive to such religious intemperance. So Sir Arthur became the prince's hatcher of strategems; he proposed to Henry, among other things, an office of public register for commercial transactions, which was granted (and which subsequently failed, testifying to the promoter's abilities);[14] but more interestingly he caught the prince's mood on the subject of recusants. A letter from Sir Arthur to the prince, dated April 29, 1610 and preserved in the Harleian manuscripts, bears witness to the writer's fervor and to the prince's evident receptivity to such schemes. (Most interesting of all perhaps is Sir Arthur's success in wedding religious piety to the profit motive.) Although the full outline of Sir Arthur's plan remains a mystery—this letter makes shorthand reference to a scheme already well under discussion—its tenor and direction leave little doubt about its general subject matter:

> When it is done, to second the same, I will be ready to acquaint your Highness with a matter, that shall bring unto your coffers, for the better supporting of your princely state, twenty thousand pounds a year at the least, and to be effected with ease, without wrong to the public, and not needing to sollicit the parliament for the same: And this shall follow in its due time, when the

> other is effected. And, in the mean time, this may suffice
> for an answer to all, that shall go about to disgrace your
> bill in parliament, that it favors more of a well-policed
> Christian state, and of the government of a wise and god-
> ly prince, rather, with mild and provident remedies, to
> prevent growing mischiefs, than afterwards to seek to
> weed them out with rigorous and bloody means, when
> they are already planted.[15]

It was perhaps this, or some such similar scheme, that Salisbury hesi-
tated over and finally told the prince, "Sure I am, if it be not tempered, it will be of ill sound in the subjects minds in this island, of
which I would be glad both father and son should have possession,
as well by the love, as the loyalty of the people."[16]

The prince's measures did sound ill in the ears of some; in October of 1610 certain "malcontents" of Hertfordshire petitioned per-
sistently against the harsh jurisdiction of the Court of Wales.[17] And
Henry was not interested solely in pursuing the matter of religious
purity only among the common folk; the nobility (as the woodcut in
The Fiery Trial of Gods Saints had hinted) had more than its share
of secret, suspected, and acknowledged Catholics.[18] When one of
these, the Countess of Shrewsbury, was implicated as an intimate of
the fugitive Arabella Stuart, Prince Henry took the opportunity (as
Sir Arthur Gorges advised) of searching out cellarages on the Shrewsbury estates—not in order to find the desperate Lady Arabella but in
order to surprise a few Catholics with perhaps a mass priest or two
among them. Henry sent Sir John Holles with armed officers on this
mission, and the prince received the following report:

> It being your pleasure and commandment I should take
> this business in charge, I accordingly have endeavoured
> therein with all diligence to give your Highness best satis-
> faction. . . . yesterday early in the morning I beset and
> entered the Earl of Shrewsbury's Abbey of Rufford,
> where after a long and a curious search in vaults, cellars,
> chambers, and garrets, I found only some crucifixes and
> old papistical books, divers trap doors to conceal and is-
> sue forth such pernicious vermin as I sought for. . . .[19]

The almost comic quality of Sir John's frustration at finding only
"old papistical books" rather than *new* (every country great house
could be expected to have in its muniment room devotional books
dating from the years before Henry VIII changed the national reli-

gion), becomes strained somewhat when we focus on the spirit of
suspicion in the prince who had given Sir John his marching orders.

The proof of Henry's zeal in hounding recusants is nowhere more
vividly portrayed than after his premature death, when stout Protestants all over the realm developed a grisly nostalgia for the prince's
stern measures. The Reverend Lewis Bayly, one of the prince's chaplains, reported that Henry, not a month before his death, complained
that "religion lay a bleeding, and no marvayle . . . when divers coun-
saillors heare masse in the morning, and then go to a court sermon
and so to the counsaile."[20] Once Henry was dead, according to the
popular perception of his symbolic power as the head of England's
Protestant community, those secret Catholics grew understandably
bold and began creeping up out of those cellars where Sir John Holles
could not find them and down out of garrets. Sir Simonds D'Ewes,
in his *Autobiography,* remarked years later with some justification
that England would not have needed Oliver Cromwell if Prince Henry
had lived: "So as had not our sins caused God to take from us so
peerless a prince, it was very likely that Popery would have been well
purged out of Great Britain and Ireland by his care."[21]

III

The Earl of Salisbury had urged the prince to temper his enthusiasm, but the prince could be tempered only by having withheld from
him the full power which he sought. If the Venetian ambassador's
idly dropped statement of June 16, 1610—"they did not desire to exalt him too high"[22] —seemed to carry little credence because it offered no hard evidence, the ambassador's fuller dispatch to the Doge
and Senate a week later did offer specifics:

> The day before yesterday, I went to wait on his Highness
> in his lodging at St. James' and congratulated him on his
> entry on the possession of the Principality. The Prince
> was pleased at this compliment, which no one else has
> paid him as yet. He has not yet received his revenues; that
> is being put off till October next, and possibly further;
> nor has the King been pleased to allow him to increase his
> household as he desired. It seems that the King has some
> reasonable jealousy of the rising sun. . . .[23]

Ambassador Correr's picture of the prince suggests a kind of political
quarantine almost, as though those in the government of England

were keeping Henry at a therapeutic distance; the apprehension of men who wished to retain their positions and their power, and the "reasonable jealousy" of Henry's own father, was not without cause. But the ambassador was quite mistaken in his prediction that Henry's revenues could be indefinitely denied him; as we shall see, the prince was able to move much more quickly than reckoned possible by those who knew his father's mind.

The sting of Henry's piety could be felt in many areas besides merely the matter of religious conformity, as Ambassador Correr went on to reveal in his June 23 communication:

> The Prince has acquired a great reputation by the recent creation of Knights of the Bath. He succeeded in rendering futile all the efforts of those who attempted to push ahead by the usual method of a good round sum. Indeed, when one of these had, by the ordinary means, secured the entry of his name on the list, the Prince complained that his blood was inferior to that of the others and caused the note to be cancelled.[24]

Great men, if they were not able to tiptoe around him without awakening his interest or his enmity, found it easier to agree with his opinions rather than face the heat of his contention. Such agreements made to the prince's face could be later rescinded or modified out of his hearing. The dispatches from the Venetian ambassador, once again, captured much of the quality of Henry's personality after June, 1610:

> *August 5.* . . . the Prince, . . . desires also to handle some of the more important affairs, and he deals with them so strictly that he easily surmounts many difficulties, for everyone is afraid of falling into disgrace with him. I am told that in the recent disagreement in Parliament he produced the results by correcting and damping the ardour of various persons.
> *November 25.* . . . he is extremely particular that everything shall be the result of his own choice. . . .
> *December 2.* The Prince has applied to Parliament for certain privileges enjoyed by his predecessors; he will meet no opposition, as everyone is anxious to please him.[25]

For Parliament, of course, he was a welcomed contrast to an unpopular king. While acting out before the people the drama of heroic vitality and forward thrust, the prince was in dozens of ways a living indictment of courtly decay, lassitude, and impiety. By every comparison, even those in which King James was obviously the superior contender, Prince Henry was granted the laurels. If King James was recognized as the most scholarly monarch ever to rule England, scholarship was by the example of Henry's fanatical delight in athletics denigrated to the level of mere effeminacy. Where the king tested his religious faith in philosophical disputation, delighting to hear opinions contrary and exotic against which he could play his wit and his wide reading, Prince Henry's single-minded and essentially mute testimony for Calvinism was held to frustrate the Devil by abstaining from the idle toys of chatter. Whereas the king loved his drink and could be remarkably and inventively profane, Prince Henry ostentatiously shunned such vices:

> Once when the prince was hunting the stag, it chanced the stag, being spent, crossed the road where a butcher and his dog were travelling; the dog killed the stag, which was so great that the butcher could not carry him off: when the huntsman and the company came up, they fell at odds with the butcher, and endeavoured to incense the prince against him; to whom the prince soberly answered, "What if the butcher's dog killed the stag, what could the butcher help it?" They replied, if his father had been served so, he would have sworn so as no man could have endured it. "Away," replied the prince, "all the pleasure in the world is not worth an oath."[26]

James could not distinguish a good counselor from a corrupt one; an efficient minister was frequently replaced by some fellow who kept his heart attending ever on himself. Prince Henry could not distinguish good men from bad either, but the people thought he could, simply because the men who served Henry *looked* more sober, more god-fearing; none of the decadent courtiers that became associated with King James's court were given any place about Prince Henry. This was perceived as a positive difference of substance between the father and son, rather than a mere difference of style.[27] Both were still Stuarts and both were possessed of the same pride in their divine right, though through the working of the Protestant myth Henry's arrogance was always read as the Christian virtue of courage and forthrightness, while King James's could be nothing more, in the popular mind, than petulance.

The perceptible difference between father and son really came down to their differing abilities to inspire and then to assume mythic personation. Prince Henry, as we have seen, both understood and actively pursued his personation; King James was baffled by the art, or more frequently perhaps frustrated that the mask he wished to don for the English became low comedy in their critical eyes. The king wished to be known by the legend *Beati Pacifici*, Blessed are the Peacemakers, but James's lofty notion of the calm ordering of chaos necessarily required something the king did not possess, the implications of bravery and courage and superior strength held in check. The king had simply too large a reputation as a coward to allow the designation *Pacificus* to work as other than a joke. Whereas Henry had never really done anything, other than constantly *suggest* the future as possibility—the eternal, infuriating luxury of the young— King James had a history which every man knew and which every man could rewrite to suit his own prejudices. A mere glance at any of King James's portraits, with only cursory comparison with those portraits of Henry that we have already examined, will tell the story of the differences in their personations. Prince Henry's portraits communicate energy, assurance, a fair measure of high voltage arrogance. King James laconically gazed out of his portraits with a kind of sodden ennui. Those large, sad eyes suggested acquiescence, and they frequently looked out with a sideway stare which inspired queasiness more than trust. His were the icons of compromise, of equivocation and fizzle. The personality behind that mask could only, it seemed, give way to the power behind Henry's personation.

Prince Henry was allowed to set up his own separate court in the months following his investiture, a fact of surpassing practical and symbolic importance. With his own household, run with his own revenue, he was all the freer to plan and initiate bolder expressions of his ambition than had been possible under the closer scrutiny of the king and Salisbury. Indeed, Salisbury found that, as Lord Treasurer and first Secretary of State, he had two centers of government from which flowed parallel, if not frequently conflicting, orders and interests.

The symbolic impact of Henry's new court, established permanently at St. James's Palace (though Henry continued to move about to his other houses, particularly the palace at Richmond), was principally a matter of tone. Henry made it clear quite promptly that his would be a godly court, the antechamber (as it were) to God's heav-

enly throneroom, for was he not as a divinely anointed prince a mir-
ror of God's will? So his Protestant myth had taught him, helped not
a little by King James's own doctrine of divine right, and so his persona continued to grow in England:

> *October 16.* The Prince's Court will be established be-
> fore Christmas, and today at Richmond he himself drew
> up certain ordinances which he will have observed. His
> gentlemen shall attend him and be present at times of
> prayers when he goes to his private chapel, in which ser-
> vice he will dispense no man. He will be properly attended
> at tennis play; and in his standing house where he is resi-
> dent, a convenient store of munitions and arms for any
> sudden occasion shall be kept. A standing table to be
> ready for the entertainment of any nobleman or stranger
> of account that may visit him upon the sudden. He will
> have his officers choose his servants without partiality or
> bribes; and the men of his guard shall be of known hon-
> est conversation and well qualified in some activity, as
> wrestling, tossing the pike, shooting or suchlike skill, and
> more than able only to wait with a halberd; and those
> places of the guard shall not be trafficked or sold. Nor
> shall those his servants who shall adjudge themselves to
> be aggrieved revenge themselves by violence or with the
> sword.[28]

> *November 25.* He is now arranging his household and ap-
> pointing his officers and gentlemen; there are infinite of-
> fers from gentlemen who vie with one another in desir-
> ing admission, and yet there is not one who dares to at-
> tempt the way of favouritism. . . .[29]

> *January 14, 1611.* His Highness, after naming the officers
> of his household and signing many excellent orders, ad-
> ministered the oath to all, and has begun to govern his
> house apart from his father's. He is delighted to rule; and
> as he desires that the world should think him prudent
> and spirited he pays attention to the regulations of his
> house and is studying an order as to the cut and quality
> of the dresses of the gentlemen of his household—which
> runs here to an incredible excess; on the other hand he
> attends to the disposition of his houses, having already
> ordered many gardens and fountains and some new build-
> ings. He is paying special attention to the adorning of a
> most beautiful gallery of very fine pictures ancient and

> modern, the larger part brought out of Venice. He is also
> collecting books for a library he has built.[30]

> "Orders for his Highness's Chapel." . . . especial notice
> shall be taken by the yoemen of the vestry of those, that
> shall omit, or at any time fail (being in the house) to re-
> pair to divine service, and to the sermons, that there shall
> be preached, to the end, that due animadversion may be
> used to such defaulters. . . .[31]

Those gentlemen who vied so earnestly to enter his service found the
discipline strict, but the richness of the promise and their own sense
of partaking in a divine plan made the rigors of Henry's service a welcomed relief from the flaccid license into which much of official England had fallen. Henry's was the *"new Star"* which had "become
Lord of the *Ascendant"*;[32] he seemed to be drawing all the world
under his influence.

As the Venetian ambassador had noted in June, Henry did have
to exercise some of his famed insistence to receive the full share of
his revenues. The king and Salisbury gave a little, pulled back a little,
gave a little again; James twice bestowed 1,000 pounds in gold on
Henry as lavish New Year's gifts in both 1611 and 1612,[33] thinking
perhaps that such abundant displays of largesse and affection might
divert Henry from the full realization of his titles. But Henry was no
child to be bribed into forgetfulness by sweets—had never been such
—and he kept the pressure constant.

The State Papers covering the period after Henry's investiture
tell the story in sums and figures which are dull only if we do not
know the energies which shaped them. On August 21, 1610 the king
grudgingly announced his intention of allowing Henry 10,000 pounds
per annum in rents and benefits, but September produced a flurry of
documents regarding the lands and revenues belonging to the Duchy
of Cornwall, the Earldom of Chester, and the Principality of Wales.
Henry was exploring fully the perimeters of his titles, nosing out every ancient grant and parliamentary precedent; he meant to have everything that by ancient order belonged to his dignity. On September 19, Charles Anthony, Engraver of the Mint, received a warrant to
make for the prince's service certain official seals necessary for the
operation of Henry's Courts of Revenue, Stannary, Courts of Devon
and Cornwall, Court of Trematon, and Office of the Sheriff of Cornwall;[34] the granting of seals, like the establishment of his separate
Court, had as much symbolic force as practical application.

By September 29, the prince's insistence had already forced James to loosen his grasp on the flow of money; the king granted to the prince certain ancient possessions which carried very healthy yearly incomes:

Principality of Wales:	£1,106	12s 7½d	per annum
Other manors in Wales:	£2,943	10s 9¼d	per annum
Duchy of Cornwall:	£2,706	3s	per annum
Chester:	£ 230	9s 10d	per annum

After only a month, Henry had managed to increase his initial yearly grant of £10,000 by over £7,000, but James allowed few of the administrative rights and jurisdictions to pass into Henry's hands along with the revenue. James retained, for example, the right to appoint the Chief Justice of Chester,[35] a matter of no little interest to those peaceful and loyal recusants who had already heard about—or felt— Henry's religious ardor.

On October 30, Henry's godly household at St. James's had burgeoned with those not too pious to eat fully their share of the prince's diet, so King James was obliged to increase Henry's revenue by £1,500 *per month;*[36] he was further obliged on January 19 of the following year to increase that monthly allowance to £1,600.[37] (The King might have remarked that those of the Puritan frame, though dainty in the matter of God's name on their lips, showed no manners at all in the consumption of flesh, fish, and fowl.) In November 1610 Henry seized the lands of Robert ap Owen and others in Wales on the grounds of late payment of lease, though the Welshmen had offered to pay any reasonable fine.[38] Though the king had withheld many of the jurisdictions over Henry's titled possessions, the prince sought to subvert that intent by eliminating the tenants-in-chief and taking possession of lands directly. On November 25, a few days after Robert ap Owen and the others petitioned Salisbury to block the seizure of their tenures, the Venetian ambassador reported on Henry's success in taking control:

> His Highness has begun to draw not only the lesser revenues of the Principality of Wales, but also other revenues the larger part drawn from land to the amount of about one hundred and sixty thousand ducats, as he exercises a certain jurisdiction in the Principality.[39]

A year later, in a letter to Sir Dudley Carleton, John Chamberlain recorded the continuing, and by now highly refined, success of the prince's acquisitive talents:

> *November 27, 1611.* The Prince hath recovered Bark-
> hampsted from Sir Ed: Carie upon the same title that he
> had Sir Warwicke Heales land, as belonging to the Duchie
> of Cornwall.[40]

Though the flow of revenue and power to Henry was slow, it was
basically continuous, but two prizes proved especially elusive and one
of those never came officially within his grasp. The first was his seat
on the Privy Council. The king made Henry wait to be sworn a Privy
Councillor until the first of October, 1611, but upon his coming into
that body, great way was made for him:

> *John Thorys to William Trumbull, October 8.* . . . the
> prince himself sat in Council on Monday last, the first
> time of his life, and is President of the Council.[41]

> *Ambassador Correr, November 11.* He will, beyond
> doubt, attend regularly, for the takes great pleasure in
> the conduct of important affairs.[42]

His influence on the pulse rate of England could only increase once
he was within the Council.

The second great office to which he aspired was Lord High Admiral. Since the days Phineas Pett had entered his service and built
the *Prince Royal,* and certainly since the time Sir Walter Ralegh had
begun educating him on the proficiency of ships and sailing, Prince
Henry had felt that the office of Lord High Admiral should belong
to him. Charles Howard, Earl of Nottingham, who had been Lord Admiral since before the Armada, was in 1611 an astonishing seventy-
five years old. He had once been an effective and dashing admiral,
most heroically commanding England's little navy against the galleons
of Spain in 1588, but since James had come to the throne, Nottingham's administration of the Royal Navy had been characterized by
waste, decay, and almost universal corruption. While the earl lived,
of course, the office was his, but many expected his death almost
hourly (he lived for thirteen more astonishing years). Henry set to
work to insure, he thought, that the office would be granted to him
on the earl's death. While he waited for the blessed event of the
Earl's demise, he found covert means to keep a proprietary eye on
his navy. In the summer of 1611, Sir John Trevor "sold" his office as
Surveyor of the Royal Navy to Richard Bingley who immediately

undertook in June, on orders of Nottingham, a strict survey of the whole navy. Master shipwright Phineas Pett refused to join in the survey "before I knew the Prince's pleasure," understanding well enough Henry's disposition. But Pett was, nevertheless, persuaded through threats to participate in the survey. When Henry finally heard of what was going forward at Chatham, he erupted in anger at Pett. Why had he not informed His Royal Highness of those proceedings? The sharp rebuke was accompanied by a warning that Pett was in the future to inform the prince instantly of all matters involving the navy.[43] And Pett was not Henry's only spy. Bishop Goodman, who knew the navy and its workings as well as any man in England, reported Prince Henry's machinations:

> I confess that the prince did sometimes pry into the King's actions and a little dislike them. A knight told me the tale that he was privily sent by Prince Henry to see how the royal navy was ordered; what defects there were, and to be a spy upon them; and no doubt but he had others in the Signet Office.[44]

Bishop Goodman added, rather mysteriously, that "some about him did put these thoughts into him, and no doubt but he had heroical intentions." With a navy at his disposal, responsive to his ambitions or his whims, a prince could do much to frighten the Spaniard on the Continent, in America, or wherever he wished. King James could see that well enough.

On one notable occasion Henry acted as his own spy, undertaking a private survey of the navy's strengths and weaknesses and charging his companions to tell no one of his activities. He took a barge from Whitehall down to Chatham with Phineas Pett and a few others, and there he went on board in succession all the ships of the line, taking down notes and observations. According to Pett's own account, the prince would "suffer" none to come near him while he made his notations, which gave rise to much speculation about his intents and purposes.[45] On the next morning, as his barge was leaving Chatham for the return to Whitehall, Henry himself commanded all the ships to salute him with a peal of ordnance. It is easy enough to imagine what dreams of conquest formed in his head as the cannon thundered.

While seeming to yield to Henry, James always kept in one thin finger of lingering control. Unexpectedly, the king announced he would bestow the admiralty on Henry's younger brother, the weak and largely ignored Charles, Duke of York. Henry contemptuously

replied that the Archbishopric of Canterbury was a far better post for
the Duke, for the archbishop's long robes could hide his wobbly and
misshapen legs.[46] James tacked; he seemed to yield for a time, even
to the point of allowing Henry to act as executor for Duke Charles
and agreeing to retire Nottingham from the service:

> *September 25, 1611.* There is a project to make the Duke
> of York High Admiral, the Prince to execute during his
> brother's minority, with a Commission of the greater
> Lords, and a subordinate Commission of Inferiors. . . .
> My L. Admiral, in recompense of his pretended resigna-
> tion, is to have 4,000£ present and a pension of 1,500£
> for life.[47]

This was a considerable concession—for all the hope the Duke of
York seemed to offer, he might be in his "minority" forever—but
Henry was not satisfied. Commissions on top of commissions was
not his idea of the best method to muster heroic action. He continued to push and within a month seemed to have won a full victory:

> *October 21.* The Prince. . . . aspires to the post of Lord
> High Admiral, and has managed so cleverly with the King
> that he has got his word for it, in spite of the fact that the
> King designed to make the Duke of York Admiral. A
> gentleman in the confidence of the Prince told me that
> in the time of the late Queen the post of Admiral was
> worth one hundred and fifty thousand crowns a year.
> . . . In time of war it is undoubtedly the greatest post in
> this kingdom. The Prince with his diligence and author-
> ity will regulate many abuses which the present Admiral,
> who is decrepit, can hardly do.[48]

It was precisely a "time of war" that Henry could see in his mind's
eye, and that coming war was chiefly his concern in surveying and
controlling the navy. The Domestic State Papers indicate that Henry
began acting in Council on the strength of his assumed victory. In
November several warrants and orders were issued for the felling and
transportation of thousands of trees: the Royal Navy was about to
go into a building boom. Henry also pushed for a general reform in
the administration of the Navy, to accompany the push to build new
ships, and on December 13 the king announced his consent for the
reform.[49] James even made a specific request that the prince be present in Council to discuss the plan, and Henry was obliging: "The
Prince in Council has dealt with the reform of the Navy and proposed

some new orders on which he has several times spoken at length." [50] That plan for reform involved primarily the rapid doubling of the war fleet, and pursuant to it, Henry commanded slightly before the middle of January 1612 all the king's master shipwrights to attend him at Greenwich to hear and discuss a plan for opening up new shipyards in Ireland.[51] Henry seemed to be everywhere at once and he was behaving in a manner befitting a Lord High Admiral.

Then on January 15, 1612, James unpredictably reversed his earlier concessions and granted to Charles, Duke of York, the office of Lord Admiral, in reversion after the death of Nottingham.[52] Perhaps the king merely wished to remind his elder son that absolute power still lay with the father, or perhaps he discovered the outline of some of Henry's "heroical intentions" and was frightened into the foolishness of bestowing the navy on Charles. Whatever his reasons, James's actions served not long to deter Henry and really only confirmed to those of the prince's household that a king so mercurial would better serve his realm by yielding his authority to a son so differently purposed.

IV

The final phase of Prince Henry's short life really commenced with the establishment of his own separate household and court at the Palace of St. James's. That contrast of character, style, and symbolism between him and his father was given a kind of geographical significance when Parliament and the rest of Protestant England watched the individually destined Henry pull away from his father's disputatious alehouse and his mother's lewd theater to establish a separate and quite godly haven dedicated to laying the plans which were intended to bring him to the head of all Protestant Christianity. To St. James's could repair those pious, those eager, those bitterly frustrated preachers and soldiers who chafed to do duty once again in some great cause. There in that place enchanted by the full, unobstructed beams of Henry's Protestant myth, the past could be misrepresented as a holy, chivalric ideal while the future could be dreamed of outside the constrictions of reality. "In this holy path you have so happily begun to walk," wrote William Crashaw to his Prince,

> your personal practice of religion and the religious government of your honorable household may be a pattern

to all the great families of these kingdoms, wherein, if
popery and profaneness found no better countenance
nor encouragement than in the Princes court, it were
happy for our church and state.[53]

But for all the holiness of the path which led him to the separateness
of St. James's, Henry could not wholly avoid being sucked occasionally into the scandal of his father's court.

In her recent biography of James I, Lady Antonia Fraser stated
flatly that Prince Henry had an affair with Frances Howard, Lady
Essex.[54] Lady Fraser was following a rumor which began only after
Henry's death and which was precipitated by anti-Stuart writers who
had never known the prince or the extent to which his personal myth
made him distinctly different from the stereotypical rakes who
crowded into the Court of James I and later into the Court of Charles I.
For the fact was, contrary to rumor both current in the seventeenth
century and perpetuated in the twentieth, Frances Howard was poison to the prince.

Indeed, most of the tribe of Howards were anathema to him, for
in them was centered the strength of the pro-Spanish party. Henry
Howard, Earl of Northampton, was the elder statesman of the clan,
a Catholic, a pensioner of the Spanish king, a bitter enemy of Sir
Walter Ralegh, and a smilingly unctuous and hypocritical stumbling
block to the prince's ambitions. Northampton's kinsman was Charles
Howard, Earl of Nottingham and High Admiral, another Howard
Prince Henry had no cause to love. The third of the triumvirate of
powerful Howards was Northampton's nephew, the Earl of Suffolk,
Lord Chamberlain and father of the notorious Lady Frances.

She had upon arrangement of her family and the king been married to the immature Earl of Essex, Prince Henry's intimate friend,
in 1606, when the earl was fourteen and she only thirteen. The marriage was not consummated at that time, and the earl was soon sent
away to the Continent alone to mature. No parallel concern for the
maturation of Lady Essex was then shown, but Frances proved herself a speedier pupil than her absent husband. By the time she was
seventeen, when her husband had returned from Europe not much
improved, she had become a common property among both gallants
and wits. Northampton, the lady's great-uncle, apparently propelled
her in Prince Henry's direction, hoping somehow to interest him in
any sort of union that might quell his anti-Catholic bias and his ambitions for accruing power. Henry was not interested. The lady was

married to one of his oldest and dearest friends, and she had, much to Henry's disgust, taken up with the king's newest favorite, Sir Robert Carr, who had by now achieved the title of Viscount Rochester.

Rochester was the young man who had won the king's affection by breaking a bone during a court tilt, and it was on Rochester that Ralegh's Sherborne estate had first been bestowed, so there was already sufficient cause for enmity between the young viscount and the young prince. This dislike could only grow as Rochester became increasingly powerful. He was made a Garter Knight in May 1611. Then he was granted an augmentation of arms and supporters in June. Next he was given the Castle of Rochester with all appurtenances in fee simple, and in July he was made Keeper of the Palace of Westminster. Early in 1612 Rochester was given 12,000 pounds outright after having already become the king's unofficial secretary, and finally in April 1612 he was sworn a Privy Councillor, having crept into the highest reaches of power where Prince Henry had already installed himself and where the prince was not inclined to welcome this handsome, ignorant, and impertinent Scotsman. The fact that Rochester had taken to his hot embrace the lascivious wife of the prince's friend gave only additional reason for Henry to hate his father's favorite.

Henry's anger was bound to express itself directly. On the day after Rochester was made a Garter Knight, Henry reluctantly accompanied his father on a hunt at Royston. James reproved Henry's sluggish lack of interest. Henry replied with sharp words of resentment, something so stinging that the king came close to violence. Eye witnesses reported that the king was "so angry that he threatened the Prince with his cane, whereupon the Prince put spurs to his horse and rode off, followed by the larger part of the company."[55] A later incident at tennis play brought Henry and the detested Rochester face to face with angry words, and then almost to blows. It was said that the prince had offered to strike Rochester with his tennis racket but was restrained by onlookers. Later, Sir James Elphington, a servant of the prince and one of that order of men who always hang about the great and powerful, eagerly ready to perform unsavory duties, approached Henry and offered to murder Rochester. Henry replied that he would do the deed himself, when he had sufficient cause. It was clear enough to all that the court and government could not hold together with these two young men vying to occupy the same place, and indeed it was perhaps only Prince Henry's premature death that saved Carr's life.

There was more of significance in Henry's subsequent treatment of Lady Essex, Rochester's paramour. The prince was, first, contemptuous toward her because of the man she had formed a liaison with:

> . . . dancing one time among the *Ladies,* and her Glove falling down, it was taken up, and presented to [Henry], by one that thought he did him acceptable *service;* but the *Prince* refused to receive it, saying publickly, He would not have it, it is *stretcht* by another, meaning the *Viscount.* [56]

But a more deep-seated attitude, the direct product of his mythologized self-perception, was at work in Henry, steering him away from Frances Lady Essex. Everyone in the court knew her to be a worn glove, and for the reasons we have examined, Henry found her charms less than overwhelming. But the fact was, he had been so thoroughly programmed to the myth of the conqueror—the myth which pictured phallic energy only in terms of power rather than in terms of love or domestic fertility—that he was, if not totally immune to the notion of romantic love and the blandishments of sexual bliss, he was so thoroughly other-directed as to make sex and conjugal union alien to his sense of self.

Indications of his disdain (perhaps *revulsion,* though that word perhaps suggests too much of the neurotic) for the sexual possibilities of his human nature began early. On this point he was apparently much the concern of his mother, who on one occasion playfully locked him into a small chamber on some ruse with a lovely young lady of the court—it could even have been Frances Howard, though we have no way of knowing that—in hopes, she said, that the imp Cupid would find his mark. [57]   Prince Henry was both chagrined and enraged. His reaction to his mother's prank suggests that his own sense of identity had been affronted by the threat of sexuality. Queen Anne's own rather frustrated libido, in fact, may have been the primary block between any close relationship between mother and son after 1603. She had scandalized the court on many occasions by appearing in masques in various stages of suggestive dishabille. For the *Masque of Blackness* she painted her body ebony and embarrassed many of the men by attempting to kiss them with her greasy lips. No one has suggested that Queen Anne's sensuality, as much as King James's several faults, drove Prince Henry from their court to establish his own at St. James's, but surely his mother's violation—or attempted violation—of his own mystique of purity must have deeply offended him.

V

Prince Henry's simple lack of interest in the sexual side of human nature—if not quite his aversion to it—became increasingly ironic as the English government manipulated a welter of possible royal matches for the prince. Henry was, by dint of his birth, a commodity of uncommon interest in every European palace where little royal princesses played their lutes, worked at their tapestries, or learned to copy out homilies in the italic hand; there was no personal myth to which Henry could dedicate himself that would free him from the commercial haggling—and the indignities—of the royal marriage market. All Henry could do, and this he did, was stay loftily above the match-making until he could no longer keep silent or watch his personation be violated by those who either did not understand his sense of destiny or disagreed with it.

The chief issue was whether Henry's bride would be Catholic or Protestant, and the complications over that issue were increased by the fact that the Lady Elizabeth, Henry's younger sister, was also on the market. James had two marriageable heirs, and the propositions for double matches were accordingly inventive. The Spanish party, led by Northampton and seconded not a little by James himself, wanted keenly to marry Henry to a Spanish Infanta; barring that match, several other princesses were available, including a daughter of Henry IV of France, the daughter of the Duke of Savoy, the sister of the Duke of Tuscany—all Catholic. There often seemed, in fact, to be no Protestant princesses at all to be considered, or so Northampton and his allies wished to make it appear. For Lady Elizabeth also there were several Catholic princes suggested, most notably the Prince of Piedmont, son of the Duke of Savoy, but as a female Princess Elizabeth was a less valuable property because of her inability to inherit while there were male heirs. So a number of Protestant princes were considered for her, including Prince Maurice of the Netherlands and the young Prince Frederick, Elector of Palatine, whom she would subsequently marry. The pro-Spanish party felt it permissible, and perhaps even wise, to strengthen alliances with Northern Europe by marrying Elizabeth to a Protestant, just so long as Prince Henry could

be successfully bound to one of the Catholic princesses. This may
have represented wise diplomatic thinking at the time, but it did not
coincide with Henry's inner myth nor with that clock ticking in his
mind.

The first flurry of excitement was over a match between the
prince and the Infanta of Spain, which the Spanish suggested as early
as November 1603.[58] James was non-committal, as his chief minister
Salisbury was utterly opposed to any union of marriage between England and Spain, but Philip III kept hinting about his Infanta through
1610, with James growing more interested with each passing year.
The Spanish king even offered in 1605 the Spanish Netherlands as
dower,[59] which the credulous chose to believe as a serious, good-
faith proposal. The assassination of Henry IV in France in 1610 considerably altered things, however, for the Spanish king took full advantage of the unsettled condition in France to contract secretly
with the Regent, Marie de Medici, to marry the Infanta to the Dauphin. When James discovered that the Infanta—Salisbury called her
that "Spanish olive"—had slipped away, he was highly incensed and
raged for a good hour at the Spanish ambassador. Philip, to placate
James, encouraged the Duke of Savoy, who was half-Spanish and
thoroughly under the control of Madrid, to offer his son, the Prince
of Piedmont, to Elizabeth; the duke later suggested that the match
be doubled by marrying Henry simultaneously to a princess of Savoy.[60]

The matches with Savoy much exercised everyone's interest.
For his own part, Henry was opposed to both. He could offer as his
reason the king's own words from the *Basilikon Doron:*

> And therefore I would rathest haue you to Marie one that
> were fully of your owne Religion; her ranke and other
> qualities being agreeable to your estate. . . . ye haue
> deeply to weigh, and consider vpon these doubts, how
> ye and your wife can bee of one flesh, and keepe vnitie
> betwixt you, being members of two opposite Churches:
> disagreement in Religion bringeth euer with it, disagree-
> ment in maners; and the dissention betwixt your Preach-
> ers and hers, wil breed and foster a dissention among
> your subiects, taking their example from your family;
> besides the perill of the euill education of your children.[61]

Though James could not bring himself to practice what he preached, his words had contributed a fair measure to Henry's inner checks. "Two religions should never lie in [my] bed,"[62] the prince was quoted as saying.

Henry gathered about him his Protestant party and encouraged the writing of reasons against the Savoyard matches. He persuaded Sir Walter Ralegh to join the pamphleteering on his side, though it took little encouragement for Sir Walter to write against what he considered a Spanish plot to enfeeble England:

> And I cannot tell, I leave it to wiser men to judge, whether the lady Elizabeth, the eldest daughter of England, were not therefore sought, both by the king of Spain and the Savoyan, by her to strengthen and revive the former pretences [to the English throne]. . . . Certainly it were a brave subject for our malicious papists to work upon. . . .
>
> It is the Spaniard that is to be feared; the Spaniard, who layeth his pretences and practices with a long hand. . . . it were an horrible dishonour to be overreached by any of those dry and subtle-headed Spaniards.[63]

Though Ralegh agreed with the prince this far, he disagreed with Henry's own developing plans for matrimony, as we shall see.

A theme which developed in the anti-Savoy literature, though not in what Ralegh wrote, owes its existence to Henry's long established fixation on the symbols of power, to the thorough exclusion of the feminine. So opposed were the anti-Spanish Protestants to seeing their prince's conquering persona married to the softness of a Catholic princess, they developed a thoroughgoing anti-feminism which extended almost unconsciously to all women, despite what religion they might practice. Marriage, even to a predestinated and sanctified Calvinist, was simply not in the programme of their young Alexander. Thus Sir John Holles, the man whom Prince Henry had sent to search for papists in the Countess of Shrewsbury's pantry, could write to Henry of the Savoyard princess as a seductive Eve, offering the fatal apple to England's Adam at the direction of that old serpent the Pope. It was only a short step from there to a lurid characterization of women in general:

> The first woman corrupted the first man, though created in perfection; and the wisest of all men forsook his God

and with Him his knowledge and gave himself up to the
idols and ignorance of his wives. A woman's tongue
caused Peter to deny his Master, and Dalila persuaded
Sampson to betray his strength and life to her. This is
the surest engine and instrument the devil hath, and the
pope and his ministers for the planting his kingdom em-
ploy no other. . . . some of that sex have already successfully prepared the way—.[64]

This last statement was Sir John's bold reference to Henry's own
mother, his evident immunity from rebuke or subsequent punishment an indication in itself that the young man to whom he spoke
shared the sentiment. The reference to Sampson was also a telling
one, for had not Henry, like the Nazarites of the Old Testament, lived
his life consecrated to a vision which demanded a kind of purity, quite
foreign to the king and the queen? And now those compromised,
impure forces were trying to clip Henry's locks by forcing him into
an unholy marriage. Sir John ended his tirade against the feminine
by holding up two more images of masculinity—Jesus and St. John—
the example of the latter particularly significant since he was be-
headed at the instigation of a seductive woman:

Christ sent before him John the masculine but the pope
delights more in Jone the feminine. . . .

What would be the result of the marriage which the Duke of Savoy
proposed and the King of Spain favored?

. . . let me by way of prospective present you more particularly the face of this court. The prince resorts to the
sermon, his Savoyard to the mass; he to his prayers, she
to her confession; either have their train; . . . where is
then that unity, that tie and knot of marriage, one bed,
one board, one flesh, one soul, one God? And, if a kingdom be divided, saith our Saviour, it cannot stand, and
those whom religion doth disjoin no art, no power, can
conjoin; and where this discord is, there God's blessing
can not come. Why should we, then, from any presumption so ever, receive a thorn into our sides?[65]

Though the arguments against the Savoyard matches were thus carried and colored, and though James dropped the proposed match between Elizabeth and the Prince of Piedmont in favor of the Palatine
Elector, a contract between Henry and the Duke of Savoy's daughter

continued to be negotiated right up to the time of his death, though
by then the prince had laid other quite definite plans.

At the height of the negotiations with Savoy, two additional
propositions were put forward for Henry. The first, with the sister of
the Grand Duke of Tuscany, had to recommend it the Grand Duke's
enormous wealth and his evident willingness to discuss a dower in
excess of £1,000,000. The sum gave James momentary pause, but
the match never had bright prospects of advancing. And Henry did
what he could to squelch it:

> *March 2, 1612.* The Prince was not disposed towards this
> match because the large dower which is offered would
> not come into his hands nor be applied for the good of
> the Crown, but would very soon be scattered by the
> King's profusion, besides which he thinks he need have no
> difficulty in finding money, as he is heir to so many
> Crowns. He says he would rather marry a subject, which
> makes people think there may be some particular one in
> his view.[66]

His threat to marry an English girl was idle; there was no one "in his
view," and the comment carried more the symbolism of his revulsion
from all the marriage proposals than his intent to carry through with
an English bride, but the statement was evidently enough to set off
a stampede of sorts among the noble women of England who had
daughters of eligible age. The Earl of Salisbury was prompted to
make a joke:

> I judge this poor man by his face to be honest, though by
> his apparel poor; which may amend, if he have but a fee
> for every virgin in London and England, that wisheth the
> Prince of Wales her maidenhead. . . .[67]

The information could have been accurate, but the smirk applied
to the weary and abstemious Henry could not have been more inappropriate.

The second proposition which was for a time seriously considered
was for the hand of Princess Christine of France. It was thought by
some of the anti-Spanish faction that such a match might serve to
break up the growing coziness between Spain and France which the
new marriage contract between the Infanta and the Dauphin had
served to cement. Sir Walter Ralegh spoke favorably of a match with
France, "seeing there is none but a catholic lady for us. . . . This

match, I say, will give the new [Catholic] league such an alarm, as
they will hardly know how to cover themselves in their own trench-
es."[68] But Henry wrote to his father on July 29, 1612, and excusing
his boldness asked the king "to stay your ambassador from moving it
any more."[69] For this "good tale ill told" Henry was severely rebuked
by his father, who was himself growing weary of his son's negative
reaction to every proposed match. The rebuke seems to have shaken
Henry; for the first time he wavered and he allowed himself to be
drawn into the discussion of the relative merits of the French and
Savoyard matches. For this compromise he would later severely ac-
cuse himself of allowing the devil into his camp, but for this once
he attempted to adjust himself to his father's demands. On October 5 he wrote the king his assent to a shocking concession; if he
married the Savoyard princess, she would be granted the right to
practice her religion, though Henry couched his surrender in angry,
pugnacious terms:

> As for the exercise of the princess' religion, your Majesty
> may be pleased to make your Ambassador give a peremp-
> tory answer that you will never agree to give her greater
> liberty in the exercise of it than that which is agreed with
> the Savoyeard, which is—to use his own word—*private-
> mente;* or, as Sir Henry Wotton did expound it, "in her
> most private and secret chamber."

But for all his attempt at compromise, Prince Henry could not keep
the demands of his higher destiny entirely out of his letter:

> If your Majesty will respect rather which of these two
> [the Savoyard princess or Princess Christine] will give
> the greatest contentment to the general body of the Prot-
> estants abroad, then I am of opinion that you will sooner
> incline to France than to Savoy.

Then, knowing that he had once again brashly thrust in his opinion,
though he was albeit violating the chastity of his myth to consider
any of these proposed matches, he hastened to head off the king's
renewed wrath:

> If I have incurred the same error that I did last, by the in-
> difference of my opinion, I hereby crave pardon of your
> Majesty, holding it better for your Majesty to resolve
> what course is most convenient to be taken by the rules
> of State, than for me, who am so little acquainted with
> subjects of that nature.

The hint of lofty detachment was coming back into his tone. With the last line of the letter he managed to regain the heights of the masculine superiority which the discussion of the two Catholic brides had made him so seriously compromise:

> And besides, your Majesty may think that my part to play, which is to be in love with any of them, is not yet to hand.[70]

With his final sentence to the king, Henry let it be known that the love motive had not triumphed over the power motive. The Puritans had not lost their hero to romance.

What was "to hand" was a secret plan which came into Henry's mind only after the signing in March 1612 of the agreement to marry Lady Elizabeth to the Palatine Elector. Prince Frederick would arrive in England that fall to claim his bride, and Henry determined secretly that he would first see his sister properly married to that promising leader of the German Protestants, and then he would accompany the couple back into Germany, there to choose a suitable consort for himself from among the ladies of the Protestant courts of the German states.[71] This was a plan which responded directly to a growing chorus of advice and hope which had arisen from Henry's Protestant constituency in England since the beginning of serious consideration of the match with Catholic Savoy:

> *Sir Edward Conway, May 3, 1612.* [I wish] that his Highness would declare his resolution not to marry but with one of the Reformed religion: "a point that would so bind and assure all the Protestants of Christendom to his Majesty and his Highness. . . ."[72]

> *Sir John Throckmorton, May 15.* God I hope has a wife in store for our brave Prince, one of his own religion the which woulde give the deade blowe to all our enimyes devices against us.[73]

If his intent to search out a bride suitable to his myth seems hopelessly vague and more like a romantic fiction of the holy grail sort, this is because Henry was more interested in setting foot on continental soil than in the real problems and practicalities of finding the next Queen Consort of England. In Europe his destiny lay; this had been the principal and most constant theme of his developing myth since Andrew Melville wrote his *Natalia* for the infant son in Scotland. For this opportunity Henry had been readying the English na-

vy; it would ferry the battalions of English soldiers behind him, when
once he located the field of battle and the conquest which God
would show him. His sister would need a proper escort out of England and into Europe after her wedding, and the prince intended to
be at the head of it. The Savoy match, the French match, all the
propositions and schemes would be quite out of the way when Henry
dipped his lance at the pope.

Sir Walter Ralegh knew of this plan and dissuaded Henry as best
he could. He pointed out sensibly that England needed a double
match with the fragmented states of Germany no more than she
needed a double match with the Spanish-dominated Dukedom of
Savoy:

> . . . you ask me, if I like of any German lady? I say, that
> I like it well enough in respect of the nation, who are
> just, and free from treachery: but the match between the
> palatine of the Rhine and the lady Elizabeth will make us
> strong enough in Germany, and, by reason of his alliance
> with the house of Nassau, better assured of the Nether-
> lands than we were. But as the merchant doth not haz-
> ard all his estate in one vessel, no more do well-advised
> princes lay all their hopes on one nation.[74]

Ralegh's mundane metaphors in support of political sensibility had
little impact on a prince who could see open before him the road by
which the highly colored dreams of his personation could finally be
realized.

VI

As secret as the prince's intentions originally were, perhaps out
of some justified apprehension that the king might put a stop to
them—though there seemed little short of God's own hand capable
of stopping this eighteen-year-old wonder—much of England and
then Europe quickly knew the wind was up and filling Henry's sails.
And even where men did not know specifically what was afoot,
there was a perceptible quickening of excitement, as during those
rare times when the very aether vibrates with the expectation of
some storm.

In Paris Monsieur Beaulieu wrote to the English agent in Brussels

that "there was great alarm here upon a rumour that the Prince of
Wales was going to Holland,"[75] and in Bourdeaux the countryside
was said to be "mightily afraid of some invasion,"

> having for a long time before together with the whole
> country of Gascony conceived no small jealousy of [Hen-
> ry's] high and generous spirit, the cause of this late fear
> being, for that the harvest quarter (at which time the En-
> glish and Scottish ships use to arrive there to provide
> themselves with wines) being then spent and the winter
> season come already and no ships arriving as they had
> wont to do, the more vigilant and wary sort did verily
> suspect that the sea ports of England had been shut up
> and all ships stayed for some great enterprize, which they
> could not think to be intended otherwise then against
> them, and that by the Prince. . . .[76]

In England, those last months before the arrival of the Palatine
Elector were characterized by an escalation of Protestant agitation
against Catholic Europe, and at the center of that aggressive talk sat
the image of Prince Henry as the conqueror knight, like a shrine to
which the national sacrifice to Mars must be addressed. They called
on Henry as though they had read his mind and knew his intentions
to go into Germany. The anonymous "French Herald" begged Henry
to lead a conquering army, rather than merely his sister, to the Continent: *"If it be not your self . . . then I see no* Generall *in the world,
when our Christian Army must come into the field."*[77] The pleading,
almost frantic voices were even turned toward James, who was asked
to release his son finally to fulfill his great mission:

> . . . you need not stirre out of your royall Whitehall;
> There we wil send you the newes of the ruine of your
> Enemies: Your arms are long enough to chastise them all
> a farre off; most especially your right Arme, the sonne
> of your thigh, the flower of your strength, the excellency
> of your dignity and power. Let's but haue him, let him
> but haue himselfe, and he will come to vs; let him goe for
> the publique good of all Christendome, for your interest,
> for his owne: We haue none else to be the head of our
> *Croisado.*[78]

Henry had been long enough in preparation, they said; study and the
schoolboy pursuits which James favored for his children were now in-

appropriate and even a dangerous frustration of God's unfolding will:

> ... you are learned enough for a Prince; and if any Prince
> in the world euer had lesse need of learning it is your
> selfe: ... Do not therefore mold any longer among your
> bookes—[79]

but equally useless were the symbolic trappings of Henry's personation, now that real war offered itself—

> no not among your tiltings and fained combats, though
> otherwise in peace, honorable, delightfull, needfull; To
> horse, to horse, the quarter is broken, the bloody Trum-
> pet hath sounded; true & mortall warre is open.[80]

If this were not enough to add fire and urgency to Henry's resolve,
other more provocative calls were forthcoming. In one, the Puritan
author promised Henry the quick following of ready soldiers that
the prince had hoped for:

> Vp then, vp, braue Prince; the eyes of all Christendome
> are now cast vpon you, to see you beginne; you shall not
> want friends and followers, euen more then you thinke,
> euen more then perhaps you looke for. ...[81]

In another, the author himself, in a fit of self-sacrificial vision, promised that he was willing to fall into step behind the prince's banner:

> And therefore renowmed [sic] Prince ... giue me leaue
> ... to wish ... that I may liue to march ouer the Alpes,
> and to trayle a pike before the walls of Rome, vnder your
> Highnesse Standard. It was my first profession, oh that it
> might be my last. The cause is Gods, the enterprise glori-
> ous, O that God would be pleased, as he hath giuen you
> a heart, so to giue power to put it in execution.[82]

The Protestant fever had reached a crescendo by October 1612
when the Elector Palatine arrived in London. The German prince
was greeted by a wave of electric anticipation which his marriage to
Lady Elizabeth could not alone have accounted for. It was rather the
thought of England's union with continental Protestantism, the clasp-
ing of hands between England's hero and Germany's, that ignited the
people. But such hope and such promise could only end in frustration and despair, for Prince Henry Stuart would be suddenly, unaccountably, dead on November 6.

Notes to Chapter 5

1. Quoted by D. H. Willson, *King James VI and I* (New York, 1967), 277.

2. *C.S.P., Venetian,* XI (1607-10), par. 3; see also par. 18 and par. 24; X (1603-07), par. 728.

3. For the crisis of the succession in Julich, see S. R. Gardiner, *History of England from the Accession of James I to the Outbreak of the Civil War* (London, 1893), II, 92 ff.

4. *The Kings Majesties Speech to the Lords and Commons of this present Parliament at Whitehall on Wednesday the xxi of March 1609* [O.S.] (London, 1610), sig. F 4. For the policy of Henry IV regarding Julich, his *grand dessein,* see Desmond Seward, *The First Bourbon, Henri IV, King of France and Navarre* (London, 1971), 189 ff. See also Maurice Lee, *James I and Henri IV: An Essay in English Foreign Policy* (Urbana, 1970).

5. *C.S.P., Venetian,* XI (1607-10), par. 870.

6. See Thomas Birch, *The Life of Henry Prince of Wales,* 198-203. The letters are in Harl. MSS. 7007, fols. 387, 398. See also *Hist. MSS. Comm. Calendar MSS. Marq. of Bath,* II (Dublin, 1907), 58-59.

7. "The Cabinet-Council," *Works,* VIII, 72.

8. Dec. 14, 1609, and Jan. 18, 1610. *Hist. MSS. Comm. Marq. of Downshire,* II, 199, 219.

9. See *The Parliamentary Diary of Robert Bowyer, 1606-1607,* ed. David Harris Willson (U. of Minn. Press, 1931), 19-21, and D. H. Willson, *James VI and I* (New York, 1956), 227-228.

10. Arthur Wilson, *The History of Great Britain, being the life and reign of King James the First* (London, 1653), fol. 51.

11. *The Diary of Walter Yonge, Esq.,* ed. George Roberts (London: The Camden Society, 1848), 22.

12. Lucy Aiken, *Memoirs of the Court of King James the First* (London, 1822), I, 387-388.

13. Helen Estabrook Sandison, "Arthur Gorges, Spenser's Alcyon and Ralegh's Friend," *PMLA,* 43 (Sept., 1928), 664.

14. *Ibid.*

15. Harl. MS. 7007, fol 357. The letter is printed by Birch, *The Life of Henry,* 188.

16. In the same letter Salisbury had acknowledged Prince Henry's desire to advance "two gentlemen" (one of them conceivably Sir Arthur Gorges) and had promised to gratify their desires, "reserving only this distinction . . . that I do not give furtherance to any suit, which may be of prejudice to his Highness . . . as I . . . do conclude my answer, that I fear me, that this will be very inconve-

nient to his Majesty, and be found directly repugnant...." Birch, 134.

17. See *Calendar of State Papers, Domestic Series,* 1603-1610 (London, 1857), 637.

18. See *The Diary of Walter Yonge,* 20. Yonge lists two of the Howard clan, Northampton and his niece, Lady Suffolk, among the suspected Catholics, as well as the Countess of Shrewsbury.

19. *Hist. MSS. Comm. Duke of Portland,* IX (London, 1923), 47.

20. *The Letters of John Chamberlain,* ed. McClure, I, 392.

21. *The Autobiography and Correspondence of Sir Simonds D'Ewes* (London, 1845), I, 48.

22. *C.S.P., Venetian,* XI (1607-10), par. 945.

23. *Ibid.,* par. 954.

24. *Ibid.*

25. *Ibid.,* XII (1610-13), par. 30, par. 115, par. 125.

26. Lucy Aiken, *Memoirs of the Court,* I, 344-345.

27. Birch offers many anecdotes of Prince Henry's purported graciousness to his English subjects: "In his removal from one of his houses to another, and in his attendance on the King on the same occasions, or in progresses, he would suffer no provisions or carriages to be taken up for his use, without full contentment given to the parties. And he was so sollicitous to prevent any person from being prejudiced or annoyed by himself or any of his train, that whenever he went out to hawk before harvest was ended, he would take care, that none should pass through the corn; and, to set them an example, would himself ride rather a furlong about" (*The Life of Henry,* 398). Birch has sanitized Henry's behavior, of course, but there was certainly a perceived difference between the Prince of Wales and his father, who used the right of purveyance to strip the countryside clean and otherwise displayed his disdain for the masses.

28. G. B. Harrison, *A Second Jacobean Journal* (Ann Arbor, 1958), 229. The original document detailing Henry's ordinances was printed in *Archaeologia,* 14 (1803), 249-61.

29. *C.S.P., Venetian,* XII (1610-13), ¶ 115.

30. *Ibid.,* par. 159. The whole matter of Prince Henry's sponsorship of the arts is interesting and important for the history and development of English taste during the seventeenth century. The Prince's interest in and influence on architecture alone (which this present work neglects) was considerable: he patronized Inigo Jones; he imported foreign architects, such as Solomon de Caus (or de Caux); he encouraged government building programs. In 1611 the English translation of Sebastiano Serlio's *First booke of architecture* was dedicated with rich appreciation to Prince Henry; in the following year de Caus dedicated his own *La Perspective* to his royal patron. Those interested in this aspect of Prince Henry's influence should consult the recently published Volume III (1485-1660) of *The History of*

the *King's Works,* edited by H.M. Colvin, D.R. Ransome, and John Summerson. Roy Strong (*The English Icon*) has interesting things to say about Henry's influence on painting.

31. Birch, 443.

32. Arthur Wilson, *The History of Great Britain,* fol. 52.

33. See *C.S.P., Domestic,* 1603-10, 654; 1611-18, 104.

34. See *C.S.P., Domestic,* 1603-10, 633.

35. See *ibid.,* 1603-10, 635.

36. See *ibid.,* 1603-10, 639.

37. See *ibid.,* 1611-18, 3.

38. See *ibid.,* 1603-10, 643.

39. *C.S.P., Venetian,* XII (1610-13), par. 115.

40. *Letters of John Chamberlain,* I, 319.

41. *Hist. MSS. Comm. Marq. of Downshire,* III, 155.

42. *C.S.P., Venetian,* XII (1610-13), par. 364.

43. *The Autobiography of Phineas Pett,* ed. Perrin, 92.

44. Goodman, *The Court of King James,* I, 250.

45. *The Autobiography of Phineas Pett,* 89-90.

46. *C.S.P., Venetian,* XII (1610-13), par. 355; Birch, 399-400.

47. *Hist. MSS. Comm. Marq. of Downshire,* III, 147.

48. *C.S.P., Venetian,* XII (1610-13), par. 355.

49. See *C.S.P., Domestic,* 1611-18, 85-86, 99.

50. *C.S.P., Venetian,* XII (1610-13), par. 404.

51. *The Autobiography of Phineas Pett,* 95.

52. See *C.S.P., Domestic,* 1611-18, 111.

53. William Crashaw, *Sermon preached at the crosse,* 2d ed. (London, 1609), sig. ¶2^v.

54. Antonia Fraser, *King James VI of Scotland, I of England* (New York, 1975), 152. Otto J. Scott in his more recent *James I* (Mason/Charter, 1976) is assertive about a sexual liaison between Henry and Frances Lady Essex, though he, like Antonia Fraser, offers no proof for such a claim.

55. The incident is described in *C.S.P., Venetian,* XII (1610-13), par. 217. Arthur Wilson has much to say about the enmity between Prince Henry and Robert Carr, though Wilson is largely responsible for promoting the mistaken notion that the two young men shared a lustful attachment for Lady Frances: see Wilson's *History of Great Britain,* fols. 55-56, 63. Rochester's rise to power can be traced easily enough in *C.S.P., Domestic,* 1611-18, 18, 40, 52, 57, 120, 127. On June 22, 1612, Thomas Viscount Fenton wrote the following observations to the Earl of Mar: "Rotchester is exceeding great with his Majestie, and if I shuld saye trewlye, greater then onye that ever I did see; kareyes it handsumlye, and begins to have a great deall of more temper; yet can he not find the rycht waye to pleis ather the Quein or the Prince, but thaye are bothe in the conceat of this Court

not weill satisfied vith him. . . ." (*Hist. MSS. Comm. E. of Mar & Kellie Supplements* [London, 1930], 41). Queen Anne apparently tried to form a strong united front with Prince Henry against the advancement of Carr; see *Hist. MSS. Comm. Marq. of Downshire,* III, 83.

56. Arthur Wilson, fol. 56.

57. "The queen, deprived of the nightly company of a husband, turned her delight to the prince, whom she respected above her other children; finding him too serious, diverted him from so much intensiveness, to an amorous gesture, in which the English court took great pride. To that purpose, she initiated him in the court of Cupid; as one night, she shut him under lock and key in a chamber, with a beautiful young lady now dead, which shewed her love to the sport; indeed, more like a bawd than a discreet mother. . . ." (Sir Edward Peyton, *The Divine Catastrophe of the Kingly Family of the House of Stuarts,* in *The Secret History of the Court of King James the First,* II, 344). It should be obvious enough from Peyton's title that he was scarcely disposed to bear any tales other than the most scandalous, though he need not be utterly dismissed as unreliable for that reason.

58. *Hist. MSS. Comm. Duke of Buccleuch & Queensbury* (London, 1899), I, 44. Sir Thomas Bodley to Ralph Winwood, 4 Nov. 1604: "We have a speech given out, among Papists in special, of a match lately moved, but I know not by whom, between our Prince and the King of Spain's two years' daughter; which is a motion so full of solecisms, as but to fill up my paper, for want of better matter, it should not so much as have been mentioned."

59. Sir Ralph Winwood, *Memorials of Affairs of State in the Reigns oj Queen Elizabeth and King James* (London, 1725), II, 100, 160.

60. An insider's account of the Spanish negotiations was written by Sir Charles Cornwallis, English ambassador to Madrid, and winsomely titled, "A relation of the marriages that should have been made between the Prince of England and the Infanta Major, and also after with the younger Infanta of Spain," in *Harleian Miscellany,* VIII (London, 1746). See also the Preface to *C.S.P., Venetian,* XII (1610-13).

61. *The Political Works of James I,* ed. C. H. McIlwain (Cambridge: Harvard U. Press, 1918), 35.

62. *C.S.P., Venetian,* XII (1610-13), xi. See also *Hist. MSS. Comm. Duke of Buccleuch & Queensbury,* I, 118.

63. "A Discourse Touching a Marriage Proposed between Prince Henry and a Daughter of Savoy," in *Works,* VIII, 240, 239. See Martin A.S. Hume, *Sir Walter Raleigh* (London, 1903), 293, and Philip Edwards, *Sir Walter Ralegh* (New York, 1953), 140.

64. *Hist. MSS. Comm. Duke of Portland,* IX (London, 1923), 45, 46. The "Speech of Sir John Holles, concerning Prince Harry's Marriage" begins on 41. The Prince's myth—or mystique—of chastity was pervasive enough to impress even the skeptical Sir Francis Bacon: "For of love matters there was wonderfully little talk, considering his age: insomuch that he passed that extremely slippery time of his early manhood, in so great a fortune and in very good health, without being particularly noted for any affairs of that kind" (*Works,* ed. Spedding, Ellis, and Heath, XII, 21). For further contemporary analysis of the marriage market, see also *Hist. MSS. Comm. Marq. of Downshire,* III, 251-253.

65. "The Speech of Sir John Holles," *Hist. MSS. Comm. Duke of Portland,* IX, 46.

66. *C.S.P., Venetian,* XII (1610-13), par. 447.

67. Birch, 138.

68. "A Discourse Touching a Marriage Proposed between Prince Henry and a Daughter of Savoy," *Works,* VIII, 251.

69. *Hist. MSS. Comm. Calendar MSS. Marq. of Bath,* II, 60. See also, Edward Edwards, *The Lives of the Founders of the British Museum* (London, 1870), I, 164.

70. Edwards, I, 165, and Mary Bradford Whiting, "Henry, Prince of Wales: 'A Scarce Blown Rose,'" *Contemporary Review,* 137 (19-30), 497-498.

71. Carola Oman, *Elizabeth of Bohemia* (London, 1938), 50-51. On this subject Sir Ralph Naunton wrote to Secretary Winwood: "It is given out by some of [Prince Henry's] confidants that he had a design to have come over with the Palsgrave and drawn Count Maurice along with him, with some strengths, and done some exploit upon the place that shot the Palsgrave's harbinger, and happily [*sic*] have seen the Lantsgrave's daughter, or I know not what. That this he meant to have done, whatsoever it was, *clam Patrem et Senatum suum;* and hatching some such secret design, ... it is now become abortive, like that of Henry the 4th in France" (*Hist. MSS. Comm. Duke of Buccleuch & Queensbury,* I [London, 1899], 118).

72. Birch, 273.

73. *Hist. MSS. Comm. De L'Isle & Dudley* (London, 1962), V, 53.

74. *Works,* VIII, 249-250.

75. *Hist. MSS. Comm. Marq. of Downshire,* III, 250.

76. W. H., *The true picture and relation of Prince Henry* (Leyden, 1634), fol. 29.

77. *The French herald summoning all true Christian princes to a generall croisade* (1611), sig. A 2^V.

78. *Ibid.,* fol. 39.

79. *Ibid.*, fols. 39-41.

80. *Ibid.*, fol. 41.

81. Edmond Richer, *A treatise of ecclesiasticall and politike power* (1612), sig. A 4^V.

82. Samson Lennard, in the ded. to his trans. of Philippe de Mornay's *The mysterie of iniquitie: that is to say, the historie of the papacie* (1612), sig. ¶iii^V.

6

Scarce Blown Rose: Death

I

At the opening of 1612, the year of Henry's death and the temporary end of Puritan hopes, the Venetian ambassador brought the prince Twelfth Night congratulations on his having entered the year which seemed to promise so much for both England and the rest of Europe. Henry was that January in the full bloom of his youth. In February he would be celebrating his eighteenth birthday, the age which Ralegh had told him the ancients held worthiest for going to war. He carried about him the aura of a personation fully realized, of complete potentiality awaiting the appearance of complete opportunity. The Venetian ambassador wrote of him that January:

> I praised his Highness in fitting terms, and in truth he deserves all praise; I have noticed that spirits athirst for glory are pleased with praise as a testimony to their worth; and when I told him that in no century, and certainly not in this, could there be found his superior, he showed his pleasure in a few modest words.[1]

The ambassador's canny understanding of Henry's vanity and his willingness to serve, as so many others had, the consuming thirst of the prince's myth, are interesting in retrospect. With a clarity that few others had exhibited, the Venetian envoy in England had gone about his business of flattery, noting with precision the amount which the occasion demanded and the degree of good effect produced. But for all his wise insight and slightly cynical calculation, the ambassador could not see the larger ironies which would mark Henry's career and his premature death. Which was the greater irony, that England should dress her prince in impossibly outsize robes and then make him believe he could stride forward to triumph in them, or that the prince thus prepared for glory should perish so unexpectedly and ingloriously, the dream of conquest no more than a hateful fiction?

Visually, the prince's arrival at the crux of symbolic power has been preserved in a miniature portrait done in his final year of life by Isaac Oliver (see Fig. 12). All trace of boyishness has vanished from the countenance, and this is no longer merely a lifeless, expressionless icon. A liveliness and individuality has entered the eyes and mouth. They communicate nothing so much as arrogance, good-natured basically, but a self-assurance and amused vitality which becomes almost an affront to sensibilities less convinced of the centrality of the self in the whirl of stars. But however much the face may have moved away from the somber dolefulness of typical English icon, Oliver still invests his portrait with the coded symbols of Henry's myth: the burnished and lively armor, the chivalric figures in the hazy background paying homage to a seated leader, the curtain pulled back as if to reveal the mental images which enlivened Henry's loosely smiling mouth. Henry bridges the gap here between romantic past and the immediate present; his eyes do not glaze over with distant dreams, nor does he peer off in rigid profile. His eyes fix steadily and bring the dream world of the background into the electrified present. It is as though the painter is saying, this is your prince, this is your quintessential Protestant hero, no longer merely the hope of the future but the immediate reality of the present.

The description which Sir Frances Bacon has left us of Henry could almost have been written to accompany Isaac Oliver's portrait:

> In body he was strong and erect, of middle height, his limbs gracefully put together, his gait kinglike, his face long and somewhat lean . . . his countenance composed. . . . His forhead bore marks of severity, his mouth had a touch of pride. . . . he seemed quite another man in conversation than his aspect promised; . . . Of praise and glory he was doubtless covetous; and was stirred with every show of good and every breath of honour; which in a young man goes for virtues. For both arms and military men were in honour with him; nor was he himself without something of a warlike spirit; he was given also to magnificence of works. . . .[2]

Though his praise was generous without being obsequious and bore the tone of accurate objectivity, Sir Francis was not able to keep an

Figure 12. Miniature of Henry by Isaac Oliver. From the Royal Collection of H.M. the Queen. Reprinted by permission of the Lord Chamberlain, St. James Palace.

occasional piece of rueful irony from slipping into his portrait ("Of praise and glory he was doubtless covetous . . . which in a young man goes for virtues"). Bacon was of that tribe of government office-holders who had learned to see Henry's brilliance through somewhat jaundiced eyes.

The death of the Earl of Salisbury in May 1612 had removed from Henry's path many of the former hindrances to his assumption of princely power. Even Salisbury's friends had not liked him very much, though he had been a man almost alone among King James's minis-ters worthy of his office and a man almost capable of bearing the in-creasing burden of it. But he died in a kind of political eclipse, hav-ing failed to discipline Parliament to James's will. The satirists leaped almost immediately on the corpse of a man they had feared too much to jeer while he lived:

> Here lyes throwne, for the wormes to eate,
> Little bossive Robbin, that was so great.
> Not Robin, good-fellow, nor Robin Hood,
> But Robin th'encloser of Hatfield wood.
> Who seem'd as sent from ugly fate,
> To spoyle the prince, and rob the state.
> Owning a mind of dismall endes,
> As trappes for foes, and tricks for friends.
> But now in Hatfield lyes the fox,
> Who stank while he liv'd, and died of the pox.[3]

With "the fox" out of the way, Henry's star could only be said to shine more brightly. He immediately pressed King James with his own nominees for the many offices which Salisbury's death had left tantalizingly vacant, and John Chamberlain wrote his office-seeking friend Carleton some well-considered advice: "But yf I might advise, I wold you could rather devise how to grow in with the Prince, and not without need yf all be true I have heard. . . ."[4]

The king left the environs of London that summer to go on a royal progress, while Henry retired to the cool precincts of Richmond, promising to join his father at the Earl of Rutland's castle of Belvoir in Nottinghamshire in August. It was an unusually hot summer in England, and Henry took some pleasure in swimming in the Thames, which activity members of his household later blamed for his sudden death. Their agony of hindsight blamed both his swimming ("for it stopt his bleeding at the nose; whereupon the bloud putrifying, engendered that fatall fever which followed") and his habit of walking by the river's side late at night "to heare the trumpets sound an eccho." "The dew then falling did him small good," wrote the Treasurer of his household and Henry's first biographer, Sir Charles Cornwallis.[5] Treasurer Cornwallis insisted that the first signs of physical malaise were already visible in Henry as early as June or July 1612, but whether here again we must discount for hindsight we cannot know. Cornwallis said that Henry was bothered by "a small kind of giddy lumpish heavinesse in his forehead." (p. 454) But if the prince was already in the grip of some malignancy, he was nevertheless behaving in a fashion typical to his personation. Having previously agreed to meet the king at Belvoir, Henry allowed the date to draw perilously close before dashing off pell mell to try his speed against the deadline. Cornwallis was somewhat exasperated, or said he was when later events suggested that Henry's mad dash may have contributed to his death:

> . . . his Highnesse neither considering the strength of his body, the greatnesse of the journey, being neere fourescore and sixteene miles, nor the extreme and wonderfull heat of the season, and notwithstanding my persuasions to the contrary, determined to ride the great journey in two dayes. . . . (pp. 457-458)

Henry joined James on his progress and together they met the Queen at Woodstock on August 26 with the full court in attendance.

Woodstock was one of Prince Henry's properties and he there feted the king and queen in magnificent style in a specially built "great summer-house of green boughs." (p.*461) The Court remained at Woodstock until the last day of August, when all returned to London to make preparations for the arrival of the Lady Elizabeth's bridegroom. Cornwallis in writing his biography found something ominous in every memory of those last four months: "Meanwhile, although the season was exceeding hot, his Highnesse did ride many and extraordinary journeyes in the same, which, as was thought, did much incline his boyling bloud towards inflamation." (p.*461)

By the beginning of October, with the Palatine's arrival only two weeks off, Henry was undeniably ill and much altered. He looked more pale and thin, was afflicted with what he described as "a cold lazie drowsinesse in his head." (p. 471) He often questioned his physician, Dr. Hammond, about his symptoms; the doctor was convinced that the prince was suffering from a fever, perhaps the one which had already been dubbed the "New Disease" and which was believed to have come to England from Hungary. "He often used . . . now and then, and in his sicknesse, to sigh often, whereof being sometimes demanded the cause by his Physician Dr. Hammond, and others neere him, he would sometimes reply, that he knew not, sometimes that they came unawares, and sometimes also that they were not without cause." (p. 471) This was strange, ambiguous talk for the prince who had made himself a reputation for sharpness and directness of speech. The symptoms grew, causing consternation among the members of Henry's household simply because the prince was behaving so uncharacteristically:

> . . . his continuall head-ache, lazinesse, and indisposition increasing, which notwithstanding because of the time he strove mightily to conceale, whereas oft before he used to rise early in the morning to walke the fields, he did lye a-bed almost every morning until nine of the clocke, complayning of his lazinesse, and that he knew not the cause; during which time, belike jealous of himselfe, he would many mornings before his rising ask of the Groomes of his Bed-chamber, "How do I looke this morning?" And at other times the same question againe; which they, fearing no danger, to make his Highnesse laugh, would put off with one jest or other. (pp. 471-472)

On the 10th of October he had two "small fits of an ague," which caused him to keep to his bed for three days, but then he insisted on struggling to his feet to make the short journey from Richmond to London, where the Palatine was looked for any day. At St. James's, where he tried to busy himself about the preparations for his sister's nuptials, a second great change was noted in him:

> . . . he began to be displeased almost with every thing, exceeding curious in all things, yet not regarding, but looking as it were with the eyes of a stranger upon them; for sundry things shewed him, which before he wonted to talke of, aske questions, and view curiously, he now scarce vouchsafed to looke upon, turning them away with the backe of his hand, and departing, as who would say, I take pleasure in nothing. (p. 472)

The Palatine prince arrived in London on October 18, with eight great noblemen of Protestant Europe in his train, including Count Henry of Nassau and Prince Maurice of the Netherlands, gentlemen whom

Prince Henry especially admired for their prior brave history of fighting the Spaniard. This was really the great moment the prince had waited for, his long-expected meeting with his brothers in the faith who with him would rid the Continent of the treacherous papists. But the lethal fingers which already gripped Henry robbed the occasion of its symbolic glory and even prevented him from extending the mundane courtesies. As the Germans came into the Great Chamber of Whitehall Palace where the king, Prince Henry, and all the English Court waited to greet them, "the Prince stirred not a foot; which was much noted." (p. 466)

He rallied enough in the week following to keep the Protestant counts company at cards and tennis play, playing one great tennis match with Prince Maurice on the twenty-fourth, which because of subsequent events became a piece of instant folklore. This was the last entire day he would spend on his feet, for on the twenty-fifth would commence the final fulmination which would cease only on November 6 with his death, after almost two weeks of terrible agony. His tennis match with Count Maurice seemed to suggest a kind of heroic warfare in itself, as though the Olympian struggle for which Henry had been prepared had unexpectedly localized in his own body:

> . . . his undaunted courage, negligently, carelesly, and wilfully (neither considering the former weake estate of his body, danger, nor coldnesse of the season), as though his body had been of brasse, did play in his shirt, as if it had been in the heat of summer; during which time he looked so wonderful ill and pale, that all the beholders took notice thereof, muttering to one another what they feared. . . . (p. 473)

The morning after the tennis bout with Prince Maurice was Sunday, and despite his weakness ("he found himselfe somewhat drousie and ill") Henry dragged himself from bed to hear one of his favorite chaplains, Robert Wilkinson, preach in the Chapel of St. James's. Mr. Wilkinson chose his text out of the fourteenth chapter of Job— "Man that is borne of a woman is of short continuance and full of trouble"—which text, said Cornwallis, "the wonderfull providence and goodnesse of God" provided to the preacher as a means of "mortification or preparation" for the death which was coming. (p. 474) The sermon, like Henry's recent illness, certainly went against the

grain of the prince's life-long personation, for the Reverend Wilkinson
dwelt on the finiteness of man, his puniness, his "miserable entry
into the world, and short continuance," all themes of mutability
which had not formed a significant portion of Henry's mythic diet
heretofore.

The prince followed that sermon with another at Whitehall, where
he went to attend the preacher with his father, and afterward they
went in to dinner together. During the meal Henry looked "exceed-
ingly ill and pale, with hollow ghastly dead eyes perceived of a great
many." The final phase commenced a couple of hours after dinner:

> . . . for all his great courage and strife to over-master the
> greatnesse of his evil, dissembling the same, the Conquer-
> or of all, about three a clock in the afternoone, began to
> skirmish with a suddaine sicknesse and faintnesse of the
> heart, usuall unto him, whereupon followed shortly after
> a shaking, with great heat and head-ache, which from
> henceforth never left him. His Highnesse finding himself
> thus suddainely taken, was forced to take his leave, de-
> parting home unto his bed; where being laid he found
> himselfe very ill, remaining all this evening in an agony,
> having a great drought, which after this could never be
> quenched but with death; his eyes also being so dimme
> that they were not able to endure the light of a can-
> dle. (p. 475)

The next twelve days would seem to rush by with savage purpose for
those who stood by his bed and for the larger country without which
prayed for his recovery, but for the prince, stricken just as he believed
himself poised for long awaited action, the days must have dragged
by with an endlessness constantly refocused by the quotidian pain.

On the second day Henry found some "intermission" from the
illness, enough to allow him to put on clothes and play a while at
cards. Messages of inquiry arrived from the court and from the Palatine Elector, and "no person surmising the least danger," Henry's
doctor Hammond sent back answers of good hopes for the prince's
recovery. Yet Henry continued to look ill and pale, "spake hollow,
and somewhat strangely, with dead sunk eyes, his drinesse of mouth
and great thirst continuing." He rested more quietly that night, and
on Tuesday morning, the third day, he seemed better when he awoke.
But soon the prince's attendants were fairly unnerved again by his
"ghastly rowling uncoath lookes" (p. 475); Dr. Hammond sent the

alarm, and King James responded by dispatching two of his personal physicians, Dr. Nasmith and Dr. Theodore Mayerne, to confer over Henry's bed at St. James's. Dr. Mayerne was French, highly regarded by James, but held in some suspicion by the other doctors and apparently the victim of their professional jealousy. Mayerne instantly recommended bleeding, but he was as instantly overruled by the two English doctors. Mayerne would later point to this moment on the third day as the crisis which his fellow doctors had bungled by refusing to open a vein.

On Wednesday, the fourth day, a fourth doctor shambled into St. James's from Cambridge, the seventy-six-year-old Master Butler. John Aubrey labeled him "one of the greatest Physicians and most capricious humourists of his time," (p. 476n) and it is clear that Aubrey celebrated him for the droll stories he could tell rather than for his powers as a healer. The sight of Henry's "cadaverous look" took some of the wit out of Dr. Butler, and he privately spoke very gloomily of the prince's chances for recovery. He also disdained Dr. Mayerne and seemed reluctant to join wholeheartedly the consultation of his fellow doctors; according to Cornwallis, Master Butler could see disaster coming and wished to put some distance between himself and the blame that was bound to fall on all those who now stood by helplessly as Henry died. Henry's fever "as yet not being continuall," Dr. Butler recommended that the treatment under way be continued without change, a transparent avoidance on his part of offering any diagnosis or suggesting any cure.

On Thursday, all symptoms intensified. The prince found it impossible to sit up and play at cards, as he had done on previous days. That night was a particularly bad one, both within and without St. James's Palace, for a display of the *aurora borealis* "about two hours or more within the night" (p. 477) filled everyone with the dread which only meteorological phenomena could induce at that time. That "lunar rainbow" was said to hang "directly crosse and over Saint James's House." On the following morning, the sixth day, Dr. Mayerne, as though following the analogy of the bloody skies of the night before, again urged the necessity of bleeding the prince. "After much adoe *pro* and *contra*," Doctors Mayerne, Hammond, and Butler concurred that a vein should be opened on Sunday, the eighth day. Dr. Nasmith demurred, and then on Sunday Dr. Butler himself repented his earlier assent and joined Nasmith in opposing the drawing of blood. Stalemate was perceived as more damning than misap-

plied remedies, and Mayerne with the aid of Hammond reassured Butler and once again the deadlock was broken. With all the doctors in
attendance the median vein in the prince's right arm was opened and
seven or eight ounces of blood taken, "during which time he fainted
not, bleeding well and abundantly, desiring and calling to them to
take more, as they were about to stop the same, finding some ease
as it were upon the instant." (p. 478) He did find some ease that Sunday afternoon, seeming to confirm Mayerne in his original opinion,
and he was visited by the king,the queen, his brother Charles, his sister and her future husband, and they all went away reasonably cheered
by his evident recovery.

On the ninth day, King James sent another eminent London physician, Dr. Atkins, to assist in the cure which Mayerne had apparently
initiated. Dr. Atkins ventured the opinion that Henry was suffering
from a "corrupt putrid fever," which did little either way towards
correct diagnosis or salutary treatment, but the king and court con-
continued to be fed with "some good small hopes" of the prince's
recovery. But that night produced in Henry "greater alienations of
braine, ravings, and idle speeches out of purpose, calling for his
cloathes and his rapier, &c. saying, he must be gone, he would not
stay, and I know not what else, to the great griefe of all that heard
him. . . ." (p. 479) It was about this time that Henry began crying
out that "this chastisement" was "a deserved punishment upon him,
for having ever opened his ears to admit treaty of a Popish match."[6]
His consent earlier that year to discuss the relative merits of two proposed Catholic brides now welled up within him like a miasma to suggest the cause of God's wrath in his present pain.

Tuesday, November 3, was the tenth day of his sickness and one
of the worst: "his boundings being turned into convulsions, his rav-
ing and benumming becoming greater, the fever more violent." Dr.
Mayerne again proposed bleeding, and when the others again expressed their hesitance and misgiving, the Frenchman delivered them
a chastening lecture. They seemed determined, Mayerne said, to let
Henry die because they were too dainty in giving him the sort of treatment that might save a "meane person." Because their patient was a
prince, Mayerne suggested, they were afraid of proceeding decisively
and boldly, and indeed he was right. They were all fearful, including
Mayerne, but his sharp words produced the action he wanted:

> . . . for easing of the extreame paine of his head, the hair
> was shaven away, and *pigeons* and cupping glasses applied

> to lessen and draw away the humour and that superfluous
> blood from the head, which he endured with wonderfull
> and admirable patience, as though he had beene insensi-
> ble of paine; yet all [was done] without any good. . . .
> For this night he became very weake, the fever augment-
> ing, the raving becomming worse than ever, in which he
> began to tosse and tumble, to sing in his sleepe, profer-
> ing to have leaped out of the bed, gathering the sheets to-
> gether, the convulsions being more violent. (p. 479)

On the eleventh day, the indignities continued. A live cock was
split up the back and applied to the soles of his feet. The cordials
were redoubled in number and quantity, all with no effect. Since
Henry was "continually molested with a number which out of their
love came to visit him," the doctors ordered that no one be admitted
to see him. It happened that this would be enforced even against his
father. That afternoon the king came back to St. James's, and being
told how matters went and how they were very likely to continue,
he determined to see his dying son but was persuaded by the doctors
to depart without visitation. Doubtless the sight of that once healthy
and muscular body, ravaged by the medieval ministrations of the doctors, would have been debilitating for the king. One visitor, however,
was admitted to the prince's chamber and his coming could only pre-
sage disaster. The Archbishop of Canterbury came in and asked
whether prayers had been read. He was answered that there had not
been any praying as yet, and the archbishop replied that more care
had been taken of Henry's mortal body than of his immortal soul.
He bent down and asked Henry if he desired that prayers be read;
the prince weakly assented, and the Dean of Rochester, one of his
chaplains, was sent for and put to the task in the sickroom. The
archbishop did not leave until he had led Henry through the confession of his faith, word by word.

The fifth of November and the twelfth day of Henry's sickness
was the seventh anniversary of the Gunpowder Plot. Parliament had
in 1606 instituted the day to be set aside for Thanksgiving for the
delivery of king, prince, and country from the treachery of the Catholics, but in England on this particular anniversary there seemed little
to be thankful for. Churches filled, rather, with those who offered
prayers for their stricken prince. Dr. Mayerne sent word to King
James that all hope for the prince was gone, except for desperate
measures, and the king responded by placing Mayerne in complete

control of Henry's treatment, "to do what he would of himselfe without advice of the rest." But Mayerne, having now the full authority which he seemed earlier to desire, shrank from the burden; "but he, weighing the greatnesse of the care and emminency of the danger, would not for all that adventure to doe any thing of himselfe, without advise of the rest, which he alwayes tooke, saying, it should never be said in after ages that he had killed the King's eldest Sonne." The king, meanwhile, for motives difficult to characterize, moved off to Theobalds north of London, to wait, some said, "the dolefull event." And the doctors, convened by their new-made chief, conferred for a third time on the advisability of bleeding and once again voted against Mayerne. They instead doubled and then trebled the cordials and applied a clyster, but Henry, perceived to be in extreme danger, was turned over to the different ministrations of the Archbishop of Canterbury, who had hurried back to St. James's. The archbishop had no cure for the sickness, only antidotes against the fear of death, and he gently probed the prince's frame of mind and his resolve. It was *contemptus mundi* that Henry heard from the archbishop; he put the prince in "mind of the excellency and immortality of the soule, with the unspeakeable joyes prepared for God's children, and the basenesse and misery of the earth, with all the vaine, inconstant, momentary, and fraile pleasures thereof in respect of heavenly joyes." With this as prelude, the archbishop told him of what exceeding great danger he was in. No one had uttered these words to the prince before, that he might die. He protested feebly, and the archbishop hurried to add that "although he might recover, as he hoped he should, yet he might also die; and that since it was an inevitable and irrevocable necessity that all must die once, late or soone, death being the reward of sinne, he asked, if it should so fall out, whether or no he was well pleased to submit himself to the will of God." Death, that universally acknowledged power, that great deity of the metaphysical seventeenth century, had never been part of Henry's myth, so it was with some effort that the prince answered the archbishop's question: "yea, with all my heart." Archbishop Abbot went on and catechized Henry, receiving satisfactory answers on the true and only church, the salvation and resurrection of his soul, and the everlasting peace of Heaven. Being assured of the prince's soul, the archbishop mercifully took leave of him for a time.

Delirium returned intermittently. He began calling for Sir David Murray, who had been in his service since his childhood in Scotland

and was "the onely man in whom [Henry] had put choise trust."
"David! David!" the prince called out, and "in extremity of pain and
stupefaction of senses confounding his speech" the prince said to
Murray when he came to his side, "I would say somewhat, but I cannot utter it!" Two additional physicians, Dr. Palmer and Dr. Gifford,
arrived that same day, and agreed with the other four that bleeding
was plainly now gone as a possibility, the prince being too weak to
sustain it. The doctors did finally agree upon diascordium as the only means left to them, and this they administered to Henry at ten
o'clock that night, along with "cooler cordials."

About midnight, as Henry was entering the thirteenth and last
day of his agony, he suddenly gripped Dr. Nasmith about the collar
and pulled him near, "speaking unto him somewhat, but so con-
fusedly, by reason of the rattling of the throat, that he could not be
understood; which his Highness perceiving, giving a most grievous sigh
as it were in anger, turned him from him. . . ." Sir David Murray,
who best knew the prince's mind and could make some sense from
the ravings, was roused and brought to the prince, asking that His
Highness say what troubled him:

> . . . his spirits being overcome, and nature weake, he was
> not able to say any thing, save that of all other businesse
> he gave order for the burning of a number of letters in a
> certain cabinet in his closet, which presently after his
> death was done.

Having seen to the destruction of what he did not wish the world to
see, he was seized by new convulsions, and Cornwallis noted at
3:00 A.M. perhaps the most horrible of the final effects visited upon
the prince *in extremis:*

> . . . his backbone, shoulders, armes, and tongue, by rea-
> son of the horrible violence of the convulsions, disjoyntly
> deviding themselves, the effect shewing that the retentive
> power was gone, the spirits subdued, the seat of reason
> overcome, and nature spent; in which extremity, fainting
> and swooning, he seemed twice or thrice to be quite gone.

Premature rumors of his death swept the city, to be succeeded by
news that he still lived. From the Tower came a small vial of liquid
and a note from Sir Walter Ralegh; he had been entreated by Queen
Anne to prepare for the prince some of his fabled "Balsam of Guiana,"
a concoction of roots, bark, and herbs, many of them collected in the

New World. The queen had once profited from a dose of Ralegh's medicine, and she believed him the wizard who might save her son. The balsam arrived at a dramatic moment; the prince was clearly dying, and though the Lords of the Council doubted Ralegh's motives and the doctors were skeptical, any last-minute measure seemed justified under the circumstances. But Ralegh's letter contained a disturbing disclaimer: he said that a draught of his medicine would surely cure the prince "except in case of poison," a statement which would engender no little doubt and discussion after Henry's death. The cordial was tasted and then administered, and Henry seemed to rally for a time. But he shortly after "became wonderfull ill againe; sight and sense failing, as also all the infallible signes of death approaching."

The Archbishop of Canterbury made his third and final assault on the prince:

> . . . first speaking aloud, putting him in mind of all those things which he had spoken unto him the day before in his perfect sense, calling aloud in his eare to remember Christ Jesus, to beleeve, hope, and trust in him, with assured confidence of mercy, to lift up his heart, and to prepare him to meete the Lord Jesus, with many other divine exhortations, thereafter calling more loud than ever, thrice together in his eare, "Sir, heare you mee, heare you mee, heare you mee? if you heare mee, in certaine signe of your faith and hope of the blessed resurrection, give us for our comfort a signe, by lifting up your hands"; which he did, lifting up both his hands together; againe he desired him yet to give him another signe, by lifting up his eyes; which having done, they let him alone. . . .

The archbishop wept and prayed "a most exceeding powerfull passionate prayer." It was just as well that he talked to God now rather than to Henry, for no amount of shouting would have reached him then. He was pronounced dead just before 8:00 P.M. on November 6, 1612. Sir Charles Cornwallis wrote: "Thus . . . lost we the delight of mankind, the expectation of Nations, the strength of his Father, the glory of his Mother, Religion's second hope!" The next day the Palace of St. James's, which had drawn all England's eyes in trust and faith, was hung with black cloth which blotted out the autumnal light.

II

A little over two weeks after Henry's death, the Venetian ambas-

sador played once again his role as reliable observer in summing up
for his principals in Venice the prince's public personation:

> He was athirst for glory if ever any prince was. He lent
> fire to the King in the affairs of Germany, and aspired to
> be head of the confederate princes who include fourteen
> of the Hanseatic towns. Many predictions centred round
> his person, and he seemed marked out for great events.
> His whole talk was of arms and war. His authority was
> great, and he was obeyed and lauded by the military par-
> ty. He protected the colony of Virginia, and under his
> auspices the ships sailed for the north-west passage to the
> Indies. He had begun to put the navy in order and raised
> the number of sailors. He was hostile to Spain and had
> claims in France. . . . His designs were vast; his temper
> was grave, severe, reserved, brief in speech. His household
> was but little inferior to the King's and kept in excellent
> order. He had few equals in the handling of arms, be it
> on horse or on foot; in fine all the hopes of those king-
> doms were built on his high qualities.[7]

The ambassador's careful catalogue offers excellent evidence of the
extent to which Prince Henry had managed to shape his life to the
frame of his public role; only occasionally in the progress of the Venetian ambassador's dispatch is one now made aware that we are
hearing described a myth which had gone to great lengths to actual-
ize itself. He was feared, loved, resented, lionized; even in death he
continued potent for both Protestants and Catholics. He had been an
eighteen-year-old youth of middling talents who had so thoroughly
wedded his life to his myth that disentaglement of the two would
forever be impossible.

Useful to us in assessing the power of his myth at the time of his
death were the things said and written in private, before the great
outpouring of public elegy began. A man writing to his friend might
be expected to touch more often those themes which told the extent
to which Henry's myth had entered the public consciousness. And
significantly, in the sources which have survived, it is the prince as
Protestant Conqueror that assumes the most forceful and telling line-
aments.

Two days after Henry's death Johannes Luntius, a Dutch Protestant in London, wrote Sir Ralph Winwood in the Low Countries
that everyone in the kingdom was vehemently affected by Henry's
death, except the Catholics ("Pontificios"),[8] and from Paris came

fuller expression that the Roman Church had much to be thankful for. After mentioning rumors that the enemies of the Protestant religion had looked forward to the death "of some great Prince," the writer continued:

> But alas! we did little apprehend, that such ominous prognostications would have lighted upon the person of that vigorous young Prince, whose extraordinary great parts and virtues made many men hope and believe, that God had reserved and destined him, as a chosen instrument, to be the Standard-bearer of his quarrel in these miserable times, to work the restoration of his church and the destruction of the Romish idoltry.[9]

Those papers which Henry had ordered Sir David Murray to burn also took on mysterious significance; John Chamberlain wrote on November 19 that they "shewed him to have many straunge and vast conceits and projects."[10]

An Englishman, John Forbes, in the German city of Middelburg, sampled the popular reaction to the news of Henry's death and wrote on November 20, "Doubtless this breach . . . doth open a great gap to the enemies of God's church and of the dominions of our gracious king and does embolden their courage to evil which . . . was yet restrained by the fear conceived of his forward courage, who now is out of their way and has left none after him of whom they have such fear."[11] It appears that Henry's death produced very real fears that Catholic armies would instantly begin forming to launch an all-out crusade against the now enfeebled Protestant states, much as Henry had intended to attack Catholicism. Fear was the prevailing emotion, a species of panic induced when the well-known mechanism of universal myth grinds to a sudden halt. From Stuttgart, a German named Daniel Buwinckhausen wrote to William Trumbull on November 26:

> The news of the death of the prince of Wales has stunned us all. It is a very great loss to us Germans also. God preserve us from many such accidents and save for us the king, queen and the rest of your royal house, which we consider as a bridle to the Spaniard. It is to be feared that this change may affect Juliers [Julich] where we fear great disorder if a remedy is not speedily employed.[12]

Prince Henry, it appears, was quite firmly rooted in the German Protestant mind as symbol, unreservedly associated with the siege of Julich which had taken place more than two years earlier.

From all around Europe dispatches brought the news of the impact of Henry's death:

> *H. Bilderbeck from Cologne, December 2.* The well-affected here are lamenting the death of the prince of Wales; the others rejoice at such news.[13]
>
> *Sir John Throckmorton from Flushing, December 3.* Yt may easelye be observed both by their discourses and countenance that our nighbors the Archdukes, and soe with them allsoe the whole pack of that Spanish faction, upon this deathe of our most exelent Prince . . . doe allredye beginne to cry out *villa gaigne.* . . . theye will teach us to daunce a newe daunce, that was never danced yeat.[14]
>
> *Sir John Digby from Madrid, December 7.* About Nov. 26 were brought, dispatched from Don Inigo de Cardenas, the tidings of the death of our most worthy prince Henry. There could scarce anything have happened whereat these people would have grieved less.[15]
>
> *Lord Roos from Florence, December 15.* It must be grievous to all men. But it seems God for our sins would not suffer us to enjoy so celestial a creature, who was too good to live upon earth.[16]

But as Sir John Digby, English ambassador to Spain, had written, all men did not grieve; the Spanish could not have grieved less, he said, and much of the reason was Henry's expansionary plans in Virginia, in Guiana, and in the opening of the Northwest Passage.

Digby wrote to King James in the summer of the next year, reporting that the Spanish had given their ambassador in London (Gondomar) instructions to ascertain whether the death of Henry had not caused a slowing of interest in the Virginia colony, "and whether bussinesses of that nature growe not muche colder since the deathe of the late Prince."[17] Such interest on the part of the Spaniards would inevitably fuel speculation among Henry's still living partisans that the Spanish had some pernicious hand in his death.

The fact was, indeed, that various of England's colonial enterprises had been guided, both in spirit and in material comfort, by Prince Henry's avid interest, and his death cast a genuine pall, especially over various of his idolaters in Virginia. That virgin land was being settled by the sort of people who most admired Prince Henry's

extreme Protestant persona. King James had more than once complained that the Virginia Company "was but a seminary to a seditious
Parliament," and that, in spite of the time and money absorbed by
it, "yet it hath not produced any other effects than that smoky weed
of tobacco."[18] The king was, of course, more accurate than even he
dreamed; in 1612, however, the Virginians had still a loyalty to the
English crown, though they looked more to Prince Henry as the temporal leader who most satisfied their spiritual ambitions. Sir Thomas
Dale, who owed his appointment as Governor to the Virginia Plantation to Henry, wrote most feelingly on his patron's death:

> My glorious master is gone, that would haue ennamelled
> with his fauours the labours I vndertake, for Gods cause,
> and his immortall honour. He was the great Captaine of
> our Israell, the hope to haue builded vp this heauenly
> new Ierusalem he interred (I think) the whole frame of
> this businesse, fell into his graue: for most mens forward
> (at least seeming so) desires are quenched, and Virginia
> stands in desperate hazard.[19]

Those who lamented his death and those who cheered either secretly or in the streets, agreed on one important detail of his life: his
name meant power. At the time, few felt inclined to separate the boy
from his myth, either because they perceived no difference between
the two or because to do so would have robbed from the embattled
Protestant minority in Europe a symbol of considerable conjuring
power. But Sir Walter Ralegh, always ready to swim against prevailing
currents and, perhaps of all men living then, the man who had both
known the prince well and had escaped from the mesmerizing aura
of his myth, wrote some final words over Henry's corpse which do
much to sum up his career, both the mythic exterior and the far less
magnificent interior. Ralegh ceased work on his monumental *History
of the World* soon after Henry's death, saying, "besides many other
discouragements persuading my silence, it hath pleased God to take
that glorious prince out of the world to whom they were directed."[20]
Whether Henry's death actually caused Ralegh to abandon the writing of his *History* is debatable; much more certain, however, is that
Sir Walter penned his famous concluding address to death on the occasion of the sudden end of the young man who had championed his
cause to the king and who so much believed himself the measure of
the world. Ralegh's great peroration on death (which I quote here at

some length) pierces so much of the mythic mask that had come to cloak Henry, turns tellingly on the difference between what a man wishes to see of himself and what death makes him see:

> *I have considered,* saith Solomon, *all the works that are under the sun, and, behold, all is vanity and vexation of spirit;* but who believes it, till Death tells it us? . . . It is therefore Death alone that can suddenly make man to know himself. He tells the proud and insolent, that they are but abjects, and humbles them at the instant, makes them cry, complain, and repent, yea, even to hate their forepast happiness. He takes the account of the rich, and proves him a beggar, a naked beggar, which hath interest in nothing but in the gravel that fills his mouth. He holds a glass before the eyes of the most beautiful, and makes them see therein their deformity and rottenness, and they acknowledge it.
>
> O eloquent, just, and mighty Death! whom none could advise, thou hast persuaded; what none hath dared, thou hast done; and whom all the world hath flattered, thou only hast cast out of the world and despised; thou hast drawn together all the far-stretched greatness, all the pride, cruelty, and ambition of man, and covered it all over with these two narrow words, *Hic jacet!*[21]

Here was a catalog far different from the Venetian ambassador's which introduced this discussion, but no less accurate in its way. "Whom none could advise . . . whom all the world flattered." Those words matched the boy who then lay encased in lead in Westminster Abbey. *Hic jacet!*

III

We cannot move on into consideration of the "Myth Prolonged" in the elegiac verse without giving some passing notice to the cause of Henry's death and the rumors which prevailed at the time. The suddenness of Henry's death, not a little aided by the ambiguities of Sir Walter Ralegh's note sent with his cordial ("except in case of poison"), did much to establish in the popular mind that the prince had been the victim of measures foul and thoughts pernicious. To her dying day Queen Anne believed he had been poisoned.

The government did what it could to squelch such rumors, starting with what appeared at the time to be a thorough and question-answer-ing autopsy, presided over by the nervous doctors who had congregated in increasing numbers about the dying prince's bed. But though the autopsy attempted resoundingly to close the door on the question of poison, and though many (John Chamberlain, for example) found this resolution satisfactory, the belief in foul play persisted for a time. Arthur Wilson, for example, writing about 1650 in his characteristically elliptical style, dropped many hints that he knew more than he was willing to divulge:

> *Jealousie* is like fire that burns all before it, and that fire is hot enough to dissolve all Bonds, that tends to the diminution of a Crown. . . . So dangerous are the paths of Greatness, that the tongue (many times) rouling aside, makes men tread awry. Strange Rumors are raised upon this sudden expiration of our Prince. . . . Some say he was poysoned with a bunch of Grapes, others attribute it to the venomous scent of a pair of Gloves, presented to him (the distemper lying for the most part in the head.) . . . the *Spaniard*, who opposed the marriage of the Prince *Palatine*, and saw their *ruin* growing up in Prince *Henries* towardly *Spirit*, were reputed (vulgarly) the *Mint-masters* of some horrid *practices;* and that a Ship of *Pocket Pistols* was come out of *Spain*, fit Instruments for a *Massacre.*[22]

Despite Wilson's shifting of the focus in this passage to the treacherous Spaniards, King James shines through even Wilson's triumphant archness as a promising suspect in the murder of his own son. Wilson's reference to tongues "rouling aside" is most definitely a reminder of the king's physical peculiarity (he was said to often befoul his dress with wine while drinking, his tongue being too large for his mouth). It was easy to remember after Henry's death what so many had noticed while he lived, that James often seemed jealous of his popularity.

But vying with James as prime suspect in the popular mind of the seventeenth century was Robert Carr, Viscount Rochester. The fact that Rochester and Frances Howard, Countess of Essex, were later successfully prosecuted for poisoning Sir Thomas Overbury made suspicion light more heavily. Rochester and Prince Henry had a quite open feud while the prince was yet alive, and Henry was surely a primary hindrance to Rochester's continued rise.

After the seventeenth century, historians managed to divide fairly evenly between those who accepted the doctor's autopsy and those who, like Arthur Wilson, credited the rumors of poisoning. In 1882 Sir Norman Moore seemed to end the matter once and for all by examining anew the autopsy report and finding there to his satisfaction enough indications to suggest "the earliest case of typhoid fever on record in England," probably contracted, Moore said, when the prince swam in the "polluted" waters of the Thames during that hot August of 1612.[23]

Dr. Moore certainly had the right idea in returning to the original autopsy report, for though the physicians of 1612 had no knowledge whatsoever of pathology, they were generally accurate describers of what their eyes beheld. And what they saw when Henry's body was opened on the day after his death, and what they wrote into their report, does considerably less than prove either the absense of poison or the presence of Sir Norman's typhoid. We know enough about heavy metal poisons now to realize that the absence of alien accumulation in the prince's stomach was meaningless and that the symptoms of heavy metal poisoning (arsenic, for example) frequently and successfully mimic the symptoms of typhoid fever and other fulminating diseases (which is precisely the reason so many poisonings in the past could go camouflaged as other dire infections).

The evidence that Henry died of natural causes is far from conclusive. On the other hand, the evidence that he had become a threat sufficiently serious to drive someone to murder is overwhelming. He had made enough personal enemies to feed our suspicions for several hours of pleasant speculation: Viscount Rochester, Frances Howard, Lord Northampton. But more importantly, by the autumn of 1612 he had become a very real threat to the entire peace of Europe. Here the suspects become more difficult to discern, but certainly King James must be listed among them because of his dedication to peace and his apparent inability to control his son; the ubiquitous Jesuits must also be marked down here, for in fact some of their secret agents were arrested in England that very October before Henry died. The fact that Henry's death should coincide exactly with the arrival of the German Protestants is suspicious in itself. It is just possible that someone in England late in 1612 understood that the Myth of the Conqueror was about to become a bloody reality, and rather than see England and all of Europe torn asunder to satisfy the implanted ambitions of an eighteen-year-old prince, someone possibly ended his career as warrior before it could get underway. This is speculation, of course, but it is speculation that deserves further investigation.

Notes to Chapter 6

1. *C.S.P., Venetian*, XII (1610-13), par. 409.

2. Francis Bacon, *Works*, ed. Spedding, Ellis, and Heath (London, 1860), XII, 19—20.

3. "Osborne's Traditional Memoirs," *Secret History of the Court of James the First* (London, 1811), I, 235-236.

4. *The Letters of John Chamberlain*, ed. McClure, I, 352. See also 357, 359.

5. These details and those events surrounding his death which follow are taken from Cornwallis' account printed by John Nichols, *The Progresses, Processions, and Magnificent Festivities of King James the First* (London, 1828), II, 454 ff.

6. *Hist. MSS. Comm. Duke of Buccleuch & Queensbury*, I (London, 1899), 118.

7. *C.S.P., Venetian*, XII (1610-13), par. 692.

8. *Hist. MSS. Comm. Duke of Buccleuch & Queensbury*, I, 117.

9. Thomas Birch, *The Life of Henry*, 406.

10. *The Letters of John Chamberlain*, I, 391.

11. *Hist. MSS. Comm. Marq. of Downshire*, III, 414.

12. *Ibid.*, 417.

13. *Ibid.*, 415.

14. *Hist. MSS. Comm. Visc. De L'Isle*, V (London, 1962), 66.

15. *Hist. MSS. Comm. Marq. of Downshire*, III, 432.

16. Birch, 371.

17. Alexander Brown, *The Genesis of the United States* (London, 1890), II, 636. As far back as 1609, the Spanish had noted with growing alarm Prince Henry's influence on the growth of English interests in America: "There has been gotten together in *20 days a sum* of money for this voyage which amazes one; among fourteen Counts and Barons they have given 40.000 ducats, the Merchants give much more, and there is no poor, little man, nor woman, who is not willing to subscribe something for this enterprise,—Three counties have pledged themselves that they will give a good sum of money, and they are negotiating with the Prince that he shall make himself *Protector of Virginia*, and in this manner they will go deeper and deeper into the business" (Don Pedro de Zuniga, Ambassador to England, to Philip King of Spain, Brown, I, 245-246). Later dispatches continued to take notice of Prince Henry's inspirational effect: "Those who are interested in this Colony [Virginia] show . . . that they wish to push this enterprise very earnestly and the Prince of

Wales lends them very warmly his support and assistance towards it"
(Don Alonso de Velasco to King Philip, 14 April 1612, Brown, II,
554).

18. H. R. Trevor-Roper, *Archbishop Laud* (London, 1940), 99.

19. Ralph Hamor, *A True discourse of the present estate of Virginia* (London, 1615), fol. 51.

20. Ralegh, *Works*, VII, 901.

21. *Ibid.*, 900-901.

22. Arthur Wilson, *The History of Great Britain, being the life
and reign of King James the First* (London, 1653), fols. 62-63.

23. Norman Moore, *The Illness and Death of Henry Prince of
Wales in 1612* (London, 1882). John Bowle in his recent *Charles the
First* (Boston: Little, Brown & Co., 1976), 31, calls Sir Norman's diagnosis "conclusive," but it can be so labeled only with peril. Since
Moore's examination of the original documents, over 90 years have
passed during which medical science has refined somewhat the diag-
nostic arts. What is needed is a contemporary expert to reexamine
the original autopsy report and to check Sir Norman's conclusion.

The Myth Prolonged

I

Godfrey Goodman, Bishop of Gloucester and a high Anglican of Romish tendencies, had been twenty-nine years old when Prince Henry died, and when Goodman came later to write his *History of the Court of King James* he remembered the young prince's keenness for the Puritan party as an unfortunate manifestation in a young man who stood so much in the eyes of his countrymen. A prince so constituted could—and did—give breath to those malcontents who looked for the present fire of Christ's return and who thought to hasten the event by burning with an uncompromising zeal. Of Prince Henry, Bishop Goodman wrote (with a fetching display of understatement), "truly I think he was a little self-willed, which caused the less mourning for him."[1] The second half of Bishop Goodman's statement may, at first glance, appear to be a bald untruth, for Prince Henry inspired a flood of elegiac display virtually unprecedented theretofore and certainly unequalled since in terms of sheer bulk. Close to fifty different volumes of memorial writing—including elegies, epicedia, epitaphs, emblems, impresa, devices, meditations, sermons—were occasioned by Henry's death, many of those volumes being, in fact, anthologies representing the poetical offerings of dozens of men in all the learned languages, both ancient and modern. Oxford and Cambridge Universities together turned out four fat compilations. Among the poets who publicly mourned were Sir William Alexander, Robert Allyne, William Basse, Richard Brathwait, Christopher Brooke, William Browne, Thomas Campion, George Chapman, John Davies, John Donne, William Drummond, Henry Goodyere, Sir Arthur Gorges, Joseph Hall, Sir Edward Herbert, George Herbert, Thomas Heywood, Hugh Holland, Henry King, James Maxwell, Richard Niccols, Henry Peacham, Walter Quinn, William Rowley, Joshua Sylvester, John Taylor, Cyril Tourneur, John Webster, and George Wither.

It might appear from this catalogue that Bishop Goodman's statement that Henry's arrogance caused him to be little mourned was
purely pique—the high Anglican taking his opportunity to denigrate
the prince who had encouraged the Puritans in their distemper—and
perhaps Goodman was only reflecting his own feeling at the time of
Henry's death; but there is an element of truth in the bishop's statement, even when it is set against that impressive outpouring of printed
pages. Insofar as Henry had not lived long enough to be known to
his countrymen as man and as ruler, he was memorialized in the only
guise by which Englishmen had consistently known him. It was not
Prince Henry they mourned; it was the sudden loss of a living national myth for which men cried out.

We can best begin to characterize the elegiac outpouring which
followed Henry's death by making comparisons with other similar
moments in English literary history. The death of Sir Philip Sidney in
1586 provided a precedent of sorts for the elegiac celebration of
Prince Henry. All the nation mourned, it seemed, for Sir Philip. In
life, as in death, he was an analogue for Henry as well as a precedent
for an elegiac outburst. Like Henry, he was young and dashing and
associated in the popular mind with a refurbished chivalry bravely
riding forth to battle the Spanish dragon. But from this point, precedents and similarities begin to pale. The elegiac poetry for Sidney
was written at the crest of national confidence, a confidence born of
deeds accomplished rather than of dreams and fantasies as yet unreal-
ized. Sir Philip had seemed the epitome of the English Golden Age;
his death was not primarily, as in the case of Henry Stuart, an opportunity for meditation on the wretchedness of human existence.
Rather, the elegiac literature written for Sidney glowed with an exu-
berant energy. It celebrated an ecstatic sense of tragedy rather than
despair. Sidney's death had proven the outer limits of man's capabilities, and it was that capacity rather than man's limits which interested the poets of 1586. Sidney's death occasioned at least one masterpiece of the genre, Spenser's "Astrophel," whereas Prince Henry's
death inspired nothing truly worthy of the word *masterpiece,* though
the poetry written for Henry, complicated as it was by the shifts and
strains in the national psyche which had intervened since Sidney's
death, may actually hold our interest longer than the purer golden
strains written for Sidney. In broad terms, the explosion of elegiac
literature at Sidney's death epitomized, without any sense of Ham-

let's irony, the rhetorical spirit of "what a piece of work is a man. . . ."
The elegies which Henry's death occasioned, on the other hand,
seem to have expressed the antithetical "man delights not me—nor
woman neither."

A second event which should have called forth an immense elegiac display— and did not—was the death of Queen Elizabeth. To be
sure a few poets wrote their summations and limned their tears, but
these elegists were largely university men, isolated from the great
body of England's poetic community which remained strangely
quiet. But the death of every important public figure did not necessarily demand the sort of elegiac outpouring which the death of Sidney had occasioned. Certainly Queen Elizabeth was almost universally loved and revered, but mere affection, as we know, has never been
the primary motivation behind elegy nor grief its primary emotion.
A nation mourns its living symbols, those who stand more for *possibility* than for *actuality,* those who in their deaths frustrate a national
goal which has seemed attainable but which has remained just beyond
grasp. At the time of her death, Queen Elizabeth's grasp was in the
wrong direction; it reached backward and held the wilted flowers of
hopes already achieved, of goals long since realized. Queen Elizabeth
was a symbol, but a dead one. Through the 1590's, when the achieve-
ments of the 1580's had fallen so suddenly to bitterness, England
found itself bound to a dying queen who could not and would not
rise phoenix-like from her own ashes. She had no heir; there was no
living symbol to lead the country forward. Her death was long expected, and when it finally came, there was no jolt of interruption,
no sting, no cause for national examination or introspection. The uni-
verse had simply wound down at last.

But with Prince Henry's death there was both jolt and sting. He
was in every way an evolving symbol; possibility in his myth far out-
weighed achievement, and hopes cut short in 1612 bled painfully.
But unlike Sidney's, Prince Henry's death actually endangered the
body politic. Sidney had been heroic embellishment to a secure
throne, so that his death was perceived as no real threat to national
stability. The elegiac literature for Sidney, like the man it celebrated,
could afford the luxury of being ornamental. But with Prince Henry's death there was a note of desperation. He was heir to the throne;
he left behind a twelve-year-old brother both weak and, worse, un-
known. In 1586 the chivalry and nationalism which Sir Philip Sidney

symbolized was celebrated by the poets for the benefit of others who could carry on that particular national myth—Sir Francis Drake, Sir Walter Ralegh, Sir Henry Lee, the young Earl of Essex. The hope which Sidney had represented clearly was not lost. But in the case of Prince Henry, hope poured out on the ground.

In the days following Henry's death, Sir John Holles, who had served the prince's ardor against English recusants and had shared his ambitions against foreign Catholics, wrote a series of letters, remarkable for their fullness of expression of one man's personal sense of loss and even more worthy of our attention in the way they anticipate the major themes and topics of the public elegiac literature. Sir John wrote first to two powerful men, the Archbishop of Canterbury and the Duke of Lennox, on November 10 and 12, and his motives should not be surprising to us nor thought wholly inappropriate. Sir John had, in losing his prince, lost his position in Henry's household and hence his income; the archbishop and the duke, he made clear, were in positions to help him find a new situation worthy of his birth and his abilities. Our tendency now may be to look at Sir John's practicality and dismiss it as mere venality, but the fact that for Holles—and for countless others—Prince Henry represented material and physical goods, as well as spiritual, should be added to the Henry myth as positive proof of its drawing power. In this young prince the stubbornly practical mind of English Puritanism could see fortuitously linked the hope of a new Jerusalem and thoroughfares brimming with the commerce of godly thrift and the spoils of holy war. But Sir John had lost this golden promise, and the tone of his letters to the archbishop and the duke suggested that the emotion he was experiencing most keenly then—not a week after Henry's death —was insult. It is as though Sir John Holles had been singled out by the malevolent fates for this mortal blow. His letters vacillated between inflated characterizations of his master who was now dead and reminders to the archbishop and the duke that Sir John never did aught to deserve this, as though in his mind national calamity and personal injury could be separated only with the greatest of effort, and even then the note of paranoia never quite disappeared. Sir John knew that England's hope had died—"the corner stone of our church, the sword and target of our king and state, the glory of Christendom and this age, the comfort of worth in men and actions" —but his attention would not stay focused there. The pain was internal—Sir John Holles had been wounded—and he looked about him in bewildered fury for the conspiracy which had deprived him of his security by depriving him of his prince. "But now I may cry out *Spes et fortuna valete!*" [Farewell hope and fortune], he wrote to the archbishop, and then moved immediately from the grand, classical gesture of grief into self-congratulation, suspicion, and petty carping: "This comfort nevertheless shall ever accompany me that I had the honour to serve so worthy a master, and of that no man's brow can deprive me, neither squinted I at any man's else." The present insult of Henry's death reminded him of past injustices and slights: "Ah! my dear master knew me his and no man's else; so was I the king's eight years, though with small fruit and acknowledgement. . . ." Then another attempt at a display of disinterested grief, followed by a most precipitous plunge into undisguised ill-will and envy: "yet nothing repent I me thereof, though peradventure I want those creeks [cracks?] to creep into which some of my fellows have."[2]

This initial reaction of anger on Holles's part was both unselfconsciously genuine and indicative of much of the tone of the elegiac poetry. It also quite obviously suggested the power of Henry's myth, that individual men immediately confused their own personal situations with the national loss, or else, that they so closely identified Henry's myth with the attainment of their own mundane ambitions that the death of the prince suggested instantly the death of personal fortunes. This suggests that Henry's myth of the conqueror was primarily a manifestation of national selfishness, and it was, at least in part. So much of what had been happening in Renaissance England had culminated in this new deification of selfishness, had camouflaged it, and had settled it symbolically in the person of Prince Henry. The cult and praise of individuals acting alone—that high doctrine of the Renaissance—had certainly contributed to the mood and spirit of selfishness; it was, after all, only one short step from exploring the limits of individual endeavor to turning those vast perimeters to personal profit and self-aggrandisement. In the year before Prince Henry's death, John Donne had written of the national mood of selfishness: "Prince, Subject, Father, Sonne, are things forgot, / For every man alone thinkes he hath got / To be a Phoenix, and that there can bee / None of that kinde, of which he is, but hee."[3] The stage literature of England had become dominated by proud, disdainful, isolated heroes, who may have ended tragically in the fictions of the time, but whose impact on social history, though great, must not always have been salutary. The literature pointed the way for men acting alone to pursue their own dreams; in the world of real men, those dreams were more often mercantile. Add to this atmosphere a strong strain of Protestantism which stressed that every man was his own priest—and in the more radical sects, his own king as well—and you have a partial explanation of some of the motivations which lay just beneath the surface of Prince Henry's myth. For all the appearance that Henry's conqueror role served the higher purposes of God, Church, and State—and, of course, it did serve those purposes also, but not purely nor totally—it seems clear enough that much of Henry's myth was underneath a disguise for acquisitiveness, materialism, and greed. Sir John Holles's anger at the shock of Henry's death was but one example of this selfishness, awaking in November 1612 to find its plans frustrated.

After he had written his two letters to potential future patrons, Sir John turned to other correspondents, to whom, because they were only friends or only country squires of limited wealth, he wrote a more modulated account of his personal feelings on the death of Prince Henry. The theme of frustrated ambition was replaced slowly by other topics which would also characterize and dominate the more formal elegiac literature. In two letters to Francis Cooke of Trusley, which followed closely the letters to the archbishop and the Duke of Lennox, the note of truculence was still there—"neither expect I in these overlooking times other comfort from my private family, patrimony and friends"—along with broadly suggestive hints of what plans had been afoot before Henry's death—"if this untimely death had not prevented his princely purpose, a few months had brought forth the comfortable fruits to the eye of the world"[4]—but there was also a powerful new theme which would find full expression in the elegiac poetry—guilt and self-accusation. To Master Cooke Sir John wrote in his second letter: "I fear me this betokeneth God's implacable vengeance upon this kingdom for the multitude and heinousness of our sins, for our hypocrisy in religion, carelessness and contempt of God and all good men, pride, luxury, abuse and unthankfulness for his great blessings and benefits."[5]

It would become an almost universal commonplace in the Prince Henry elegies that England's own sinfulness had caused the young man's death. This was, of course, quite genuine guilt which had only misapplied itself and avoided in the end the necessity of facing the truth. The national mood of self-accusation, first enunciated quite unconsciously by Sir John Holles in his letters to his friends, arose,

as did much of Prince Henry's myth, out of that same attitude of
selfishness which we were discussing earlier. So many men realized,
perhaps only subconsciously, that a great coalescing of personal ambitions had first constructed for Henry a role too vast for any man to
fill—except symbolically—and then perhaps had driven the young
prince too frantically in his attempt to achieve that goal. In that sense
the sins of England had been great, and the complicity in Henry's
death also great for all those who had contributed to the construction of his myth or in the flattery which made him believe the myth
was real. But Sir John Holles's sense of guilt, though generated from
this powerful source, was not simultaneously analytical; he realized
in some vague way that Henry's blood was symbolically on all their
hands. Beyond this he could only interpret the guilt he felt in the
Protestant frame-work of sin and retribution. Sir John, and so many
of the poets then writing, postulated sins of commission and sins of
omission, and ironically, Holles felt that the gravest omission had been
the failure to purify religion in England. Everyone, his logic went,
must therefore rededicate himself to rooting out the last vestiges of
papacy in his own heart and in the country. So out of the sense of
frustration and guilt arose even more heated dedication to the impossible goals and dreams which had given birth to the frustration
and guilt in the first place. This was—and became even more so in
the vast outpouring of elegiac literature—self-flagellation which fed
its own need for self-inflicted pain.

A corollary to the theme of self-flagellation was a florid restate-
ment of Henry's doctrinal purity and the belief that whereas the
country had flagged in purifying itself of all paganism, Prince Henry
had not tired nor despaired in his service of Reformed Religion, and
he would have, had not God cut short his mission, established the
holy city of Jerusalem. For this theme, the persona of Josiah was
most useful, for the Old Testament king had been anointed for rulership while still a boy and he had purged the Temple and harrowed
out the heathen with vigor and zeal. The similarities between Josiah
and Henry were appealing. Sir John Holles wrote to Francis Cooke
on this theme, immediately after expressing his sense of shame for
the sins of England: "And much of this ill had this worthy prince reformed, if God had spared him life. But Josias must be received to
his fathers that he stand no longer in the gap to keep back the sword
of wrath. Good men must die and wicked men live."[6] On November 28, Holles wrote similarly to Sir John Digby in Spain, showing

that he had been meditating further on the Josiah personation of his dead prince: "so precious was he to all nations, either as loved or feared, and to this church and country I may say even another Josias: and by this time I suppose you have in the place where you live [Madrid] discovered much base metal, seeing the papists among us, like the beasts of the forest, at this sun setting, begin already to whet their teeth, and to promise themselves their *regnabo* [I shall rule] by our *regnavi* [I did rule]."[7] As we have already seen in other letter writers at the time of Henry's death, here was that form of Protestant paranoia which believed that with the symbol of conqueror destroyed, the Catholics and their worst henchmen would have no reason to delay their assault on English liberty. Holles, who had other reasons to be bitter toward Henry's father, openly doubted King James's abilities to hold back the traitorous Catholics: "Oh that the King had as well power to believe as to hear Cassandra and while time serveth to lance this exuberated, mortal, impostume, which grows in the vitals of his State. My noble master saw it and would have cured it, he stood rooted in his own virtues like a rock in the midst of the ocean whom force feared and fraud dared not to approach."[8] In language increasingly metaphorical, Holles captured the two simultaneous movements which would characterize much of the elegiac literature: as Prince Henry became progressively more saintly in retrospect, England became more hopelessly rotten with sin and the weak prey to all the Catholic world. "He was the stay and comfort of our tottering church, the king and kingdom's right arm, the glory of Christendom, the encourager of all good, both of actions and men. . . . now that our hedge is broken down all passengers will pull off our grapes; our sea banks be overwhelmed and who or what shall defend us from the overflowing, all devouring, tyranny of pope and Spaniard? A prey we are to all nations and, methinks, I see Troy's walls broken down to receive in Sinon's horse, and that verse verified *Invadunt urbem somno vinoque sepultam* [They invaded a city buried in sleep and wine]."[9]

The next logical step in the mourning process flowed directly from the sense of guilt and reproach—a deep feeling of *contemptus mundi*, which sometimes became self-loathing—and in this too Sir John Holles in his correspondence pointed the way for the elegists. The theme first appeared in his letter to Sir Robert Mansfield on November 14, in which Sir John relied on the far from original metaphor of bodily sickness to suggest his sickness of soul (the microcosm) and the sickness of the entire world (the macrocosm): "Since 12 of the clock of Saturday night [the night after Henry's death] . . . I have kept my chamber, was entering into a hot ague for which I purged and let blood;. . . ." His illness at the time seemed genuine enough, though the psychological basis for it cannot be doubted; yet Sir John, like any poet of the time, was immediately aware of the philosophical and literary analogies to be drawn: "but no mortal hand can cure the everlasting comfortless sickness of my soul, which while I live I shall suffer for the loss of my most dear master, with the destruction of church, kingdom, and all worth of actions and men."[10] Henry's symbology was powerful enough to function vicariously as life-force for many people, and when that symbol suddenly ceased to exist, a growing despair was both a natural and genuine result.

The combination of preacherly rebuke for all England's sinners and the morbid contempt for life (which would make repentance from sin a somewhat superfluous impulse—not the first nor the last of several ironies arising from the Henry elegies) was perhaps most graphically combined by Joshua Sylvester in his *Lachrymae lachrymarum*. In verse which maintains a high level of savage invective, Sylvester excoriated all the sins of the time, and the sinners, naming as participants in Henry's death every group of Englishmen he could identify as in some way guilty of collective faults. This blamefixing, from which he did not seem to exclude himself, was set on the printed page within frames of human skeletons (see Fig. 13), the insistently visual *mementoes mori* for all those sinners who thought they might slip away unconfessed. The grim minuet of Sylvester's skeletons, dancing to the harsh music of his poetic denunciation, suggests much about the impulses which were channeling into the elegiac literature written for Henry.

The final elegiac theme, which in the case of Prince Henry was first enunciated in the correspondence of Sir John Holles, was the cataloguing of the young man's virtues. This classical, wholly conventional ploy was supposedly a step toward consolation: to remember the virtues and goods which the dead brought to and bestowed on the world was one way of lessening the pain of his death. For John Holles, as no less for the popular imagination generally, Henry could be remembered, for example, as the author and supporter of the Virginia plantation and the Northwest Passage exploration. He opened "the passage to virtue with reward of merit." He was known for wisdom, courage, justice, moderation, and (as Sir John was at pains to

mention in several letters) "secrecy." Good men of all professions
were welcome to him, and he loved "true prophets" among his advisors. All men of learning "he countenanced and comforted." Sometimes oxymoron was the only device for capturing the quality of his
virtue: "He was frugally bountiful." He was a great, a judicious, and
a "silent" searcher into men's motives, a curious and practical observer of all new inventions and designs. He was seldom angry. He
never uttered foul word or oath "in his life." This princely "inside"
was matched by a majestic outside: his able, graceful body was never
wearied by labor or exercise, whether on horseback or on foot. He
favored public works, such as Lambeth Bridge, the reconstruction of
Richmond and St. James's. He entertained the best engineers and
architects of Christendom. But above all, he upheld religion both at
home and abroad.[11] As Holles wrote to a gentleman in the Low Countries on November 27: "Nay this sun was too glorious, too usefull,
to be confined within our horizon—the United Provinces, those of
our religion in France, Germany, nay through the whole Christian
world, resent with us this great desolation, the scars and marks
whereof, I fear me, will appear ere long in characters too legible."[12]

II

The thematic movement in Sir John Holles's correspondence in
the month following Henry's death—from selfish fury to guilt and
self-reproach to *contemptus mundi* to the relaxation of tension
through memory of the prince's virtues—is a fairly accurate program
for following the development of the elegiac poetry written for Prince
Henry. That poetry written closest to his death tended to be more
often dyspeptic, violently anti-Catholic; the more distance a poet
was able to put between himself and the quenching of his and the
nation's hopes in Henry's death, the more he was likely able to focus
on the prince's virtues and lay aside self-laceration and aggressive anti-
clericalism. This tendency in the elegiac poetry may simply have been
the result of the natural impulses of differently tempered poets: the
hot-headed and more intensely self-interested would more normally
rush into print, while the coolly philosophical and more selflessly
meditative might naturally wait several months while they contem-
plated the meaning of Henry's death. But even with this latter group
the humors agitated by the prince's sudden death were volatile; de-
corum was difficult to maintain when the mind might unpredictably

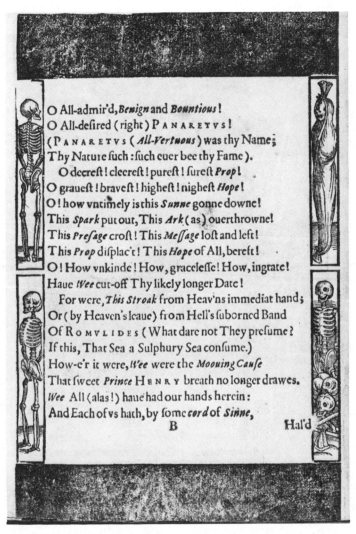

O All-admir'd, *Benign* and *Bountious* !
O All-defired (right) P A N A R E T V S !
(P A N A R E T V S (*All-Vertuous*) was thy Name;
Thy Nature fuch : fuch euer bee thy Fame).
    O decreft ! cleereft ! pureft ! fureft *Prop* !
O graueft ! braueft ! higheft ! nigheft *Hope* !
O ! how vntimely is this *Sunne* gonne downe !
This *Spark* put out, This *Ark* (as) ouerthrowne !
This *Prefage* croft ! This *Meffage* loft and left !
This *Prop* difplac't ! This *Hope* of All, bereft !
O ! How vnkinde ! How, graceleffe ! How, ingrate !
Haue *Wee* cut-off Thy likely longer Date !
    For were, *This Stroak* from Heav'ns immediat hand;
Or (by Heaven's leaue) from Hell's fuborned Band
Of R o m v l i d e s (What dare not They prefume ?
If this, That Sea a Sulphury Sea confume.)
How-e'r it were, *Wee* were the *Moouing Caufe*
That fweet *Prince* H e n r y breath no longer drawes.
Wee All (alas !) haue had our hands herein :
And Each of vs hath, by fome *cord* of *Sinne,*
                        B   Hal'd

Figure 13. Joshua Sylvester's *Lachrymae Lachrymarum,* 3rd ed., 1613, sig. B, whole page. S.T.C. 23578, British Museum Department of Printed Books. Reproduced by permission of the British Library Board.

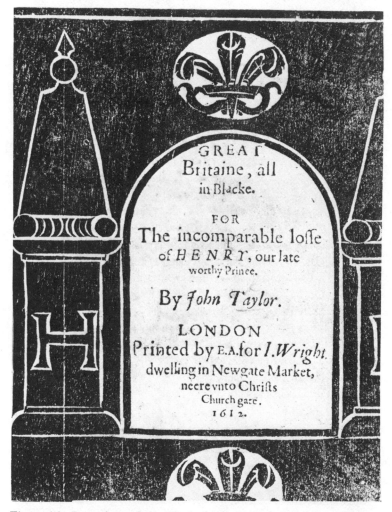

Figure 14. Page from John Taylor's *Great Britaine, all in Blacke,*
sig. A. S.T.C. 23760, British Museum Department of Printed Books.
Reproduced by permission of the British Library Board.

stumble once again into bitter disappointment. Contempt, anger, loathing could then flood out and swamp what had begun as a sweet-spirited *ubi sunt*. It seemed at times that the rehearsal of Henry's virtues, rather than calming and soothing men's wounds, served only as smarter lashes to their sense of guilt and shame. To utter his perfection was only to remind themselves once again of how close they had all come to personal Edens.

Much of the disconcerting quality of the verse may be attributable to a grinding sense of peculiar Protestant penance in the poetry, as though the writing of an elegy was in itself expiation for some of the national sin. If the necessity for writing elegies was looked upon as a Christian duty and therefore more comforting to the soul's salvation in direct proportion to the pain involved, pain of a different sort for subsequent readers could hardly be insubstantial. Men at the time, curiously enough, seemed well aware of the penitential quality of their writing and of the necessity to get that painful duty over and done with. John Thorys, one of that myriad who tried exorcising their personal demons by way of an elegy to Henry, wrote to William Trumbull on January 7, 1613: "But that my nephew Thwayts had a copy of my poetry about the prince's death I would have sent one to you of purpose; among others it was fortune to be one of the first as well as one of the worst. Mine was done before I slept, next day after he died."[13] There may have been a fair measure of braggadocio in Master Thorys's announcement, but there was also the tell-tale mark of Puritan discipline—"before I slept"—which attached itself to the meaning of Henry's death as a self-induced pain meant to give meaning to the meaningless.

Much of what is now familiar to us in the personation of Henry continued in the elegies, thus effectively limiting many of the poets to aggressive, anti-Catholic outbursts, for they continued to place over Henry's visage the masks of great conquerors and godly warriors.[14] The Alexander parallel in death, as during the prince's life, was a reoccuring motif. So was the mask of Edward the Black Prince, who was memorialized along with Henry in the elegies as the one who frighted France. Josiah, as we have already noted, made much headway as a popular personation for Henry, primarily because of the Old Testament figure's violent zeal in putting paganism to the sword, although the symbolic fact of Josiah's death in godly battle was made much of. Prince Henry was also displayed for the grieving public as a parallel to Scipio Africanus, as the God of War himself, as Henry V, as Julius Caesar, as Hector defending Troy. Important for all this impulse toward personation—the unflagging impulse which had accompanied Henry from the moment of his birth and now stood vainly hovering over his corpse, trying to reinstill those dead limbs with borrowed personality—was the outright acknowledgment of Henry's primary value as show, as display. He had come to mean so much to England precisely because he had been capable of donning the robes of Alexander or of successfully impersonating a youthful Hercules or a new Edward the Black Prince. The surprising recognition that Henry's essence was theatrical is given explicit utterance in only a few elegies, though the assumption may be the essential artistic principle behind all of them. Thomas Heywood wrote in his elegy:

> This Vniuerse imagine a Theater,
> Nations spectators, and this land a stage.
> Was euer Actor, made by the Creator,
> That better scean'd his part vnto his Age?
> 'Mongst all compos'd of fire, aire, earth and water,
> So grauely yong, and so vnmellowed sage:
> > Whose Trunke the Tombe exacts, as of a detter,
> > Subiect or Prince, none euer acted better.[15]

And John Webster observed, lest any impute theatrical show to emptiness, that Henry knew the difference between the mock drama of court jousts and the more important spectacle of the world's larger stage: the prince "knew that battailes, not the gaudy show / Of ceremonies, do on Kings bestow / Best Theaters, t'whom naught so tedious as Court sport. . . ." "Wee hop't much of him," Webster said, "Wee stood as in some spacious Theater."[16]

It may be objected with good reason that both Heywood and Webster, since they were dramatists, were merely following the dominant metaphors of their own occupation in characterizing Prince Henry. But I had rather think that Heywood and Webster were simply more perceptive, by reason of their dramatic training, in recognizing a fellow actor, even though his stage was the whole world rather than the Globe or the Swan. And the two dramatists were not alone in sensing the theatrical basis behind Henry's national role.

Even a clergyman like Daniel Price, a man who by no means possessed an affinity for plays or playhouses, unconsciously evoked the metaphors of the theater in his meditations on Henry's life and death published in his *First Anniversary:* "All the *world* were sate, to see, & harken, how his Highnesse hopefull, youthfull age should be *em-*

ployed, for in HIM, a *glimmering light* of the *Golden* times appeared.
. . ."[17] Interestingly, the metaphorical presentation of all the world
sitting to watch Prince Henry perform his illusion of the past made
immediately present reveals even more of the temper which produced
Henry's myth. The contentedness with which Reverend Price and his
ten thousand brethren were willing to settle back and watch the theatrical performance of their prince suggests the extent to which Henry had become almost the sole agent of movement and action in a
culture grown torpid and dangerously compressed. Out of the claustrophobia and funneling down of the society during the 1590's had
arisen, not new national energies expressed in national movements,
but a single symbol fueled by a single myth, whose trajectory was
aimed at smashing through barriers, demolishing limits, performing,
in short, the violent liberation from constraint which all of England
seemed to need. The theatrical metaphor was inevitable, for Henry
in his masks, in his heroic and grand posturing, allowed for England
a vent for bottled spleen, a catharsis for inhibited ambition. "All
lines of expectation met in this *Center,*" the Reverend Price wrote,
still thinking unconsciously of the stage metaphor and recapitulating,
incidentally, that portion of Henry's myth which emphasized the pre-
dominance of sight and the principle of psychological perspective:
"His *Magnetique* vertue drewe all the *eies,* and *hearts,* of the *Protestant* world. . . . he stood like a *Center,* vnmoved, the *circumference*
of his estate, being drawne aboue, beneath, about him. . . ."[18] In
remembering Prince Henry, Reverend Price proposed that sight and
appearance formed the essential principle of his power; this principle
was at heart theatrical: "There is no honest *subiect* that ever saw
him, but will forever care to *carry* the resemblance of his *Princely*
feature in their best composed *memory,* his piercing *eye,* gratious
smile, graue *frowne,* and divine *face* composed of *modesty* and *maiestie.*"[19] What his death meant, then, was that he could no longer be
seen; and no longer beheld by the admiring theatergoers of the world,
he and the play he enacted were lost. No appearance, no play, no salvation: "What in the *world* shall make shewe to sence of *stabilitie,*
what creature is a fixed *starre,* if such a *Prince* must die. . . . our *eies*
cannot now behold him, . . . our *lookes* must be *limited* to a meaner
light, & we must rather humble our selues to the *twilight* of inferior
things then celestiall *spirits.*"[20]

    With this theatrical principle behind Henry's myth in mind, we
can see readily how at his death presentations of either grief or of

Henry's living virtues tended to form themselves in florid, self-con-
sciously theatrical images. Sir Arthur Gorges's *Olympian Catastrophe*
was a perfect example of this tendency carried to its most extreme—
and quite readable—conclusion. Gorges constructed a Spenserian
world of knights and jousts, presided over, incongruously, by three
goddesses—Bellona, Minerva, and Juno—who quarreled in the fashion
of the judgment of Paris over who had bestowed the greatest gifts on
valiant Prince Henry.[21] (Significantly, Venus was replaced by a god-
dess of war, soft love never having been a part of Henry's myth.)
Henry's death, then, was presented in the framework of medieval
trappings, theatrically embellished to the point of enwrapping the reality of the prince's death in a shroud of fantasy. But whereas Gorges
went to great lengths to dramatize and mythologize the figure of
Henry himself, George Chapman in his *Epicede* gave over his stage to
Fever, who spoke as wickedly and theatrically as any Machiavellian
character on the English stage.[22] The theatrical urge was evident in
many of the elegies. Richard Niccols used three weeping women, the
allegorized figures of England, Wales, and Scotland, to speak long
monologues which alternated between decorous tears and unladylike
spite for Rome.[23] George Wither imagined "A Supposed Inter-locu-
tion betweene the Spirit of Prince Henry and Great Britaine,"[24] and
Henry Peacham made Death a character in his little elegiac drama,
though unlike Chapman's figure, Peacham's Death was a quite decent
chap genuinely chagrined that he had caused such general woe ("HEN-
RIE the good, the great, vnware I hit / With deadly dart before the
timely day").[25]

III

Those poets and writers who shared, while Henry lived, the aims,
motives, and assumptions of the dominant Protestant myth of the
prince as conqueror, could only, once the prince was dead, defiantly
restate their allegiance to that myth, though the body which it in-
habited and on which it depended for symbolic sustenance was dead
and decaying. Two motifs which had been supremely important for
Henry as living myth became even more important at his death: the
motif of limitlessness and the motif of chastity (which was, in fact, a
rejection of the alternate fertility myth).

Some of the poets tried to hold steady in their minds the image
of Henry thrusting always forward across the bounds which the world

and Satan threw up in his path. It was perhaps in that spirit that
John Taylor published van de Passe's well-known engraving of Henry
(see Fig. 14; cf. Fig. 6), poised to strike with the javelin, and wrote
his own accompanying verses in which he identified the prince as
England's *"Achilles* and *Vlisses."*[26] There was in this gesture something of the forlorn, celebrating what could have been, holding in
cupped hands a wisp of smoke. For most of the elegists, the remembered personation of Henry as unbounded force combined readily
with their theatrical impulses to produce extended versions of the
borders the prince would have crossed, had he lived. Spain and France
and Rome, under this spell of limitlessness, became too small a world
for Henry to have conquered; the globe spread flat before the march
of his imagined, now lost, military might:

> Heroick *Chiefetain,* who our Hearts didst fill
> With Valour, Hands with Weapons, Heads with Skill
> To manage Martiall deeds; we did expect,
> By thine auspicious *Leading,* to haue checkt
> The proudest *Saracen,* or *Mahumetan,*
> Tam'd the *Barbarian,* and wilde *Indian:....*[27]

Christopher Brooke analogically compared Henry to the king of beasts,
hunting unchecked across the whole surface of the earth:

> We look't HEE should haue impt the wings of FAME;
> Charm'd Death, ruld FATE, and made proud Fortune yeeld,
> And Lion-like haue forrag'd o're the EARTH
> To hunt his prey, and Crowne his NAME and BIRTH.[28]

But perhaps the most theatrical treatment of the theme of hurtling
power occurred in William Drummond's *Teares, On the Death of
Moeliades* (which Drummond glossed as an anagram for *Miles a Deo*),
in which the poet dared to voice what so many of the Protestant party had thought—that it would have been far better had Henry died in
bloody battle than in an ignoble sickbed—and like many others,
Drummond extended the geography of Henry's ambition to include
the Moslem world:

> Moeliades, *ô that by* Isters *Streames,*
> *Amongst shrill-sounding Trumpets, flaming Gleames*
> *Of warme encrimson'd Swords, and Cannons Roare,*
> *Balls thicke as Raine pour'd by the* Caspian *Shore,*
> *Amongst crush'd Lances, ringing Helmes, and Shields,*
> *Dismembred Bodies rauishing the Fields,*

> *In* Turkish Blood *made red like* Marses Starre,
> *Thou ended hadst thy Life, and Christian Warre!*[29]

It is surely significant that a mild-mannered and even-tempered Calvinist like Drummond of Hawthornden could become so curiously and salaciously bloodthirsty in an elegy for a dead, eighteen-year-old prince, but such was Henry's myth, and such the anger engendered when the myth collapsed. George Wither was no less extreme in following the theme of Henry's boundlessness, though in Wither's poem it was the English who would level the earth for Henry's sake; for Henry they would have depopulated the earth rather than allow him to be held in check (and worthy of attention, once again, is the implicit antagonism to fertility in Wither's images of the Henry myth):

> But were this deare, beloued, Prince of ours
> Liuing in any corner of this All,
> Though kept by *Romes* and *Mahomets* chiefe powers;
> They should not long detaine him there in thrall:
> We would rake *Europe* rather, plaine the *East;*
> Dispeople the whole *Earth* before the Doome:
> Stampe halfe to powder, and fier all the rest;
> No craft, nor force, should him deuide vs from:
>   We would breake downe what ere should him confine,
>   Though 'twere the *Alpes,* or hilles of *Appenine.*[30]

For those less bloody-minded though no less convinced of the validity of Henry's illimitable force, they could say with William Alexander, "For O, to what strange hight had his perfections flowne, / Had they as first, still by degrees proportionablie growne!"[31]

There was, of course, one crushing irony which sat down heavily on all the imagery of boundless power: the fact was, Henry had been limited irredeemably by death itself. But it was the struggle with this terrible contradiction which so much vexed the poets into their theatricalism and their flaming assaults on the Catholic Church, as though their own boundless and indecorous outbursts in the elegies might somehow take up the power which had resided mythically in Henry, and by extending that power verbally and metaphorically, prove against all hope the truth of Henry's ability to fly over every barrier. Even in death his disciples might drink the communion of his blood, like Drummond, strengthened to go forth and carry on the Protestant crusade. In this way, the elegies became something like a sacramental elevation of the host, wherein the real presence of the body and blood of their myth might transubstantiate the realm of death to enter again the pulsating realm of possibility. If during Henry's life, art had been almost indistinguishable from politics, art now became in the fact of his death almost indistinguishable from religion. The irony here is that the religious and sacramental basis behind the elegies so closely mimicked the central mysteries of Catholic rite, the religion most of the elegists had sworn to hate.

Not all the poets allowed themselves to wander unconsciously into the paradox of celebrating the boundlessness of a prince who had been bounded by death. They developed rather a pseudo-otherworldliness which allowed them to think—or speak, at least—of death as yet only another field of conquest for their conqueror prince. It was a neat enough trick, learned from the conventions of classical elegy, and it may actually have worked to soothe some of the hurt. But whether or not it functioned as consolation, this extension of the boundlessness theme into the suburbs of heaven can add to our understanding of the Henry myth, for in postulating heaven as the last conquest for Prince Henry, they characterized earth as too small for his ambitions:

> For frowning *Neptunes* liquid field of feares,
> And this poore mote of dust that all vpbeares,
> To his great mind seem'd too too small a space:.... [32]

It was Daniel Price who most thoroughly explored the philosophical implications of this other-worldly theme in his *Second Anniversary.* The heaven to which Prince Henry had ascended was clearly for Price an extension of the geographical acquisitiveness of Henry's earthly myth; where once again Henry was imagined as too mammoth a force in too small a space:

> ... celestial kingdomes, were his *aime,* & *hope,* a *king-dome* that hath no *end* for *termination,* no *confines* for *limitation,* farre aboue *principalities* and *powers,* where-in no man can *resolue* whether his sanctified *ambition* were more *high* or more *happy.* For had his desires lev-el'd, at the *regaining* of a *neighbour* kingdome, which either by match hath beene *conioyned* or by *prowesse* hath beene *conquered,* the *example* had not wanted *fol-lowers,* nor the *enterprise honours.* [33]

Reverend Price could still evoke the persona of Alexander the Great, but for slightly different purposes; an overweening ambition was still the theme, but the direction had altered:

> It was the speech of *Philip* to his sonne *Alexander*, . . .
> Sonne seeing *Macedonia* is not a place *fit* for thee, thou
> maist finde a more *competible* and *compacious* kingdome.
> The *world* is not capable of vs, it is a limited finite small
> *compasse,* the *soule* though it be but the inmate of the
> *body,* is a celestiall *transcendent creature,* and being
> rightly guided, is ever ascending *vpwards*. . . .[34]

Daniel Price's philosophical meditations on Henry's death and
the similar poetic musings of the elegists were not simply Christian
solace or classical *sententia,* nor was this evident straining upward to
follow the flight of Henry's soul a mere conventional development
of the *contemptus mundi* theme, though all three elements may be
said to intermingle here with what I believe to be the primary impulse: for all its appearance of otherworldliness, the Reverend Price's
statement that "the *world* is not capable of vs" is at heart still this-
worldly. Though Price and the elegists spoke of heaven, their metaphors and imagery were bound in rock and soil, as were the normal
patterns of cause-effect logic which fed ambitions and by which the
ambitions plotted their worldy courses. If Price and his fellow Protestant mourners seemed to become increasingly otherworldly and
anti-materialistic, it was only because their efforts to keep alive the
Henry myth necessitated their elevation of it to a realm where it was
hoped it could escape the ravages of time. The myth kept alive and
aloft could quickly descend to find a new home in a new living embodiment, should such a being appear (as perhaps he did in Oliver
Cromwell), where it would soon show again its true heart of acquisitiveness and materialism. For many, of course, the trick of keeping
the myth alive by making it seem to transcend hateful reality was
simply an impossible feat. For them there was far more bitterness
and irony in realizing that a prince mythologized as limitless had so
soon found his resting place in a casket shockingly small. For them,
one particular epitaph might speak with stinging truth:

> *Looke here within this little place he lies,*
> *Eu'n he that was the* Vniuersall Hope:
> *And almost made this Ile* Idolatrize,
> *See, hee's contented with a little scope.*[35]

Part of the struggle in getting Prince Henry symbolically airborne
was due, in part, to the implications of the second major theme in
the recapitulation of his Conqueror myth—the motif of chastity. For
the Puritans, Henry's life-long rejection of the love motive became

doubly important to them in the contemplation of his death, for
without the defilement of sex he could seem more saint-like and, to
more than one writer, a type of Christ. Some of the poets reveled in
the fact that though "the courtliest dames / . . . shot *Eye-bals* wrapt
in CVPIDS fire," Prince Henry's "steel'd Brest"[36] was immune to
their advances and their provocations. No, *"Bellona* was his GOD-
DESSE, whom he sought / With Knightly valour, more then courtly
grace: / . . . . ARMES had his *Hart;* when LOVE had scarse his
Heele."[37] The prince may have fired all the women of the court with
the love motive—"O *Rose!* of thousand *Damsels* late desired, / Whose
crimsin hew their snowie bosomes fired"[38] – but he was nevertheless
free himself from lust or desire or even the flicker of an eyelid. In
him, the elegists said or implied, the power motive never paled:

> . . . *Musiks* wanton part though He could grace,
> As well as euer yet could Carpet knight,
> And could adorn a Dance to please the sight
> Of the most choise and curious Damsells eyes; . . .
>
> .   .   .   .   .   .
>
> But, running, swimming, and such exercise,
> As much more Masculine, hee more did prize.[39]

But for all the celebration of masculinity and the unnecessary deni-
gration of the feminine, the Puritan elegists had entered another
ironic trap. Male chastity might be fitting and even powerful for
saintly figures, but with Prince Henry dead and the desire keen to
keep his myth alive, the poets discovered that the other side of chastity was sterility.

The problem of fruitlessness nagged at them. Many of them, in
using the conventional elegiac *topos* of "nature-spoiled," found that
they could, without putting too fine a point on it, suggest a general
fertility which was lost at Henry's death. But this solution was pat-
ently false and rang hollowly. Some chose to face the issue squarely
and then deny its importance or else suggest ways around its seriousness: "That euen though chyldlesse dead, thou shalt not barren be, /
If Phoebus helpe to procreat posteritie for thee."[40] The poet was
here suggesting the conventional notion that in poetry the prince
could live on, and that Henry's inspiration of so much verse surely
represented a fertility more important than any man could achieve
in his corruptible flesh. But this solution was as hackneyed and un-
convincing as suggesting that all of nature was now dead and dying
because Henry was gone. Others, like Walter Quin, found it easier to

admit simply that fertility was just another might-have-been:

> But when the world of all his Vertues rare
> The wished fruit to gather did expect. . . .
> .   .   .   .
> Vntimely death then from vs did him take, . . .[41]

It was perhaps the anti-fertility of Henry's myth and its resultant pressure on the elegists, who needed desperately to procreate that myth
into a new generation, that led Ruth Wallerstein to comment that
"many of the elegists fail in their statements of grief and of faith,
through aridity."[42] She was right; England's poets found themselves
trying to invest with new life the sterile dust of masculine and Puritan aggressiveness.

Though most were content to simply walk safely around the trap
of Henry's essential sterility, there were among the elegists those
who had urged on Henry while he lived a different personation—native fertility god—and had warned him against the pride of crossing
boundaries and transgressing limits. These poets, too, were writing,
and some of them stubbornly insisted on returning to the rich imagery of fertility which they had constructed for the prince, who had
in turn rejected it for lance and battlehorse and symbolic conquest.
Now in the sterility of his death, the proffered images of sexual whole-
ness and abundance became perhaps the most devastating irony of all:

> His high-erected thoughts look't downe upon
> The smiling valley of his fruitfull heart.
> *Honour* and *Curtesie* in every part
> Proclaim'd him, and grew lovely in each lim,
> He well became those vertues which grac'd him.
> He spread his bounty with a provident hand;
> And not like those that sow th'ingratefull sand. . . .
> He was not like the mad and thriftlesse Vine,   .
> That spendeth all her blushes at one time:
> But, like the *Orange* tree, his fruits he bore;
> Some gather'd, he had greene, and blossomes store. [43]

The moderate Anglicans had their myth too, though Henry had never given them any aid in keeping it alive; for the reason of Henry's
indifference to the mask of fertility, perhaps, their elegies sometimes
struck a forlorn note quite apart from any grief for the death itself:
"despight all injustice [thou] wouldst have proved / So just a *Steward*
for this Land. . . ."[44]

While most of the poets were describing, in the conventional *topos,* nature subverted or blasted by Henry's death, Joseph Hall (who had been among those moderate voices who had warned Henry of the dangers in the conqueror myth) could not resist mentioning a meteorological irony. During the winter following Henry's death, unprecedented rainfall had saturated England while the temperatures had held temperate; grass grew in December, hedges blossomed, the last roses of summer were succeeded by unseasonable buds. Though Hall likely did not intend his rhetorical flourish as sarcastic commentary on the barrenness of the Henry myth, the question he asked in one little poem did provide exactly that counterpoint: "Did euer WINTER *mourne* in *greene?"*[45]

Most interesting of this latter group was George Chapman, whose countering of the conqueror myth we examined in Chapter Four. In his *Epicede,* Chapman depicted a "fertility failed" in Henry. He had been England's *"Day-star,"* now fallen from the sky leaving a hole in heaven through which poured the "second deluge" (which became for Joseph Hall a witty image), "in which are ouer-flowne / The seeds of all the sacred Vertues, set / In his Spring-Court. . . ."[46] The imagery of agricultural fertility continued, closely associated with a version of Henry never really encouraged by the prince himself: he had brought regeneration to those lying in "graues of vice, / Digg'd in their old grounds, to spring fresh on those / That his diuine Ideas did propose, . . ."[47] It was not the celebration of the prince's virtues which commented ironically on the Henry myth; it was Chapman's stubborn faith in the symbols of fertility. But though every nobleman in England thirsted "to plant his sonne neer him / As neer the *Thames* their houses," the young crops were not deeply enough rooted nor sturdy enough against the buffets of the world: "And how the wilde Bore, Barbarisme, now / Will roote these Quick-sets vp? What hearb shall grow, / That is not sown in his inhumane tracts?"[48]

Such imagery was, of course, giving Henry more than his due, and Chapman later rather bluntly acknowledged the fiction of his own fertility myth. With a quite sobering honesty Chapman acknowledged that "men now are scarce to warmnesse fir'd / With loue of thee; but rather colde and dead,"[49] and it seems clear enough that the lack of life-sustaining warmth was a product of Henry's failure to fertilize with the love motive his own home soil. Near the end of his *Epicede,* Chapman too came to the bleakness of Henry's final legacy—

"who now dyed fruitlesse"[50]—though he tried valiantly to suggest that Henry's virtues, his affection for learning, and his support of scholars and poets would live on in after ages. These and his other hyperbolic attributes would, as a matter of fact, soon die the death of the forgotten, as England would learn to hate the very name of Stuart.

IV

Henry's myth did live on for a while. Men, however, cannot grieve long for what is out of sight, and soon the prince was memorialized in the histories as simply "hopeful Prince," an empty phrase and a brief one which masked so much that had been full of meaning.

If there was one continuing effect of Henry's myth, it rested onerously on James's second son, the weakling brother who now became the Prince of Wales. Henry and Charles had been worlds apart in temperament, personality, and in personation, and if Protestant England looked for Charles to step into the mythic robes of Henry—as surely they did—they were much disappointed in an heir who drew his own sense of self from such different reservoirs. Perhaps, in fact, it was the appallingly aggressive persona of his brother—with all the suggestion of cruelty and force—which contributed to Charles's own growing personation as victim. The Conqueror Prince gave way to the Martyr King. How else, in the push and pull of metaphor, could the succession of myths have worked their own terrible logic?

Occasionally, something would happen in the affairs of men to bring Henry's myth pushing impudently back into the national consciousness. One such event was the birth in 1614, to Henry's sister Elizabeth and her husband the Palatine Elector, a first son and heir to the Protestant union of German states. Elizabeth, in an act of devotion to the memory of her dead brother, promptly named the child Henry Frederick, and in England some could not resist returning for a time to the symbolic implications. One such was Henry Peacham, who had done much during Prince Henry's life to feed his myth, and who published a long poem significantly titled, *Prince Henry Revived*. Here at last in the little German prince was the succession longed for, the fruit born of fertility, and Peacham presented to the eyes of England a drawing of the baby (see Fig. 15) surrounded by the devices, mottoes, and Latin inscriptions which made explicit the continuity—or the hoped for continuity—of England's Henry in Ger-

Figure 15. Peacham's engraving from verso of title page, *Prince Henry Revived*. S.T.C. 19514, British Museum Department of Printed Books. Reproduced by permission of the British Library Board.

many's Henry. In Peacham's Latin verse at the foot of the portrait, the conqueror personation was begun afresh; like Prince Henry lying encradled in Scotland in 1594, Elizabeth's little boy was already "CAESAR," growing strong to overwhelm with his fame the heights of Olympus. England, it seemed, was determined to have its conqueror.

Its conqueror would come, fulfilling in ways unforeseen the myth that England's Protestants found so strangely attractive, but he would not come as a German Prince. Indeed, none of the Stuarts or their descendants would fill the role that had begun as the birthright of a Stuart prince. It would, in the end, take a Protestant from the ranks of Parliament, a man who understood the power offered to anyone who could fulfill the myth and a man who did not shrink from grasping that power. Oliver Cromwell would show them soon enough the meaning of barriers overridden.

Notes to Chapter 7

1. Godfrey Goodman, *The Court of King James the First,* ed. John S. Brewer (London, 1839), I, 251.
2. Both letters are printed in *Hist. MSS. Comm. Duke of Portland,* IX (London, 1923), 33-34.
3. "The First Anniversary," ll. 215-218.
4. *Hist. MSS. Comm. Duke of Portland,* IX, 34.
5. *Ibid.*
6. *Ibid.,* 34-35.
7. *Ibid.,* 37.
8. *Ibid.*
9. In Holles' second letter to Francis Cooke, *ibid.,* 35.
10. *Ibid.*
11. *Ibid.,* 8-11, 33-39.
12. *Ibid.,* 36-37.
13. *Hist. MSS. Comm. Marq. of Downshire,* IV (London, 1940), 9.
14. Obviously my purpose in this chapter is to examine the elegiac literature in the light of Prince Henry's life. For better or for worse, I am interested in the elegies as expressions of mythic biography, so I have not paused to evaluate this literature *as* literature. That has been done already by Ruth Wallerstein in her excellent *Studies in Seventeenth-Century Poetic* (U. of Wisconsin Press, 1950), 59-96. Barbara Kiefer Lewalski's recent *Donne's Anniversaries and the Poetry of Praise* (Princeton, 1973) adds to the work of Wallerstein on the Prince Henry elegies. I have found Professor Lewalski instructive on various points, particularly her discussion of Daniel

Price. Interested readers may wish to consult also E. C. Wilson's catalogue of the elegiac literature and his discussion of it in *Prince Henry and English Literature* (Ithaca, 1946). See also John Philip Edmond, "Elegies and Other Tracts Issued on the Death of Henry, Prince of Wales, 1612," *Publications of the Edinburgh Bibliographical Society*, 6 (1906), 141-158.

15. *A Funerall Elegie, upon the death of the late most hopefull and illustrious Prince, Henry*, printed as the third of *Three elegies on the most lamented death of Prince Henry* (London, 1613), sig. B.

16. *A MONVMENTAL COLVMNE, Erected to the liuing memory of the euer-glorious HENRY, late Prince of Wales*, printed as the second of *Three elegies* (1613), in *The Complete Works of John Webster*, ed. F. L. Lucas (London, 1927), III, ll. 90-92, 47-8.

17. *Prince Henry, his first anniversary* (Oxford, 1613), fol. 4.

18. *Ibid.*

19. *Ibid.*, fol. 5.

20. *Ibid.*, fol 3.

21. *The Olympian Catastrophe* in *The Poems of Sir Arthur Gorges*, ed. Helen Estabrook Sandison (Oxford, 1953).

22. *An Epicede or funerall song on the most disastrous death of Henry, Prince of Wales* (1612) in *The Poems of George Chapman*, ed. Phyllis Brooks Bartlett (New York, 1941).

23. *The Three Sisters Teares. Shed at the late Solemne Funerals of the Royall deceased Henry, Prince of Wales* (London, 1613).

24. *Prince Henries Obsequies; Or Mournefull Elegies vpon his Death*, in *Juvenilia: Poems by George Wither*, Part II (Manchester: The Spenser Society, 1871).

25. *The Period of Mourning. Disposed into sixe Visions. In Memorie of the late Prince* (London, 1613), sig. B 2^V.

26. *Great Britaine, all in Blacke. For the incomparable losse of HENRY, our late worthy Prince* (London, 1612), sig. A.

27. Henry Burton, "Elegie," in Joshua Sylvester's *Lachrymae Lachrymarum, or The Spirit of Teares Distilled for the vn-tymely Death of the incomparable Prince Panaretus*, 3rd ed. (London, 1613), sig. G 3^V.

28. *Two Elegies, Consecrated to the neuer-dying Memorie of the most worthily admyred; most hartily loued; and generally bewayled Prince; Henry* (London, 1613), sig. C. The second of the *Two Elegies* is by William Browne of Tavistock and is printed with separate title page.

29. *Teares, On the Death of Moeliades* (Edinburgh, 1613), in *The Poetical Works of William Drummond of Hawthornden*, ed. L. E. Kastner (Manchester, 1913), I, 76, ll. 39-46.

30. "Eleg. 24," *Prince Henries Obsequies,* printed in *Juvenilia,* Pt. II, 389.

31. "An Elegie on the Death of Prince Henrie" (Edinburgh, 1612), in *The Poetical Works of Sir William Alexander, Earl of Stirling,* ed. L. E. Kastner & H. B. Charlton (Edinburgh & London, 1929), II, 529, ll. 81-82.

32. "Epit. 6" by"[Ignoto]," in *MAVSOLEVM, OR The Choisest Flowres of the Epitaphs, written on the Death of the neuer-too-much lamented PRINCE HENRIE* (Edinburgh, 1613), sig. [2^V].

33. *Prince Henry his second anniversary* (Oxford, 1614), fol. 21.

34. *Ibid.,* fol. 26.

35. George Wither, "An Epitaph Vpon the most Hopefull and All-vertuous *Henry,* Prince of *Wales,"* in *Prince Henries Obsequies, Juvenilia,* Pt. II, 400.

36. Christopher Brooke, *Two Elegies,* sig. [B 4^V].

37. *Ibid.*

38. Hugh Holland, "Elegie on the vntimely Death of the Incomparable Prince, Henry," in Joshua Sylvester's *Lachymae,* 3rd. ed., sig. D 2.

39. Sir William Cornwallis, in Joshua Sylvester, *Lachrymae,* sig. [E 4].

40. William Alexander, "An Elegie," in *The Poetical Works,* II, 530.

41. "Epit. 1," in *MAVSOLEVM, OR The Choisest Flowres,* sig. [1].

42. *Studies in Seventeenth-Century Poetic,* 63.

43. John Webster, *The Complete Works,* III, 275-76, ll. 34-40, 43-46.

44. *Ibid.,* ll. 285-286.

45. *"Of the Rain-bowe, that was reported to be* seene in the night, ouer St. IAMES, before the Princes death; and of the unseasonable *Winter, since,"* *The Collected Poems of Joseph Hall,* ed. A. Davenport (Liverpool, 1949), 149.

46. "An Epicede," *The Poems of George Chapman,* 256.

47. *Ibid.,* ll. 135-138.

48. *Ibid.,* ll. 139-140, 144-147.

49. *Ibid.,* ll. 308-09.

50. *Ibid.,* l. 631.

Bibliography

Primary Sources

[Listings follow the practice of Pollard and Redgrave's *A Short-Title Catalogue, 1475-1640.*]

Abbot, Robert. *The true ancient Roman Catholike.* London, 1611.

Alexander, William, Earl of Stirling. *An elegie on the death of Prince Henrie.* Edinburgh, 1612.

Alexander, William, Earl of Stirling. *A Paraenesis to the prince.* London, 1604.

Alexander, William, Earl of Stirling. *The poetical works of Sir William Alexander, Earl of Stirling.* Ed. L. E. Kastner & H. B. Charlton. Two volumes. Edinburgh & London, 1921-29.

Allyne, Robert. *Funerall elegies upon the most lamentable and untimely death of the thrice illustrious Prince Henry.* London, 1613.

Allyne, Robert. *Teares of joy at the happy departure of Frederick and Elizabeth, prince and princesse Palatine.* London, 1613.

Bacon, Francis, Viscount St. Albans. *The Works of Francis Bacon.* Ed. James Spedding, Robert Leslie Ellis, & Douglas Denon Heath. Fifteen volumes. Boston, 1860-64.

Barclay, John. *Joan. Barclaii Sylvae.* London, 1606.

Basse, William. *Great Brittaines sunnes-set bewailed.* Oxford, 1613.

Baudius, Dominicus. *Monumentum consecratum honori &c memoriae serenissimi Britanniarum principis.* Lugduni, 1612.

Benvenuto, Italiano. *Il passagiere.* London, 1612.

Blenerhasset, Thomas. *A direction for the plantation in Ulster.* London, 1610.

Bowyer, Robert. *The parliamentary diary of Robert Bowyer, 1606-1607.* Ed. David Harris Willson. Minneapolis & London, 1931.

Brathwait, Richard. *The poets willowe, or the passionate shepheard.* London, 1614.

Brinsley, John. *Ludus literarius; or the grammar schoole.* London, 1612.

Brooke, Christopher. *Two elegies, consecrated to the memorie of Henry, Prince of Wales.* London, 1613.

Broughton, Hugh. *A comment upon Coheleth or Ecclesiastes.* [London] 1605.

Broughton, Hugh. *Familia Davidis, quatenus regnum spectat.* Amsterdam, 1605.

Broughton, Hugh. *A replie upon the R. R. F. Th. Winton for heads of his divinity in his sermon and survey.* Amsterdam, 1605.

Brown, Alexander, ed. *The Genesis of the United States. A series of historical manuscripts now first printed.* Two volumes. London, 1890.

Burhill, Robert. *Pro Tortura Torti contra Martinum Becanum Jesuitam.* London, 1611.

Cambridge University. *Epicedium cantabrigiense in obitum Henrici principis Walliae.* Cambridge, 1612.

Campion, Thomas. *Songs of mourning bewailing the death of prince Henry.* London, 1613.

Carey, Robert, Earl of Monmouth. *Memoirs of Robert Cary.* Ed. G.H. Powell. London, 1905.

Caus, Solomon de. *La perspective avec la raison des ombres et miroirs.* London, 1612.

Chamberlain, John. *The letters of John Chamberlain.* Ed. Norman Egbert McClure. Two volumes. Philadelphia, 1939.

Chapman, George. *An epicede or funerall song; on the most disastrous death of Henry Prince of Wales.* London, 1612.

Chapman, George. *Euthymiae raptus; or the teares of peace.* London, 1609.

Chapman, George. *The poems of George Chapman.* Ed. Phyllis Brooks Bartlett. New York, 1941.

Charron, Pierre. *Of wisdome, three bookes.* Trans. Samson Lennard. London, n.d. [before 6 Nov. 1612].

Charron, Pierre. *Of wisdome, three bookes.* Trans. Samson Lennard. London, n.d. [after 6 Nov. 1612].

Cheeke, Gulielmus. *Anagrammata, et chron-anagrammata Regia, nunc primum in hac forma in lucem emissa.* London, 1613.

Chester, City. *Chesters triumph in honor of her prince.* London, 1610.

Chetwind, Edward. *Votivae lachrymae; a vow of teares for the loss of Prince Henry, in a sermon preached in the city of Bristol December 7, 1612.* London [1612].

Clapham, Henoch. *A briefe of the Bibles history, drawne first into English poesie.* London 1603.

Clapham, Henoch. *Doctor Andros his prosopopeia answered, of removing of Catholike scandale.* Middelburg, 1605.

Cleland, James. *Institutes of a young noble man.* Ed. Max Molyneux. New York, 1948.

Clifford, Anne. *The Diary of the Lady Anne Clifford.* Ed. V. Sackville-West. London, 1923.

Coke, Roger. *A detection of the court and state of England during the four last reigns and the Inter-Regnum.* Two volumes. London, 1694.

Collectanea curiosa. Ed. John Gutch. Two volumes. Oxford, 1781.

Colman, Morgan. [*The genealogies of King James I. and Queen Anne*] [London? 1608].

Cooper, Thomas. *Nonae Novembris aeternitati consecratae in memoriam admirandae illius liberationis principis et populi Anglicani à proditione sulphurea.* Oxford, 1607.

Cornwallis, Sir Charles. *An account of the baptism, life, death, and funeral of the most incomparable Prince Frederick Henry, Prince of Wales.* London, 1751.

Cornwallis, Sir Charles. *A discourse of the most illustrious prince, Henry.* London, 1641.

Cornwallis, Sir Charles. *The life and death of our late most incomparable and heroique prince, Henry prince of Wales.* London, 1641.

Cornwallis, Sir Charles. *A relation of the marriages that should have been made between the Prince of England and the Infanta Major, and also after with the younger Infanta of Spain. Harleian Miscellany,* VIII. London, 1746.

Coryate, Thomas. *Coryats crambe, or his colwort twise sodden and now served in with other macaronic dishes, as the second course of his crudities.* London, 1611.

Coryate, Thomas. *Coryats crudities; hastily gobled up in five moneths travels.* London, 1611.

Cotton, Robert Bruce. *An answer made by command of Prince Henry to certain propositions of war and peace, delivered to his highness by some of his military servants.* London, 1655.

Craig, Sir Thomas. *Ad serenissimum Britanniarum principem Henricum.* Edinburgh, 1603.

Crashaw, William. *The sermon preached at the Crosse Feb. xiiij. 1607.* Second edition. London, 1609.

Crashaw, William. *A sermon preached in London before the right honorable the Lord Lawarre, Lord Governour and Captain General of Virginea.* London, 1610.

Daniel, Samuel. *The complete works in verse and prose of Samuel Daniel.* Ed. Alexander B. Grosart. Five volumes. London, 1885-96; reprt., New York, 1963.

Daniel, Samuel. *The tragedie of Philotas.* London, 1607.

Davies, John, of Hereford. *Microcosmos; the discovery of the little world.* London, 1603.

Davies, John, of Hereford. *The muses-teares for the losse of Henry Prince of Wales.* London, 1613.

D'Ewes, Sir Simonds. *The autobiography and correspondence of Sir Simonds D'Ewes.* Two volumes. London, 1845.

Digges, Thomas & Dudley Digges. *Foure paradoxes, or politique discourses: two concerning militarie discipline, written long since by Thomas Digges, two of the worthinesse of warre and warriors, by Dudley Digges, his sonne.* London, 1604.

Drayton, Michael. *The works of Michael Drayton.* Ed. J.W. Hebel. Five volumes. Oxford, 1931-41.

Drummond, William, of Hawthornden. *The poetical works of William Drummond of Hawthornden.* Ed. L.E. Kastner. Two volumes. Manchester, 1913.

Drummond, William, of Hawthornden. *Teares on the death of Meliades.* Edinburgh, 1613.

Du Faur, Gui, Seigneur de Pibrac. *Tetrastica. Or, the quadrains of Guy de Faur.* Trans. Joshua Sylvester. London, 1605.

Eudes, Morton. *Catholique traditions or a treatise of the belief of the christians of Asia, Europa, and Africa in the principal controversies of our time.* Trans. Lewis Owen. London, 1609.

Extracts from the accounts of the revels at court. Ed. Peter Cunningham. London, 1842.

Fennor, William. *Fennors descriptions, a relation of divers speeches.* London, 1616.

Fennor, William. *Pluto his travailes, or the divels pilgrimage to the college of Jesuits.* London [1611].

Fletcher, Robert. *The nine English worthies.* London, 1606.

Franchis, Joannes Maria de. *Of the most auspicious marriage betwixt Frederick, Count Palatine, and Elizabeth.* Trans. S. Hutton. London, 1613.

French Herald. *The French herald, summoning all true christian princes to a generall croisade.* London, 1611.

Gheyn, Jakob de. *The exercise of armes for caliures, muskettes and pikes.* The Hague, 1607.

Goodman, Godfrey. *The court of King James the First.* Ed. John S. Brewer. Two volumes. London, 1839.

Gordon, John. *Anti-bellarmino tortor, sive Tortus retortus.* London, 1612.

Gordon, Patrick. *Neptunus Britannicus Corydonis.* London, 1614.

Gorges, Sir Arthur. *The Olympian catastrophe dedicated to the worthy memory of the most heroicall lord Henry.* Ed. Randall Davies. Kensington, 1925.

Gorges, Sir Arthur. *The poems of Sir Arthur Gorges.* Ed. Helen Estabrook Sandison. Oxford, 1953.

Gwinne, Matthew. *Vertumnus sive annus recurrens Oxonii xxix. Augusti anno. 1605. Coram Iacobo Rege, Henrico Principe, Proceribus.* London, 1607.

H., W. [William Hammond?]. *The true picture and relation of Prince Henry.* Leyden, 1634.

Hakewill, George. *Scutum regium.* London, 1612.

Hall, Joseph, Bishop. *The collected poems of Joseph Hall.* Ed. A. Davenport. Liverpool, 1949.

Hall, Joseph, Bishop. *Contemplations upon the principal passages of the holie storie. The first volume.* London, 1612.

Hall, Joseph, Bishop. *Epistles. The first volume.* London, 1608.

Hall, Joseph, Bishop. *The Peace of Rome.* London, 1609.

Hall, Joseph, Bishop. *The works of Joseph Hall.* London, 1625.

Hamor, Ralphe. *A true discourse of the present estate of Virginia.* London, 1615.

Hannay, Patrick. *Two elegies on the late death of Queene Anne.* London, 1619.

Harbert, William. *A prophesie of Cadwallader.* London, 1604.

Harington, Sir John. *Nugae Antiquae.* Two volumes. London, 1804.

Harrison, John. *A short relation of the departure of Prince Frederick from Heydelberg.* London, 1619.

Hayward, John. *The lives of the III. Normans, kings of England.* London, 1613.

Henry Hudson the Navigator. Ed. G. M. Asher. London, 1860.

Henry, Prince of Wales. *The funeralls of the high and mighty prince Henry.* London, 1613.

Henry, Prince of Wales. *Great Brittans mourning garment. Given at the funerall of Prince Henry.* London, 1612.

Henry, Prince of Wales. *Londons love to the royal Prince Henrie.* London, 1610.

Henry, Prince of Wales. *Mausoleum; or the choisest flowres of the epitaphs on the death of Prince Henry.* Edinburgh, 1613.

Henry, Prince of Wales. *The order and solemnitie of the creation of Prince Henrie, Prince of Wales.* London, 1610.

Henry, Prince of Wales. *Sundry funeral elegies on the untimely death of the Prince.* London, 1613.

Henry, Prince of Wales. *A true report of the baptisme of Henry Fredericke, Prince of Wales.* London, 1603.

Henry, Prince of Wales. *A true reportarie of the baptisme of Frederik Henry, Prince of Scotland.* Edinburgh [1594?].

Herring, Francis. *Pietas pontificia, seu, conjurationis illius prodigiosae, et post natos homines maximè execrandae, in Iacobum primum.* London, 1606.

Herring, Francis. *Popish pietie.* Trans. A. P. London, 1610.

Heywood, Thomas. *A funerall elegie upon the death of Henry, Prince of Wales.* London, 1613.

Historical Manuscripts Commission. *Calendar of the manuscripts of the Marquis of Bath.* Four volumes. London, 1904-1968.

Historical Manuscripts Commission. *The manuscripts of His Grace the Duke of Portland.* Ten volumes. London, 1891-1931.

Historical Manuscripts Commission. *Report on manuscripts in various collections.* Eight volumes. London, 1901-14.

Historical Manuscripts Commission. *Report on the manuscripts of Lord De L'Isle and Dudley.* Five volumes. London, 1925-1962.

Historical Manuscripts Commission. *Report on the manuscripts of the Duke of Buccleuch and Queensberry.* Three volumes. London, 1899-1926.

Historical Manuscripts Commission. *Report on the manuscripts of the Earl of Mar and Kellie.* London, 1904.

Historical Manuscripts Commission. *Report on the manuscripts of the Marquess of Downshire.* Four volumes. London, 1924-1940.

Historical Manuscripts Commission. *Supplementary report on the manuscripts of the Earl of Mar and Kellie.* London, 1930.

Holland, Hugh. *Pancharis, the first booke.* London, 1603.

Homer. *Homer, prince of poets: translated in twelve bookes of his Iliads.* Trans. George Chapman. London [1610].

Horatius Flaccus, Q. *Quinti Horatii Flacci poemata.* Ed. John Bond. London, 1606.

Hubbard, William. *Great Brittaines resurrection.* London [1606?].

Hume, David. *Illustrissimi principis Henrici justa.* London, 1613.

James VI and I. *Britannia triumphans. Sive icon quater maximi Monarche Iacobi Primi.* London, 1607.

James VI and I. *Correspondence of King James VI of Scotland.* Ed. John Bruce. London, 1861.

James VI and I. *The Kings majesties speach to the Lords and Commons of this present Parliament at Whitehall on Wednesday the xxj. March 1609.* London, [1609].

James VI and I. *Letters to King James the Sixth.* Edinburgh, 1835.

James VI and I. *The political works of James I.* Ed. Charles H. McIlwain. Cambridge, Mass., 1918.

James VI and I. *A princes looking glasse.* Trans. William Willymat. Cambridge, 1603.

James VI and I. *Secret history of the court of James the First.* Ed. Sir Walter Scott. Two volumes. Edinburgh, 1811.

Jonson, Ben. *Ben Jonson.* Ed. C.H. Herford, Percy Simpson, and Evelyn Simpson. Eleven volumes. Oxford, 1925-52.

Jonson, Ben. *The masque of queenes celebrated from the house of fame.* London, 1609.

Julius, Alexander. *In Henricum Fridericum primo genitum Iacobi, Walliae principem lachrymae.* Edinburgh, 1612.

Juvenalis, Decius Junius. *Junii Juvenalis et Auli Persii Flacci satyrae.* Ed. Thomas Farnaby. London, 1612.

Leigh, William. *Great Britaines, great deliverance, from the great danger of popish powder.* Second edition. London, 1609.

Lescarbot, Marc. *Nova Francia, or the description of that part of New France which is one continent with Virginia.* Trans. Pierre Erondelle. London, 1609.

Lydiat, Thomas. *Emendatio temporum, compendio facta ab initio mundi.* London, 1609.

Lydiat, Thomas. *Recensio et explicatio argumentorum productorum libello emendationis temporum compendio factae.* [Oxford] 1613.

Manningham, John. *The diary of John Manningham.* Ed. John Bruce. London, 1868.

MS. Harleian (British Museum) 7007.

MS. Jones (Bodleian Library) 44.

MS. Royal (British Museum) 16.E.XXXVIII.

Marcelline, George. *The triumphs of King James.* London, 1610.

Marcelline, George. *Les trophees du roi Jacques I.* [London ?] 1609.

Markham, Gervase. *Cavelarice; or the English horseman.* London, 1607.

Maxwell, James. *The laudable life, and deplorable death, of Prince Henry. Poemes.* London, 1612.

Melville, Andrew. *Principis Scoti-Britannorum natalia.* Edinburgh, 1594.

More, George, Esquire. *Principles for yong princes.* London, 1611.

Morgan, Nicholas. *The perfection of horsemanship, drawn from nature, art, and practise.* London, 1609.

Mornay, Philippe de. *The mysterie of iniquitie: that is to say the historie of the papacie.* Trans. Samson Lennard. London, 1612.

Mornay, Philippe de. *A worke concerning the trueness of Christian religion.* Trans. Sir Philip Sidney and Arthur Golding. Third edition. Ed. Thomas Wilcocks. London, 1604.

Morton, Thomas. *The encounter against M. Parsons by a review of his last sober reckoning.* London [1610].

Moysie, David. *Memoirs of the affairs of Scotland.* Ed. James Dennistoun. Edinburgh, 1830.

Murray, Sir David. *The tragicall death of Sophonsiba.* London, 1611.

Narratives of voyages toward the north-west. Ed. Thomas Rundall. London, 1849.

Nethersole, Sir Francis. *Memoriae sacra Henrici Walliae principis laudatio funebris.* Cambridge, 1612.

Niccols, Richard. *The three sisters teares, shed at the funerals of Henry, Prince of Wales.* London, 1613.

Nichols, John. *The progresses, processions, and magnificent festivities of King James the First.* Four volumes. London, 1828.

Osborne, Francis. "Some traditional memorials on the reign of King James the First." *Secret history of the court of James the First.* See under James VI and I.

Osborne, Francis. *The works of Francis Osborne.* London, 1673.

Owen, John. *Epigrammatum Joannis Owen Oxoniensis, Cambro-Britanni, libri tres.* London, 1612.

Oxford University. *Eidyllia in obitum fulgentissimi Henrici Walliae Principis.* Oxford, 1612.

Oxford University. *Justa Oxoniensium.* Oxford, 1612.

Oxford University. *Luctus posthumus sive erga defunctum Henricum Walliae Principem Magdalenensium officiosa pietas.* Oxford, 1612.

Parliamentary debates in 1610, from the notes of a member of the House of Commons. Ed. Samuel Rawson Gardiner. London, 1862.

Pasquale, Carlo. *False complaints, or the censure of an unthankfull mind.* Trans. W. C[ovell]. London, 1605.

Peacham, Henry, the Younger. *Graphice or the most auncient and excellent art of drawing and limming.* London, 1612.

Peacham, Henry, the Younger. *Minerva Britanna or a garden of heroical deuises.* London, 1612.

Peacham, Henry, the Younger. *The period of mourning in memory of the late Prince, together with nuptial hymns for the Prince Palatine and Elizabeth.* London, 1613.

Peacham, Henry, the Younger. *Prince Henrie revived; or a poeme upon the birth of the hopeful young Prince Henry Frederick.* London, 1615.

Pett, Phineas. *The autobiography of Phineas Pett.* Ed. W. G. Perrin. *Publications of the Navy Records Society,* 51. London, 1918.

Peyton, Sir Edward. "The divine catastrophe of the kingly family of the House of Stuarts." *Secret History of the court of King James the First.* See under James VI and I.

A poetical rhapsody, 1602-1621. Ed. H.E. Rollins. Cambridge, 1931.

Price, Daniel. *The creation of the Prince.* London, 1610.

Price, Daniel. *The defence of truth against a booke falsely called, the triumph of truth by Humphrey Leach.* Oxford, 1610.

Price, Daniel. *Lamentations for the death of the late illustrious Prince Henry and the dissolution of his religious family. Two sermons.* London, 1613.

Price, Daniel. *Prince Henry, his first anniversary.* Oxford, 1613.

Price, Daniel. *Prince Henry, his second anniversary.* Oxford, 1614.

Price, Daniel. *Recusants conversion, a sermon preached at St. James, before the prince on the 25 of February 1608.* Oxford, 1608.

Price, Daniel. *Spirituall odours to the memory of Prince Henry. In foure sermons.* Oxford, 1613.

Price, Sampson. *Londons warning by Laodicea's luke-warmnesse. A sermon.* London, 1613.

Public Records Office. *Calendar of state papers and manuscripts, relating to English affairs, existing in the archives and collections of Venice.* Thirty-seven volumes. London, 1864-1939.

Public Records Office. *Calendar of state papers, domestic series, of the reign of James I, 1603-[1625].* Four volumes. London, 1857-59.

Public Records Office. *Calendar of the state papers relating to Scotland.* Two volumes. London, 1858.

Purchas, Samuel. *Purchas his pilgrimage.* Fourth edition. London, 1626.

Quin, Walter. *Corona virtutem principe dignarum.* London, 1613.

Quin, Walter. *Sertum poeticum in honorem Jacobi sexti.* Edinburgh, 1600.

Ralegh, Sir Walter. *The history of the world.* London, 1614.

Ralegh, Sir Walter. *The works of Sir Walter Ralegh.* Eight volumes. Oxford, 1829; reprt., New York, 1965.

Reliques of ancient English poetry. Ed. Thomas Percy. Three volumes. London, 1812.

Rhodes, John. *A briefe summe of the treason intended against the king and state.* London, 1606.

Rich, Barnaby. *The fruites of long experience; a pleasing view for peace. A looking glass for war, or call it what you list.* London, 1604.

Rich, Barnaby. *A souldiers wishe to Britons welfare.* London, 1604.

Richerius, Edmundus. *A treatise of ecclesiasticall and politike power.* London, 1612.

Rogers, Thomas. *Gloucesters myte for the remembrance of Prince Henrie.* London, 1612.

Saluste du Bartas, Guillaume de. *Bartas: his deuine weekes and workes.* Trans. Joshua Sylvester. London, 1605.

Saluste du Bartas, Guillaume de. *Posthumus Bartas.* Trans. Joshua Sylvester. London, 1607.

Saluste Du Bartas, Guillaume de. *The third dayes creation.* Trans. Thomas Winter. London, 1604.

Scott, Thomas. *Vox coeli, or newes from heaven.* [Utrecht?] 1624.

Serlio, Sebastiano. *The first booke of architecture.* Trans. Robert Peake. London, 1611.

Sharpe, Leonell. *Oratio funebris in honorem Henrici Walliae principis.* London, 1612.

Smyth, William. *The black-smith. A sermon.* London, 1606.

Sparke, William. *Vis naturae et virtus vitae explicatae, comparatae, ad universum doctrinae ordinem constituendum.* London, 1612.

Spenser, Edmund. *Works. A variorum edition.* Ed. Edwin Greenlaw, Charles Grosvenor Osgood and Frederick Morgan Padelford. Nine volumes. Baltimore, 1932-49.

Stow, John. *The annales of England. Continued unto 1631.* London, 1631.

Strachey, William. *For the colony in Virginea Britannia. Lawes divine, morall and martiall.* London, 1612.

Sutcliffe, Matthew. *An abridgement or survey of Poperie.* London, 1606.

Sylvester, Joshua. *Lachrymae lachrymarum.* Third edition. London, 1613.

Sylvester, Joshua. *The parliament of vertues royal.* London, 1614.

Taylor, John. *Great Britaine all in blacke. For the incomparable losse of Henry, our late worthy Prince.* London, 1612.

Temple, William. *A logicall analysis of twentie select psalmes.* London, 1605.

Tooker, William. *Duellum sive singulare certamen cum Martino Becano Jesuita.* London, 1611.

Tourneur, Cyril, *et al. Three elegies on the most lamented death of Prince Henrie.* London, 1613.

Trial. *The fierie tryall of Gods saints.* London, 1611.

The voyages of Captain Luke Foxe and Captain Thomas James in search of a north-west passage. Ed. Miller Christy. Two volumes. London, 1894.

Wake, Sir Isaac. *Rex Platonicus: sive de potentissimi principis Iacobi Britanniarum Regis, ad illustrissimam Academian Oxoniensem adventu August 27 Anno. 1605.* Editio secunda. Oxford, 1607.

Ward, John. *The first set of English madrigals.* London, 1613.

Webster, John. *The complete works of John Webster.* Ed. F. L. Lucas. Four volumes. London, 1927.

Webster, John. *A monumental columne erected to the memory of Henry late Prince of Wales.* London, 1613.

Wedderburn, David. *In obitu summae spei principis Henrici lessus.* Edinburgh, 1613.

Weldon, Sir Anthony. *A cat may look upon a king.* Amsterdam [London] 1714.

Weldon, Sir Anthony. Anon. *A cat may look upon a king, answered paragraph by paragraph.* London [1720?].

Weldon, Sir Anthony. "The court and character of King James." *Secret history of the court of James the First.* See under James VI and I.

Weldon, Sir Anthony. "A perfect description of the people and country of Scotland." *Secret history of the court of James the First.* See under James VI and I.

Wilbraham, Roger. *The journal of Roger Wilbraham.* Ed. Harold Spencer Scott. London, 1902.

Willet, Andrew. *An harmonie upon the first booke of Samuel.* London, 1607.

Willymat, William. *A loyal subjects looking-glasse.* London, 1604.

Wilson, Arthur. *The history of Great Britain, being the life and reign of King James the First.* London, 1653.

Winwood, Sir Ralph. *Memorials of affairs of state in the reigns of Queen Elizabeth and King James I.* Three volumes. London, 1725.

Wither, George. *Juvenilia: poems by George Wither.* Three volumes. Manchester, 1871.

Wither, George. *Prince Henries obsequies.* London, 1612.

Wright, Edward. *Certaine errors in navigation.* London, 1610.

Yonge, Walter. *The diary of Walter Yonge, Esquire.* Ed. George Roberts. London, 1848.

Secondary Works

Adamson, J. H., and H. F. Folland. *The Shepherd of the Ocean.* Boston, 1969.

Aiken, Lucy. *Memoirs of the Court of King James the First.* Two volumes. London, 1822.

Akrigg, G. *Jacobean Pageant.* London, 1962.

Artin, Tom. *The Allegory of Adventure: Reading Chretien's "Erec" and "Yvain."* Lewisburg, Pa., 1974.

Bell, H. E. *An Introduction to the History and Records of the Court of Wards and Liveries.* Cambridge, 1953.

Bergeron, David M. *English Civic Pageantry.* London, 1971.

Bergeron, David M. "Prince Henry and English Civic Pageantry." *Tennessee Studies in Literature,* 13 (1968), 109-16.

Birch, Thomas. *The Court and Times of James the First.* Two volumes. London, 1849.

Birch, Thomas. *The Life of Henry, Prince of Wales.* London, 1760.

Bowle, John. *Charles the First.* Boston, 1976.

Bradner, Leicester. *Musae Anglicanae.* New York, 1940.

Chidsey, Donald Barr. *Sir Walter Ralegh: That Damned Upstart.* New York, 1931.

Clark, George T. *Some Account of Sir Robert Mansel and of Admiral Sir Thomas Button.* Dowlais, 1883.

Clowes, William Laird, *et al. The Royal Navy: A History from the Earliest Times to the Present.* Five volumes. London, 1887-1903.

Durst, Paul. *Intended Treason.* South Brunswick & London, 1970.

Edmond, John Philip. "Elegies and Other Tracts Issued on the Death of Henry, Prince of Wales, 1612." *Publications of the Edinburgh Bibliographical Society,* 6 (1906), 141-158.

Edwards, Edward. *The Life of Sir Walter Ralegh.* Two volumes. London, 1868.

Edwards, Edward. *The Lives of the Founders of the British Museum.* Two volumes. London, 1870.

Edwards, Philip. *Sir Walter Ralegh.* New York, 1953.

Fraser, Antonia. *King James VI of Scotland, I of England.* New York, 1975.

Gardiner, Samuel R. *History of England from the Accession of James I to the Outbreak of the Civil War.* Ten volumes. London, 1894-96.

Grant, W. Leonard. *Neo-Latin Literature and the Pastoral.* Chapel Hill, 1965.

Greenblatt, Stephen. *Sir Walter Ralegh: The Renaissance Man and His Roles.* New Haven, 1973.

Harris, William. *An Historical and Critical Account of the Life and Writings of James the First.* Second edition. London, 1772.

Harrison, G. B. *A Second Jacobean Journal.* Ann Arbor, 1958.

Hume, Martin A. S. *Sir Walter Raleigh.* London, 1903.

Hurstfield, Joel. *The Queen's Wards.* London, 1958.

Land, Robert Hunt. "Henrico and Its College." *William and Mary College Quarterly Historical Magazine,* n.s., 18 (1938), 453-498.

Lee, Maurice, Jr. *James I and Henri IV.* Urbana, 1970.

Lewalski, Barbara Kiefer. *Donne's Anniversaries and the Poetry of Praise.* Princeton, 1973.

Lindsay, B. N., and J. W. Williamson. "Myth of the Conqueror: Prince Henry Stuart and Protestant Militancy." *Journal of Medieval and Renaissance Studies,* 5 (1975), 203-222.

McElwee, William Lloyd. *The Wisest Fool in Christendom.* London, 1958

Moore, Sir Norman. *The Illness and Death of Henry Prince of Wales in 1612.* London, 1882.

Murdoch, W. G. Blaikie. *The Royal Stuarts in Their Connection with Art and Letters.* Edinburgh, 1908.

Newton, A. Edward. *The Greatest Book in the World.* Boston, 1925.

Oman, Carola. *Elizabeth of Bohemia.* London, 1938.

Oppenheim, Michael. *A History of the Administration of the Royal Navy.* London, 1896; reprt., Hamden, Conn., 1961.

Orgel, Stephen. *The Jonsonian Masque.* Cambridge, Mass., 1965.

Rowse, A. L. *Sir Walter Ralegh.* New York, 1962.

Sandison, Helen Estabrook. "Arthur Gorges, Spenser's Alcyon and Ralegh's Friend." *PMLA,* 43 (1928), 645-674.

Scott, Otto J. *James I.* New York, 1976.

Seton, Walter W. "The Early Years of Henry Frederick, Prince of Wales, and Charles, Duke of Albany, 1593-1605." *Scottish Historical Review,* 13 (1916), 366-79.

Seward, Desmond. *The First Bourbon, Henri IV, King of France and Navarre.* London, 1971.

Starnes, DeWitt T., and Ernest W. Talbert. *Classical Myth and Legend in Renaissance Dictionaries.* Chapel Hill, 1955.

Statham, Edward Phillips. *A Jacobean Letter Writer: The Life and Times of John Chamberlain.* London, n.d.

Steeholm, Clara and Hardy. *James I of England, the Wisest Fool in Christendom.* New York, 1938.

Strong, Roy. *The English Icon: Elizabethan and Jacobean Portraiture.* New York, 1969.

Thiébaux, Marcelle. *The Stag of Love.* Ithaca & London, 1974.

Thompson, Edward. *Sir Walter Ralegh.* New Haven, 1936.

Trevor-Roper, H. R. *Archbishop Laud.* London, 1940.

Waith, Eugene M. *The Herculean Hero.* New York, 1962.

Wallace, Willard M. *Sir Walter Raleigh.* Princeton, 1959.

Wallerstein, Ruth. *Studies in Seventeenth-Century Poetic.* Madison, 1950.

Wedgwood, C.V. *Poetry and Politics under the Stuarts.* Cambridge, 1960.

White,Terence Hanbury. *The Book of Beasts.* London, 1954.

Whiting, Mary Bradford. "Henry, Prince of Wales: 'A Scarce Blown Rose.'" *Contemporary Review,* 137 (1930), 492-500.

Williams, Franklin B., Jr. *Index of Dedications and Commendatory Verses in English Books Before 1641.* London, 1962.

Williamson, Hugh Ross. *Sir Walter Raleigh.* London, 1951.

Willson, David Harris. "The Earl of Salisbury and the 'Court' Party in Parliament, 1604-1610." *American Historical Review,* 36 (1931), 274-294.

Willson, David Harris. *King James VI and I.* New York, 1967.

Wilson, Elkin Calhoun. *Prince Henry and English Literature.* Ithaca, 1946.

Index

213